The Judicial Politics of Economic Integration

The Judicial Politics of Economic Integration analyses development strategies and regional integration in the Andean Community (the former Andean Pact), focusing on the establishment of the Andean Court of Justice and its case law, as well as the intellectual underpinnings that made such an impressive reform possible. The court is a transplant taken from the European integration process and it materialises the visions, expectations, and dreams of the transnational development movement of 'integration through law'. The book discusses the outcomes of the Court in light of the debates about judicial reform in the process of development and regional integration. Although clearly confirming several earlier claims that 'one size does not fit all', Osvaldo Saldías provides new insights into how legal transplants adapt and evolve, and how we can learn much more about legal reform from a project that presumably failed than from successful copies. The Andean Court of Justice is a remarkable example of an institution capable of adapting to political and economic challenges; therefore, in times of a severe European economic crisis we should not forget that we might improve our understanding of European integration by looking at developments in other regions.

An interesting new study with an international focus, this book will be a fascinating read for students and scholars of Law and Latin American Studies.

Osvaldo Saldías is based in the School of Law at the Humboldt University of Berlin.

The Judicial Politics of Economic Integration

The Andean Court as an engine of development

Osvaldo Saldías

LONDON AND NEW YORK

First published 2014
by Routledge
2 Park Square, Milton Park, Abingdon, Oxfordshire OX14 4RN

Simultaneously published in the USA and Canada
by Routledge
711 Third Avenue, New York, NY 10017

A GlassHouse Book

Routledge is an imprint of the Taylor and Francis Group, an informa business

First issued in paperback 2015

© 2014 Osvaldo Saldías

The right of Osvaldo Saldías to be identified as author of this work has been asserted by him in accordance with sections 77 and 78 of the Copyright, Designs and Patents Act 1988.

All rights reserved. No part of this book may be reprinted or reproduced or utilised in any form or by any electronic, mechanical, or other means, now known or hereafter invented, including photocopying and recording, or in any information storage or retrieval system, without permission in writing from the publishers.

Trademark notice: Product or corporate names may be trademarks or registered trademarks, and are used only for identification and explanation without intent to infringe.

British Library Cataloguing in Publication Data
A catalogue record for this book is available from the British Library

Library of Congress Cataloging-in-Publication Data
Saldias, Osvaldo.
The judicial politics of economic integration : the Andean Court as an engine of development / Osvaldo Saldías.
  pages cm
Includes bibliographical references.
ISBN 978-0-415-82970-0 (hbk) – ISBN 978-0-203-40514-7 (ebk)
1. Comunidad Andina–Economic policy. 2. Tribunal de Justicia del Acuerdo de Cartagena. 3. Law–Andes Region. 4. Andes region–Economic integration. I. Title.
KG736.A5S24 2013
347.28'01–dc23   2013011067

ISBN 978-0-415-82970-0 (hbk)
ISBN 978-1-138-91512-1 (pbk)
ISBN 978-0-203-40514-7 (ebk)

Typeset in Garamond by
Cenveo Publisher Services

Contents

Table of Cases		vii
Foreword		ix
1	Introduction	1
2	The rise of a model: The European Court of Justice as an engine of integration	8
	Neofunctionalism 9	
	Intergovernmentalism 33	
3	The saga of European legal integration: The court and its case law	43
	Forging the European judicial archetype 43	
	Integration and international public law 46	
	The transformation of the preliminary ruling procedure: the case law 47	
4	The politics of judicial design: professionals and legal experts	58
	Brief notes on the transplant approach: aims and limitations 59	
	Three Andean puzzles around the establishment of the Andean Court of Justice 61	
	Epistemic communities and advocacy coalitions: an overview 63	
	The Andean-European network 66	
	Conditions for the action of networks: using windows of opportunity 72	
	Assessing the efficacy of legal networks: a counterfactual inference 76	
	Expanding the Andean network: bringing the judges in 79	
5	The Andean Court of Justice: charting the course for its case law	84
	The origins of the Andean Group 84	
	The Andean institutional setting: an overview 88	
	The Andean Court of Justice 90	
	Common policy on intellectual property: the case of the patents 101	
	Establishing a common market by expansive interpretation 108	

6	What legal engineers do not get: rights politics and the pitfalls of concept stretching	113

Assessing empirical variations between the courts 114
Neofunctionalism and the Andean engine of integration 117
Intergovernmentalism and the kite model 118
Towards an alternative explanation 119
Two competing regulatory models: decentralised vs. centralist 123
Explaining expansive jurisprudence in regional integration: rights politics 130
South American scholarship and the community of fate 131
Concept stretching and theory building 134

7	Epilogue and excursus: the Andean way towards constitutionalisation	137

The foundational period (1969–72) 138
The period of institutional expansion and stagnation (1972–96) 139
Towards constitutionalisation (1996 onwards): an excursus 140

Bibliography   145
Index   163

Table of Cases

Andean Court of Justice

(available at www.tribunalandino.org.ec)

Sentencia 1-IP-87 *Aktiebolaget Volvo c/ Colombia*	81, 82, 109
Sentencia 1-IP-88 *Stauffer Chemical c/ Colombia*	102, 103, 106, 110, 127
Sentencia 2-IP-88 *Cavelier c/ Colombia*	81, 102
Sentencia 3-IP-88 *Daimler-Benz A.G. c/ Colombia*	102
Sentencia 3-IP-89 *Ciba Geigy A.G. c/ Colombia*	103, 104, 105, 127
Sentencia 7-IP-89 *Ciba Geigy A.G. c/ Colombia*	103, 104
Sentencia 1-IP-90 *Aluminio Reynolds Santo Domingo c/ Colombia*	109, 123, 124, 127
Sentencia 3-IP-93 *Sociedad de Aluminio Nacional c/ Colombia*	111, 112
Sentencia 6-IP-94 *Laboratorios Ecuatorianos c/ Ecuador*	106, 107

European Court of Justice

Case 3/62 *Commission v. Luxembourg* [1963] ECR 445	79, 112
Case 26/62 *Van Gend en Loos* [1963] ECR 1	17, 47, 49, 54, 79, 91
Case 6/64 *Costa v. ENEL* [1964] ECR 585	17, 47, 50, 79, 91
Case 26/69 *Stauder v. City of Ulm* [1969] ECR 419	55
Case 6/72 *Continental Can* [1973] ECR 215	79, 112
Case 4/73 *Nold, Kohlen- und Baustoffgroßhandlung v. Commission* [1974] ECR 491	56
Case 8/74 *Dassonville* [1974] ECR 837	79, 108, 110, 111, 126
Case 45/86 *APS* [1987] ECR 1493	107
Case C-215/88 *Fleischhandel* [1989] ECR 2789	107
Case C-300/89 *Commission v. Council* [1991] ECR 2687	107
Case 106/77 *Administrazione delle Finanze dello Statu v. Simmenthal SpA* (II), ECJ Case 106/77 (1978) ECR 629	51, 95, 96
Case 294/83 *Parti Écologiste "Les Verts" v. European Parliament.* case 294/83 ECJ [1986]	52

Case 22/70 *Commission v. Council (AETR/ERTA)*, case 22/70 [1971]
  ECR 263, par. 17, 31   53
Case 804/79 *Commission v. UK*, case 804/79 [1981] ECR 1045,
  par. 17, 18   53
Opinion 1/94 on the WTO Agreements (GATS and TRIPS) [1994]
  ECR I-5267   53
Case 1/58 *Stork v. High Authority* [1959] ECR 17   54, 131
Cases 36, 37, 38 and 40/59 *Geitling v. High Authority* [1960]
  ECR 423   54, 131
Case 40/64 *Sgarlata and others v. Commission* [1965] ECR 215   54, 131

German Constitutional Court

Case 2 BvL 52/71, *Internationale Handelsgesellschaft*, 29.05.1974,
  known as the *Solange* ruling   56
Case 2 BvR 197/83 *Wünsche Handelsgesellschaft*, 22.10.1986   56

Supreme Court of the United States

William Marbury v. James Madison, Secretary of State of the United States,
  5 U.S. 137 (1803)   140

Foreword

The book you are about to read was completed in March 2013. Since I started thinking about the central idea of testing European theories in the Andean region, much has happened. The world experienced its deepest financial crisis in decades, several EU states entered into a whopping budget crisis, and the European Monetary Union is currently struggling to regain its credibility. In South America, Brazil is beginning to claim a place among the global superpowers, and the Venezuelan authoritarian – albeit democratically elected – president Hugo Chavez died before being able to assume his fourth term.

The world is changing and, as power appears to be shifting at the global level, the public debate seems to have forgotten the initial purpose that motivated several regions to initiate process of regional integration. With the public fear of losing part of the wealth that economic integration has produced, several theoretical cleavages about what really drives regional integration seem to become less fashionable.

However, the legacy of Ernst Haas' neofunctionalism, the objections of intergovernmentalism, and the resurrection of neofunctionalism through the narrative of the European Court of Justice (ECJ) as an 'engine of integration' are still a pillar of the education of political scientists and legal scholars interested in European integration. The meta-theoretical quarrel about the drivers of integration is still unsolved at the present moment. Moreover, scholars of European integration have not yet noticed that the nature of the European Union is perceived differently in other regions compared to the European self-image. While James Caporaso was asking whether European integration was a singular case, a $n=1$, a whole generation of Latin American scholars understood the Andean Community to belong to the same category as the EU.

European academics would be surprised to know that European Community law, Andean law and MERCOSUR community law are treated and taught in Latin American universities as one single legal discipline: in Spanish we know it as *Derecho de la Integración*. Having studied, researched and taught in Germany, I could not possibly imagine a European university course teaching European law, along with MERCOSUR law, or the law of any other regional organisation as if they were part of the same disciplinary field. I have always found it most intriguing why this difference has remained largely unnoticed. I address these issues, and the implications for Andean legal integration, in Chapter 4.

Nonetheless, the main challenge of this book is to understand more the role of supranational courts in regional integration schemes. With the hope of understanding better the role of the Andean Court of Justice, I was resolved to use the analytical toolkit of European studies without suspecting that I would up ending learning much about the European Court of Justice itself. Although the debate between the two European grand theories cannot be entirely solved by the comparison with the Andean case, there are questions that tell us much about regional integration as a research field, and community law as a legal discipline. The research shows that Euro-centred research is often blind to numerous assumptions about law, about political institutions, and about international politics.

If there is a main lesson to be drawn from the Andean saga, it is the idea that legal transplants are much less a tool for solving legal problems than a magnificent chance for improving our knowledge about legal change. Legal engineering should not be regarded as an answer to social problems; rather, legal engineering should be viewed as part of the question that guides us towards understanding how law interacts with politics and social reality.

This project started as a PhD dissertation at the Otto Suhr Institute for Political Science of the Free University of Berlin. I rewrote and complemented much of its content during post-doctoral research in the KFG Research Group at the same university, as well as my research stay in Chicago as a visiting scholar at the Weinberg College of Arts and Sciences at Northwestern University, and as a visiting faculty at the American Bar Foundation.

The project has been accomplished thanks to many people that helped me during my research. First of all, I am deeply grateful to my PhD supervisor, Tanja A. Börzel, for her unconditional support, guidance and motivation. Academics like her are the reasons why I considered a career as an academic in the first place; where ordinary people see closed doors, Tanja sees chances and possibilities. This project would not have been possible without her encouragement. I am also deeply indebted to Karen Alter, who has been a generous mentor to me since we discovered we were both researching the Andean Court of Justice simultaneously. It was a coincidence and also a marvellous feeling to know that I was in such a good company.

I am also deeply thankful to Ingolf Pernice, spokesperson of the Research Training Group 'Multilevel Constitutionalism: European Experiences and Global Perspectives' at the Humboldt University of Berlin, who gave me a wonderful environment in which to develop my ideas. Thanks to Daniel Thym, Julia Wunderer, Rüdiger Schwarz and all the staff that make such an outstanding project possible. The academic and the human quality that I experienced have shaped much of my life decisions, and I will never forget the many friends I have made there. Thanks to Manuel, Benjamin, Chia, Christian, Isabelle, Tillmann, Thorsten, Yoan and Ruslana for your friendship.

I also owe much to the American Bar Foundation, particularly its directors Robert Nelson and Terence Halliday. I will always cherish the privileged experiences that I had in Chicago at the Foundation and working with its researchers and staff; thank you Lucinda, Eileen, Anne and Gabriele for making me feel so welcome. In addition I would like to thank the people at the Weinberg College for Arts and Science, as well as the Roberta Buffett Center for International and Comparative Studies at Northwestern University for their support during my stay in Chicago.

I also wish to express my gratitude to Laurence R. Helfer for his advice and encouragement. When I was just a junior researcher in Berlin, Larry generously invited me to one of his famous round tables at Vanderbilt; I still remember that wonderful experience as if it was yesterday. I cherish the deep and fantastic discussions with Larry and Karen Alter about the ACJ, which resulted in the three of us writing together.

Special thanks go to the Heidelberg Center for Latin America in Santiago de Chile, and the people that make such a wonderful academic project possible. To Walter Eckel and Isabel Aliaga, who gave support not only to me but to my family when times were not too easy. I shall never forget their unconditional help.

I am also thankful to the Max Planck Institute for Comparative Public Law and International Law in Heidelberg, especially to its Director Armin von Bogdandy, and Mariela Morales, for their academic, intellectual and bibliographic support. I also thank two anonymous reviewers for their helpful comments and critique.

Finally, but most importantly, this book would never have seen the light if it were not for my family: my wife Monica, my inspiration and source of strength, and my children Daniela, Laura and Gabriel. They all suffered as a result of the extended working hours this project demanded. And last but not least, my parents, who always encouraged me to follow my passion. Thank you.

Chapter 1
Introduction

Scholars of regionalism often overlook the fact that the idea of regional integration has been in place in Latin America for more than 200 years (Emmes and Mols 1993: 47). During the independence war against the Spanish crown in the nineteenth century, the young states that were emerging shared the cultural *mestizo* legacy, originated by the blending of the European monarchical tradition with the native aboriginal societies. At the very beginning, the conquerors imposed the Spanish order; their brethren – the *criollos* – inherited much of their status, as Latin American freedom fighters rapidly understood that the fate of one state would have a decisive impact on their neighbours' struggle against the colonial power. With such an extended experience, it might appear as a paradox that social scientists have insisted so much on the need for Latin America to learn from European integration. The most probable reasons are that Europe has been a remarkable example of deep integration. Furthermore, most of the integration endeavours in Latin America, if not all, have not lived up to their expectations; and yet, it is impossible to overlook the persistence with which Latin American states pursue economic regional integration.

Why do states in Latin America still persevere in their attempts to reach some sort of regional integration? A popular line of argument seems to be that states are actors with emotions. We find commentators of different linguistic backgrounds coming up with particular explanations for the reasons that account for the persistent attitude towards regional integration; ideas like *noción de pertenencia* (Hirst 1992: 27), *Zusammengehörigkeitsbewusstsein* (Emmes and Mols 1993: 51), or *voluntad política en favor de la integración* (JUNAC 1979: 27) are just some of them.

The debate on Latin American integration since the 1950s has predominantly centred around the idea of 'terms of trade' and the need for solidarity in the region (Mols 1993: 3). Much of the insights came from the United Nations' Economic Commission for Latin America and the Caribbean (ECLAC) – widely known in the Spanish-speaking world as CEPAL (Comisión Económica para América Latina y el Caribe) – which aimed at dismantling

Latin American economies' dependence on industrial countries (Herrera 1976). This came to be known as the 'dependence theory' (Emmes and Mols 1993: 163). According to that strategy, Latin American countries might benefit from scale economies by expanding their targeted markets and protecting the region from extra-regional trade. This orientation came to an abrupt halt with the Latin American debt crisis in the 1980s, a period known as 'the lost decade of Latin America' (Blanco 1997; Mols 1993). Contrary to the import substitution approach, Latin American countries began looking to global markets as the source of dynamic growth, convinced that without external financing internal growth was not viable over time (Franko 2007: 236). Regional integration became an attempted function of improving Latin America's appeal to international investors who seek 'large markets endowed with credible institutional guarantees' (Mattli 1999b: 155).

The list of regional arrangements in Latin America is long. Those that are still ongoing include ALADI,[1] CAFTA,[2] CARICOM,[3] Group of Three,[4] PICAB,[5] and NAFTA.[6] Most of them are created with traits of strong negative integration (Scharpf 1995; Patrice 2007). All attempts made to integrate Latin American states have nevertheless scored below the expectations.

MERCOSUR[7] is also a good example. It is an integration scheme established by Argentine, Brazil, Uruguay and Paraguay with a view of establishing a southern cone common market. Member states agreed to implement it by the end of 1994. Nevertheless, the fulfilment of the promises had to be repeatedly postponed (Sangmeister 2001). Today, it is an 'imperfect customs union' at best (Mattli 1999b: 155), and the jurisdiction of its dispute settlement body has been questioned as Argentina recently took a long-running dispute with Uruguay to the International Court of Justice, just as the Permanent Body was also claiming jurisdiction over the conflict (Schmidt and Pavón Piscitello 2007). Although it is an ongoing project, it seems to hold both permanent promise and constant pitfalls for the member states (Franko 2007: 263).

The idea of a Central American common market is also an example of frustrated integration, as it was interrupted by armed conflict between two member states, a war that the integration scheme was unable to impede

---

1 Asociación Latinoamericana de Integración.
2 Central American-United States of America Free Trade Agreement.
3 Comunidad del Caribe.
4 Free Trade Agreement between Colombia, Mexico and Venezuela.
5 Programa de Integración y Cooperación Económica entre Argentina y Brasil.
6 North American Free Trade Agreement (TLCAN).
7 Established by the Treaty of Asunción on 26 March 1991. Venezuela joined in 2006, and in 2012 Bolivia signed a protocol adhesion to MERCOSUR, which establishes a four-year transition period towards full membership.

(Mattli 1999b). Moreover, as will be discussed in Chapter 4, one ambitious project, the Central American Economic and Social Community, never saw the light, despite its sophisticated institutional design.

All these institutional arrangements share one distinct characteristic: not one of them has ever accomplished its goals in terms of implementation. The inefficacy of these schemes is twofold: on the one hand, main landmarks are never achieved in time. Some goals have, in fact, never been achieved. States have not complied with their own commitments. On the other hand, the newly established institutions that are supposedly charged with the role of attaining the goals have not been able to fulfil their expectations either.

Overall, it seems to be very obvious that regional integration has never been successful in Latin America. Despite ambitious goals and iteration, setbacks clearly dominate achievements in the history of Latin American regional integration. Why is that so?

The question becomes especially puzzling if we consider how, in several cases, institutions that were important in European integration were emulated without comparable success. Notions of supranationality were incorporated into the jargon of regional policy-makers, yet the outcomes do not even come close to European levels of integration. In the cases of CARICOM and the Andean Community (CAN), institutions were established in the image of the European Court of Justice (ECJ) committed to the aim of pulling member states into compliance with their own promises. Up to today, however, neither of those regional arrangements has been able to implement its common market. Moreover, integration as a political process was severely curtailed by the withdrawal of Venezuela from CAN; and war between member states has been a problem both for CAN and CARICOM.

What are the reasons for these repeated failures? Why are Latin American integration schemes persistently missing their own goals? Two circumstances exacerbate the mystery around this puzzle. First, the impressive number of attempts is matched by equal numbers of alleged failures. Unless this rate of non-success is observable in other regions too, one could speculate that there are factors – not to say problems – that are particular to Latin America. This assumption has implications, though. It would mean that all the staunch attempts to reach a European-fashioned integration are inherently doomed to failure. However, it can equally be argued that the European path of integration is an outcome so extraordinary that it cannot possibly be repeated elsewhere. This latter assertion would imply that integration *à l'européen* is not attainable at all and should not even be attempted elsewhere.

A look at global tendencies reveals that the opposite is currently happening: numerous international organisations are emulating EU institutions (Börzel and Risse 2009). As scholars of European integration began making the claim of being able to explain and predict integration in several regional settings, there were several attempts to launch regional integration in Latin America, the Pacific, North America and Asia during the 1960s

(Rosamond 2000: 69; Fawcett 1995). This book delves into the case of the Andean Community and its Court of Justice against the backdrop of praise from numerous scholars for its institutional sophistication and intensive emulation of EU institutions. The importance of arbiters or dispute settlement bodies that have jurisdiction over regional disputes is especially interesting; they hold states accountable for their commitments, since all treaties establishing regional organisations are mere promises of working towards integration (Mattli 1999b: 12).

The Andean Court of Justice was modelled after the ECJ and the procedures are not only equivalent (Frischhut 2003: 274) but nearly identical. The spirit driving this reform was the widely known role played by the ECJ in developing European community law and the alleged success in making national law permeable to European law. This was especially due to the mechanisms of the preliminary references and the doctrines of supremacy and direct effect.

However, the performance of this judicial mechanism within the Andean region has been far from successful. On the one hand, until 2009 its case law had never been thoroughly vetted. On the other hand, 28 years after its foundation, the Andean Community has not been able to achieve its main goal of establishing a common market. Indeed, what exists today is an imperfect customs union ('unión aduanera imperfecta'; Taccone and Nogueira 2005: 51). Although the Cartagena Agreement has opened the possibilities for further South American states to join – especially the member states from the ALALC – this has proven very unattractive. To be sure, MERCOSUR[8] countries and Chile[9] applied for associate status, yet no Latin American state has up to now expressed its intention to become a full member. The literature is consistent: the process of Andean integration is usually dismissed as a failure (Helfer *et al.* 2009: 2; Mattli 1999b: 12, 42).

However, what makes the case of the Andean Community so special for regional studies is that it incorporates a number of features that are commonly regarded as the key factors that led Europe to deepen its own integration process so impressively. Ernst Haas, a European scholar puzzled by Latin American integration, suggested that we should pay attention to indicators of progressive integration when evaluating regional integration in non-European settings (Haas 1961: 367). Of course, Haas assumed these levels to be particularly low in Latin America generally. Unfortunately, he did not include the paradoxical Andean case in his research; thus, by 1979, the organisation showed

---

8 Decision 613, Asociación de la República de Argentina, de la República Federativa de Brasil, de la República del Paraguay y de la República Oriental del Uruguay, Estados Parte del MERCOSUR, a la Comunidad Andina, 7 June 2005.

9 See *Acta de Constitución de una Comisión Mixta* CAN-Chile, signed November 2006.

extremely high indicators due to the establishment of conflict resolution at supranational level, yet with meagre results.

Considering that the European Court of Justice played a prominent role in European legal integration, and that the Andean Community emulated the European judicial polity-design together with its substantive legal doctrines, why has Andean integration not been able to advance? Why has the ACJ not become an engine of legal integration like its European counterpart? The question is circumscribed to Andean legal integration; however, it strives for generalisations, as the European model of dispute settlement is becoming an inspiration for other settings, especially MERCOSUR (Dreyzin de Klor 2007; Schmidt and Pavón Piscitello 2007; Sanguinetti 1994).

As none of these settings has reported a successful outcome, scholars are still busy determining whether the European Union is indeed a case of $n=1$ (Caporaso 1997). Discussions on factors or necessary conditions for successful integration are recurring; causal propositions and explanations are abundant, as suggested by Latin American literature. There are a number of general explanations for the constant Latin American unsatisfactory outcomes. They range from endogenous factors like corruption, bureaucracy and marginalisation, to exogenous factors such as interference caused by the World Bank, the International Monetary fund, or even the Reagan Administration (Mols 1993: 26; Hirst 1992: 30; JUNAC 1979: 144). The frenetic search for explanations even led some writers to postulate an inherent Latin American disposition towards failure, supposedly due to an under-evolution caused by lack of technology, narrow markets, and unfair income distribution, or an alleged *morbus latinus* (Wöhlcke 1989).

There are also several specific explanations for the failure of the Andean Community to achieve its goals. Some arguments are deduced from the general proposition that apply to regional integration in Latin American generally; other explanations point specifically to the Andean Community.

Arguments that deal with the Andean Community as an instance of Latin American integration tend to follow different strands. Institutionalist explanations assume that institutions constrain actors' behaviour to the extent that actions become consistent with formal rules and procedures. Although literature on Latin American politics[10] refers to different currents of institutionalists and some variety of institutionalisms, explanations on the outcome of regional integration have not delved into the hindrances of institutionalism. Hence, and stated in a broad sense, for these scholars 'institutions matter' (see Ortiz 2004; Díaz Barrado 1999; Tangarife 2001a; Camacho Omiste 2001).

In contrast with institutionalist explanations, some scholars have suggested that it is the Latin American context in general, and the Andean context in particular, that is responsible for the disappointing outcome of

---

10 This is especially the case for scholarship on Democracy in Latin America (Ortiz 2004).

regional integration. Contextualist explanations point to local particularities that are able to hinder or suppress outcomes expected by policy-makers. Arguments that focus on special contextual factors frequently use variables like corruption, poverty, democratisation, political instability and the lack of rule of law. Such views regard contextual variables as given and sufficiently important to influence the performance of regional institutions (for instance, Haas and Schmitter 1964; Haas 1967; Bondia García 1999; Blanco 1997).

Other available explanations use international coordination approaches and game theories to explain the outcome of regional integration in the Andes. According to such explanations, Andean actors are assumed to be essentially rational, although there are also some normative constraints that make them want to attain superior goals. The interests of individual governments sometimes differ from the overall regional interest, which is deemed to be normatively superior. Therefore, authors frequently rebuke member states for following their self-interest instead of the regional goal. This perspective assumes that a certain *will* has to be present so as to do what is appropriate. When the logic of appropriateness fails, it is due to a 'lack of political will' to do the right thing (Andueza 1985a: 31).[11] According to this kind of explanation, non-compliance with Andean law, or lack of implementation of an Andean common market, originates from the attitudes of state leaders who put minor national interests at the forefront and neglect the general regional common good (for instance, Emmes and Mols 1993; Sobrino 2001; JUNAC 1979; da Cruz Vilaça and Sobrino 1996).

In this book, I divide the narrative on the Andean saga into functional chapters. Each tells a story of contextualised problem-solving, and each has its own underlying middle-ranged theory. However, the meta-theoretical conversation between neofunctionalism and intergovernmentalism runs through the whole book. This exercise is part of my conviction that we can learn much about European integration when we look at other regions. The same is true for Latin American scholarship, in that the study of regionalism must be theory-driven. The analytical added value of comparative research only increases a sound methodological approach.

Hence, Chapter 2 showcases the theoretical debate around European integration. Haas' neofunctionalism, intergovernmentalism and (neo)neofunctionalism have been engaged in incredibly passionate academic quarrels, while Chapter 3 explores the saga of the European Court of Justice. Chapter 4 introduces the functional strategies that led a professional Andean-European network of lawyers to adopt the postulations of Haas' neofunctionalism and to transplant the ECJ into the Andean Pact (later, the Andean Community). Chapter 5 delves into the institutional setting of the Andean Community, its Court of Justice and its judicial procedures. Its case law is represented here

---

11 On conditions that spark willingness for integration, see (Mattli 1999b).

through the comparative lens of the European experience. To my knowledge, this is the first project where the ACJ is analysed through the lens of the 'engine of integration'. The main findings and its analysis can be found in Chapter 6, where I also lay down the main claims about our current knowledge of the ACJ.

There are analytical and methodological ways to avoid the dangers and pitfalls of unsound comparisons. This is especially true when it comes to comparing courts across regions. Chapter 7 dares an excursus about current development in the Andean region. Although I claim that transplanting the ECJ into the Andean Community produces neither further integration nor the constitutionalisation of economic law, there seem to be interesting trends towards institutionalising human rights, democracy and the rule of law between the member states. It appears that Andean governments are trying to harness political power at the regional level and to provide new sanctioning mechanisms in order to enforce them. That last is a subject for a book that has yet to be written.

Chapter 2

The rise of a model

The European Court of Justice as an engine of integration

According to many legal scholars, the European Court of Justice (ECJ) is a true engine of European integration. The legal narrative of the constitutionalisation of the Treaty of Rome portrays the ECJ as the major factor that allowed EC law to permeate national law and subordinate it to European Community law (see, for instance, Alter 2001; Burley and Mattli 1993; Stone Sweet 2004a). This chapter focuses on the theoretical debates around European integration mainly during the 1990s, and how law began to resonate as a possible explanation of integration outcomes. In order to understand the arguments about causality in regional integration that resonated among policy-makers and use it in a later stage of the book, the chapter resorts to the analytical toolkit of possibly the most prominent theoretical account of that time: neofunctionalism. This approach, sometimes referred to as the official theory of European integration, provided the intellectual underpinnings for the establishment of its brethren, the Court of Justice of the Andean Community. According to this view, regional integration is most likely in 'low politics' areas, like market integration or legal integration. Hence, framing 'law' as a technical matter provides the opportunity for supranational organs to exploit unintended consequences and shift more competences towards the community. Neofunctionalists claim that this is how an activist ECJ managed to introduce its famous doctrines of direct effect and supremacy of EC law. The importance of this causal narrative about 'integration through law' is that it would find a fertile ground in the Andean Community in times when the first signs of stagnation became visible.

This chapter focuses on the noted neofunctionalist–intergovernmentalist controversy, which is frequently labelled as the 'great debate' in EU studies and, despite its spectacular tone as a dialogue at a meta-theoretical level, its helpfulness has sometimes been questioned (Rosamond 2005: 242–3). The relevant explanations that have been given for the case of European integration in general are presented here, and the role of the ECJ in particular. These arguments are picked up in Chapter 4 in order to extrapolate them into the context of legal engineering in the Andean Community.

Neofunctionalism

The questions that drive the neofunctionalist enquiry

The main questions that have driven research on the European Union are related to the process of international cooperation and the formation of international communities. The puzzle was posed as early as the 1950s when Ernst Haas asked about 'how and why states cease to be wholly sovereign, how and why they voluntarily mingle, merge, and mix with their neighbours so as to lose the factual attributes of sovereignty while acquiring new techniques for solving conflict between themselves' (Haas 1970: 610; Burley and Mattli 1993: 53). With his question he began challenging the dominant models in international relations, which assumed, in those days, that national states were primarily interested in their own survival within a hostile international environment.

The work of neofunctionalists began with a 'sympathetic critique' of functionalism, and it owes much of its dynamism and reputation to the success of European integration, along with which it became 'a distinctive, if not always coherent, body of concepts, hypotheses, assumptions and beliefs pertaining to political integration on the regional and global levels' (Pentland 1973: 100). It strived for an explanation for the process of formation of political communities within the international system (Haas 1964a: 7, 8; Rosamond 2000: 50; Wiener and Diez 2004: 8), and initially applied to the big six in Europe (Belgium, France, Italy, Luxembourg, the Netherlands and West Germany), focusing on the dynamic process of integration rather than on any static features (Rosamond 2000: 68; Haas 1968: 11).

Because early neofunctionalism attempted to professionalise social science, it insisted on explaining, classifying and generating hypotheses, as well as generating rules of procedures and schemes of interpretation for studies on international cooperation and integration. Thus, the methodological question required theorists to agree on *what* exactly had to be explained, and *how* it could possibly be operationalised in this field. For such ends, it was of great importance that research projects established a dependent variable, the explanandum, and as a consequence, general propositions could be empirically tested. These were precisely the kind of problems of systematicity that propositions derived from international relations theories were not able to solve (Rosamond 2005: 240–1; Pentland 1973: 103; see also Mattli 2005: 331). In this regard, for neofunctionalism, integration is the framework's dependent variable.

By generating testable hypotheses, it is easy to formulate propositions about the conditions under which it would be possible to advance regional integration; furthermore, if such conditions are present in a different context, integration should be predictable. Viewed in this manner, neofunctionalism is more than a sophisticated description of European integration (Rosamond 2000: 69), and rather a general analytical framework, under which Europe is a case that scores extremely high. In turn, if the hypotheses are confirmed, the framework might unveil its predictive qualities within and across regional settings (Haas 1964a: 49, 1970: 610).

The history of neofunctionalism is thus one of 'theory-building' and evaluation that resonates the norms of social science (Rosamond 2005: 251). Yet, at the same time, its theory–practice interface and its linkage to the 'Monnet method' of integration, together with a strong normative transnational agenda for preventing wars (Haas 1961: 366; Wiener and Diez 2004: 7; Schmitter 2005: 265; Moravcsik 2005: 350), gave neofunctionalism its label of being the 'authorised version' of European integration (Rosamond 2000: 50–1) or the 'quasi-official ideology' in the Commission (Wiener and Diez 2004: 13–14).

In what follows, I present a neofunctionalist discussion that offers a possible explanation for the outcome of Andean legal integration. I lay down the general conditions that have been postulated as necessary in the case of European integration in general, and European legal integration in particular.

General conditions for regional integration

The framework addresses the plausibility of predicting regional integration, and suggests that the likelihood of successful integration is tied to the conditions present in each setting. In 1961, Haas postulated three necessary background conditions that he observed in Western Europe: (a) pluralistic social structures, (b) substantial economic and industrial development, and (c) common ideological patterns among participating units (Haas 1961).

Viewed from a neofunctionalist perspective, pluralism entails 'a situation of full mobilisation of all segments of society with strong interest groups and political parties, and leadership by elites competing for political survival and dominance under rules of constitutional democracy' (Mattli 2005: 229–30; see also Haas 1958). Accordingly, the notion of pluralism necessarily breaks down the traditional nation state into several units, represented by governmental officials, political parties, and all the groups that could represent an interest that has a stake in the integrative process (Schmitter 2005: 256; Haas 1961: 366). This departure from the holistic view of sociological functionalism, which considers national actors in integrating systems as an undifferentiated whole, is a cornerstone of the incremental logic of neofunctionalism, because different interest groups would unite and reunite in different subsequent temporary coalitions so as to achieve their individual goals (Haas 1968: xxv; Pentland 1973: 121–2). In this logic, every group will receive a little, few groups would be deprived, while few groups would receive a sudden large gift (Haas 1968: xxiv). 'The acceptance of measures of economic integration by political institutions is possible because of the sharp fragmentation of interests and beliefs within each nation', and this fragmentation is increased by the action of supranational institutions (Haas 1968: 312). Hence, actors begin to face changing incentives, and the pattern of transnational interaction becomes complex as all participants 'appear as *differentiated* actors, a plurality of negotiating units (classes, status groups, subregions, *clienteles*, bureaucratic agencies, ideological clusters, etc.)' (Schmitter 1971: 260).

Furthermore, pluralism follows democratic principles in that it links authorities with organised interest representation. In other words, elites and authorities necessarily have to consider the interests and preoccupations of organised groups (Lindberg 1966: 240). Hence, 'the greater the increase in internal pluralism within and across member states, the more likely are transnational groups to form and are regional identities to emerge' (Schmitter 2003: 62).

In terms of economics, neofunctionalism sees additional requirements for a successful integration. Certain socio-economic structures are requisites for integration inasmuch as the rate of transaction within the region is contingent upon the levels of interdependence. In modern industrial areas, the transaction rates are likely to be high, which in turn is advantageous for more cooperation. Moreover, as economic interaction increases, the number of economic sectors that can provide functional tasks increases too, raising the pressure for more integration and increasing the odds for spillover to occur (Pentland 1973: 121). Hence, a sustained market pressure for integration becomes a demand condition (Mattli 1999b: 20), as it requests a specific response from authority. The response, what Mattli calls 'supply', comes from political leaders and market authorities. Formulated in theoretical terms, supply conditions are those under which 'political leaders are willing and able to accommodate demands for functional integration at each step of the integration process' (Mattli 1999b: 3).

Walter Mattli complemented much of the framework in his *The Logic of Integration* and suggested that coordination between members of the group will bring in re-distributional issues; given that coordination is a game played over time, the leader can ease these distributional issues and act as a 'paymaster' (Mattli 1999b: Ch. 4). Therefore, a key supply condition for successful integration is the presence of an undisputed leader among the group of countries seeking to reach a successful integration. The leader constitutes a focal point in the coordination of rules, regulations and policies; and, of course, it will be that leader's governance structure that will be applied (Mattli 1999a).

However, beyond distributional issues, economic difficulties are an important background condition for integration, because they spark willingness for integration. Nevertheless, says Mattli, economic difficulties by themselves cannot guarantee successful integration because of collective action problems. Coordination is especially difficult in the case of an integration scheme, because it is not limited to mere removal of trade barriers. States have different and, to some extent, opposing interests that can collide. So, coordination problems arise regarding the choice of certain courses of action (Mattli 1999a: 4, 13).

The theoretical importance that neofunctionalism sees in economics and industrial development lies in the observation that some sectors within national economies are best suited as a haven for integration because they maximise the so-called spillover effect. In other words, states that aim at advancing a regional integration scheme should strategically look for the functional sector with the most 'inherently expansive' tasks, and in the 1950s, there was a consensus that the economic sector fulfilled such requirements (Pentland 1973: 121).

The same potential for spillover effects can be found in issues related to law, especially international agreements. Human behaviour entails much uncertainty. Therefore, no contract or agreement can predict all consequences that a contractual relationship brings about. The possibility that unforeseen consequences shape legal relations is considerable.

The conjugation of background conditions and the spillover effect led neofunctionalists to promote the idea of 'automatisation' of the integration process. They suggested that, because of the spillover effect, technical economic tasks would get politicised, spurring political decisions that could address technical needs (Rosamond 2000: 71). This notion of 'technical self-determination' is a functionalist legacy and it led neofunctionalism to come very close to postulate the inevitability of spillover (Pentland 1973: 119; Haas 1967: 315). However, despite the considerable appeal of the idea of automatisation, neofunctionalists never stopped viewing regional integration as agent-driven processes; neofunctionalism is not a deterministic theory (see Rosamond 2000: 70). The involvement of certain actors, then, is necessary for spillover to occur in regional integration. Moreover, an outcome of maximised spillover effect is possible as long as actors have at least a vague hope of reaping economic benefits from the process. For this purpose, the expectation of benefits can be vague or obscure, so as to allow for everyone to expect benefits. If actors estimate that they will not have the chance of making any sort of profit whatsoever, they will probably not agree to a political union (Haas and Schmitter 1964: 708; Schmitter 2005: 118).

It would be reasonable to object that this argument for expansion and interdependence should be plausible only for those particular contexts, where economic benefits are realistic. These would be mostly the case for regions that enjoy conditions of development comparable to Western Europe. Since these patterns are frequently not present in other regional settings, integration should be hard to attain elsewhere. This means that it would not be realistic to theorise about a universal process of integration. Haas had to concede, in 1961, that regions lacking the European environmental factors would probably not be able to imitate its success (Haas 1961: 389).

This objection, however, did not discourage neofunctionalists from producing theory-derived propositions that could be empirically tested and eventually falsified. They began suggesting possible 'functional equivalents' that would make it possible to use the newly gathered insight in areas less developed than Europe (Haas and Schmitter 1964: 274; Nye 1965; Pentland 1973: 121). Contexts and environment could now be taken into consideration as intervening factors, as long as the observer could assume that the observed phenomenon represented an equivalent solution to a problem-oriented question. Hence, if similar conditions, albeit specific to a given context, could lead to integration, they could be regarded as functional equivalents (Rosamond 2000: 70).

This insight also called for new evidence available in different regional settings. Based on the Latin American experience with the Latin American Free Trade Association (LAFTA), Haas and Schmitter refined the existing framework in 1964, and introduced the role of background conditions into the analysis of regional integration (Haas and Schmitter 1964; Rosamond 2000: 71). Neofunctioanlists could, thereafter, problematise specific socio-economic conditions that relate to the probability of integration to progress. The link between spillover and increasing levels of integration was reformulated as a 'hypothesis about the likelihood of integration when certain specified conditions are present' (Pentland 1973: 119; Haas 1967: 327–31; Schmitter 1969b: 164).

Experts and the limits of the national state

Neofunctionalism assumes that national states themselves represent the main barrier for the formation of an international community (Haas 1958, 1964a, 1964b). Therefore, many aspects of human needs can be best satisfied outside the political domain: 'weaving an ever-spreading web of international institutional relationships on the basis of meeting such needs. They would concentrate on commonly experienced needs initially, expecting the circle of the non-controversial to expand at the expense of the political, as practical cooperation became coterminous with the totality of interstate relations. At that point a true world community will have risen' (Haas 1964a: 6).

Neofunctionalism also embraces, on the one hand, a traditional functionalist assumption that there is an antagonism between technicians, experts, or professionals, who would administer 'things' (Pentland 1973: 70) and, on the other, politicians or diplomats, who would mainly rely on their understanding of the world as being a constant balancing of power. In such a cleavage, functionalists would see politics as 'identified with the pursuit of power and with residual infantile behaviour traits', whereas technical management will lead to progress and the common good. A corollary of this is that societies, where authority is exercised by politicians, parliaments or diplomats, will be dominated by disharmony. Conversely, authority exercised by technicians or groups of professionals will predominantly show harmony, because the attainment of general welfare would be one of its immediately realisable goals (Haas 1964a: 9, 13).

In its first phase, the history of European integration – a proto-integration period, according to Antje Wiener and Thomas Diez – had a strong normative agenda: trying to prevent future wars. This was also its function, and it was to be achieved by constraining states through a network of transnational organisations (Wiener and Diez 2004: 4). Furthermore, while rendering warfare impossible, these interwoven networks would perform all the traditional welfare functions of the nation state (Pentland 1973: 70). However, at the same time, a central point of functionalist theory was the idea of functional domains that allow the circumventing of direct clashes of political interests (Burley and Mattli 1993: 44; Mitrany 1966: 99).

It follows from those assumptions that, for cooperation to be successful, it should be sought in 'low key' areas like economic and social plans (Burley and Mattli 1993: 56), as opposed to political fields that could 'start a disputation'; logically, 'any working arrangement would raise a hope and make for confidence and patience' (Mitrany 1966: 99). This logic relies on key sectors driving integration; such sectors are typically 'low politics' areas like, for instance, market integration (Rosamond 2000: 51–2). Furthermore, the objectives of integration are portrayed by their advocates as neutral in substance, closely linked to technical or knowledge-based topics, which would be impossible to achieve in an arena dominated by politics (Burley and Mattli 1993: 72).

So much for the initial theoretical assumptions. However, economics and politics are impossible to separate on absolute terms, and therefore every economic decision will inexorably acquire a political significance, allowing for a gradual interpenetration of both dimensions (Burley and Mattli 1993: 72). Leon Lindberg suggested, 'There is no paradox between the progress of economic integration in the Community and sharpening political disagreement; indeed, the success of economic integration can be a cause of political disagreement' (Lindberg 1965: 80).

Although this focus on fields that are allegedly apolitical takes much inspiration from functionalism's strong divide between technical and political matters, neofunctionalism sees a certain connection between economics and politics. Therefore, issues in technical areas will always coalesce with political issues.[1] Although these clashes are expected, the actual consequences cannot be foreseen by any of the actors. Still, technocratic state officials will recognise the functional linkages and growing transnational activities, increasing their support for more integration and ceding authority to the regional level (Moravcsik 2005: 352–3; Rosamond 2000: 59). At this point, unforeseen consequences arise because events have developed beyond any planned action. In turn, by performing the necessary agency, actors can exploit such unintended consequences. The result is deepening integration in the original

---

1 According to Haas, 'the purely economic decisions always acquire political significance in the minds of the participants' (Haas 1968: 152).

sector, as well as the incorporation of a functional related sector to the process. In this way, both automatic processes and deliberate entrepreneurial activities of agents converge to spark further and deeper integration, making it irreversible (Lindberg 1966: 243; Rosamond 2000: 58–9).

Together with expansion, deepening is also inherent in neofunctionalist reasoning, and ever-deeper economic integration is one of the finest examples for such a functional spillover. The way in which the European Community for Steel and Coal transitioned to the European Monetary Union is the most noted example of deepening through politicisation: here, politics follows economics (Rosamond 2000: 60). Making decisions on allegedly technical and neutral issues allows reaching outcomes that would not be possible in 'pure' political matters. But, since there is no absolute divide between 'technical matters' and politics, following neofunctionalism, the decision will eventually acquire a political significance (Haas 1964b: 65; Burley and Mattli 1993: 72). 'The supranational style stresses the indirect penetration of the political by way of the economic because the "purely" economic decisions always acquire political significance in the minds of the participants' (Haas 1968: 65).

These ideas can eventually be materialised through the engagement of administrators and technicians, who can work along with voluntary groups of professionals in order to attain general welfare through the performance of technical and economic tasks. For instance, the establishment of a free trade area should, according to that logic, create pressure for the formation of a customs union, and subsequently for a common market and, finally, for a monetary union (cf. Balassa 1962). Progressively, such persistent pressure will begin touching upon wider aspects of the existing societal system. Conflict is inevitable as long as interests are not regarded as in need of being reconciled, but rather 'integrated' in a higher level of actors' perceptions.[2] The nation state, on the other hand, has unnaturally taken that place. As a result, 'Our social activities are cut off arbitrarily at the limit of the state and, if at all, are allowed to be linked to the same activities across the border only by means of uncertain and cramping political ligatures' (Mitrany 1966: 42).

As mentioned earlier, this is where neofunctionalists interested in market integration converge with earlier functionalists concerned with security issues: both see the nation-state as 'the chief barrier to rational organization for human welfare' (Pentland 1973: 81), obstructing any possible progress as the state is allegedly 'too weak to secure us equality and too strong to allow us liberty' (Mitrany 1933: 141; Pentland 1973: 81). Creative work is severely curtailed by arbitrary state boundaries; the activities of statesmen, parliamentarians and diplomats are consequently concerned with collective security,

---

2 Functionalists see this trait in the pre-national Guilds. Occupational groups allow for a sense of participation in the task of solving practical problems, which is closely linked to creativity, thereby leading societies towards happiness and peace (Haas 1964a: 8).

and such concerns have to do with power instead of creativity. Security issues are treated with a direct and confrontational political approach, limited by lingering nationalism, and favouring confrontation and disruption. The predominant end result is disharmony.

On the other hand, the natural grouping of humans, united in associations by occupation or fields of expertise, ignores such territorial boundaries (cf. Farrell and Héritier 2005: 274). The peace-making contribution of such groupings lies in the tasks of managing scarce resources by means of creative solutions; in other words, this means welfare rather than order (Haas 1964a: 11). By handing tasks over to these groups, the jurisdiction of 'rightful' authorities is replaced by jurisdiction based on a function: the task. Since such functional jurisdictions bluntly ignore national borders, territorial jurisdiction will become superfluous, as they would only deal with the local dimension of the general problems (Haas 1964a: 11).

International organisations, Haas says, are the ideal entities to fulfil these tasks because they feature the functions that will allow an indirect approach to community-building (Haas 1964a: 11). Similarly, Mitrany's view of a peaceful world system is one of functionally specialised global organisations run by experts (Schmitter 2005: 256; Mitrany 1966). Transnational cooperation and integration can be best achieved through transnational ties among experts – as opposed to politicians – because they would actively look for solutions to technical problems (Farrell and Héritier 2005: 274). Furthermore, as such international bodies of like-minded professionals attract people's new expectations on welfare, they build new structures as well as sentiments: loyalties begin to develop (Haas 1964a: 13).[3]

Law as a technical task

In neofunctionalist terms, the incremental logic of technical tasks that is able to expand itself equally applies to the realm of legal integration. In such an analysis, it is the logic of the law that serves as function for the expansion. The agreed objective of a common market will demand that the authority charged with the accomplishment of that particular objective overcomes any obstacle to fulfil its mission. In doing so, the authority's jurisdiction will expand so as to deal with difficulties arising from the fact that the task collides with countervailing interests. These conflicting boundaries define the parameters within

---

3 In sum, and in Engle's words, 'these three features – a reliance predominantly upon functional units, an expectation of an eventual system of government made up primarily of interlocking functional units, and the assumption that in functional cooperation certain dynamic behavioural mechanisms of an "institution-building" and a "consensus-building" nature are at work – constitute, then, the ideal type of the functionalist theory at the international level (Engle 1957: 58; cited by Haas 1964a: 14).

which the functional logic works; this is functional spillover in action (Burley and Mattli 1993: 65).

Anne-Marie Slaughter and Walter Mattli were the first to look specifically at the law in neofunctional terms. In their research, they focused on the activity of the European Court of Justice as the main actor driving legal integration ahead. Rulings like *Van Gend & Loos*, or *Costa v. ENEL* are major examples of such logic, where law fulfils a technical task in the service of market expansion (Burley and Mattli 1993: 65–6). As is explained in Chapter 3 on the ECJ, the *Costa* case and its doctrine of supremacy of European law is an indispensable step towards overcoming conflicts that arise because of expansive pressure (Mancini 1989: 600). Because member states could easily circumvent the decisions of the ECJ by simply enacting new national statutes, and invoke the legal principle according to which the newest law derogates older legislation, the Court had to take another gradual step. In order to realise the full benefits that *Van Gend en Loos* could provide, the supremacy clause had to be established (Weiler 1991: 2414). The same functional logic also affects cognate fields, broadening the scope of Community law and spilling over to such fields as health, social, sports and environment (Burley and Mattli 1993: 66).

The new version of neofunctionalism claims that transnational incrementalism led to a progressive shift in actors' loyalties and expectation, as Haas predicted in 1958 (cf. Haas 1958: 12). Law has an inherent quality of producing such effects – as long as it is perceived as law – when it commands courses of actions and provides remedies when these prescriptions are not abided by. According to Burley and Mattli, a 'major function of a legal rule is to provide a clear and certain standard around which expectations can crystallize' (Burley and Mattli 1993: 67). Applied to a judicial process at EC level, this means that, although member states can certainly fight a court action filed by an individual wanting to advance his or her individual interests by means of a European rule, once a ruling has been acknowledged as pertaining to actual law, the same member states will begin using the arguments contained in it and will thereby shift their legal standpoints when it comes to a next round in Luxembourg. There is no evidence that the opposite might happen: that is to say, that member states might try to get a prior precedent to be declared overruled (Rasmussen 1986: 275–81). Political spillover accounts for this dynamic.

The empirical findings provided by ECSC, the EEC and Euratom led earlier neofunctionalists to construct a framework for the study of regional integration, with a basic logical argument: namely that when two or more states agree to advance integration in a certain sector, they appoint a supranational bureaucracy that can monitor the process. But, in order to achieve the full benefit of integration in a given sector, related sectors have to be considered and included in this process. This circumstance produces pressure on cognate sectors to join the integration process, rendering the expansions of the scope of integration a function for achieving the benefits of integration in the original sector. Hence, functional linkages are created among different sectors. Automatic processes begin at this point. The first of them is the increase in transnational transactions between actors within the integrating sector (Rosamond 2000: 58). Given that European integration was launched in the economic sector, neofunctionalists focused on transnational economic activities for establishing their framework (Stone Sweet 2004b). These activities would lead actors within the specific sector to gather at regional level in new groups that represented their interests. Even the sponsoring 'high authority' would encourage these actors to form new regional groups, and permanently advocate for the advantages that could be drawn from integration, especially by exploiting the inevitable 'unintended consequences' that occur when external effects arise during the pursuit of common tasks (Schmitter 2005: 256; Haas and Schmitter 1964: 708).

The concept of spillover

Neofunctionalism assumes that benefits of integration become visible to domestically located interest groups. These groups, in turn, will lobby their governments to influence them and reap the benefits (Rosamond 2000: 59). This assumption relies on heavy rationalistic and utilitarian notions of actors' behaviour; actors are assumed to drive the process as rational maximisers of their narrow self-interest (Mattli 2005: 330; Rosamond 2000: 66). It presupposes that interest groups are in a position to identify those agents that can deliver solutions and satisfy their needs, regardless of ordinary ambiguities that faceless agents might show (Rosamond 2000: 66; Lodge 1978).[4]

It is at this point where the interest groups change the target of their efforts for the satisfaction of several expectations, commanding their loyalties towards the new agent. This is what Haas understood under 'shift of loyalties'; that is to say, the actors' obedience to the injunction of authority of symbols and institutions, to whom they turn for the satisfaction of their important expectations. His words became a seminal statement for integration studies: 'political actors in several distinct national settings are persuaded to shift their loyalties, expectations, and political activities towards a new and larger center whose institutions possess or demand jurisdiction over the pre-existing national states' (Haas 1961: 366; 1958: 12).[5] Neofunctionalism, however,

---

4 In this regard, Haas claimed that the 'good Europeans' were those who created in the regional community nationally constituted interest groups willing to use supranational means to their benefit (Haas 1958: xiv).
5 It should be noted that Haas was not concerned about the behaviour of mass population, but rather about the elites (Haas 1964a: 45–6). The whole project of European integration was an elite-driven project and, since the elites were to benefit most from integration, it would be precisely them who would be more likely to shift their loyalties towards Europe (although

does not focus on the interests of societal and business elites, but on the role they play in the process; when pursuing the fulfilment of their needs and interests, these elites can strategically use the new supranational institutions and, because of the spillover effect and the link between policy fields, advance further integration in an unintended way (Wiener 2003: 17–18). To be sure, this shift does not imply an immediate repudiation of the nation state or the government, because 'dual loyalties' are perfectly possible (Haas 1958: 14–15; Risse 2005: 295).[6] Furthermore, if the process of dual loyalties is persistent and satisfactory over time, 'the central institutions could ultimately acquire the symbolic significance of end value' (Haas 1958: 14–15).

The mechanism presupposes technocratic state officials recognising the functional linkages and growing transnational activities, increasing their support for more integration and ceding authority to the regional level (Moravcsik 2005: 352–3; Rosamond 2000: 59).

The concept of spillover seems to be the most characteristic and, at the same time, the most disputed contribution of neofunctionalism, and was introduced to depict the mechanism that drove progress in regional integration. In general, spillover stands for pressure that neofunctionalists claimed to see during the process of integration, which demands further integration (Rosamond 2000: 51, 60). Emphasising the pressure exerted over actors, it can be defined as a situation where 'imbalances created by the functional interdependence or inherent linkages of tasks can press political actors to redefine their common tasks' (Nye 1971). Thus, achieving the full benefit of integration in a given sector is assumed to be desirable. But this full benefit that comes along with integration in a given sector can only be achieved by incorporating related sectors into the process (Rosamond 2000: 60). Centralised institutions will increase support for integration; but, at the same time, they will not be able to satisfy the needs of the new clients, thus provoking a spillover into a linked sector not yet integrated, and become the focus of demands for more integration (Haas 1991: 23; Farrell and Héritier 2005: 274; Pentland 1973: 118–19). Partial results within a sector lead to dissatisfactions; pressure arises, then, to expand the scope of integration by means of centralising further action (Haas 1958).

Because modern industrial economies are interdependent (Mutimer 1989; Schmitter 2005: 268), advancing integration within a single sector will create 'a situation in which the original goal can be assured only by taking further

---

Thomas Risse calls this into question; Risse 2005: 297). According to Risse: 'If this were the case, farmers should be the most ardent supporters of the EU, throwing their tomatoes at Euro-sceptics rather than at bureaucrats in Brussels' (Risse 2005: 305).
6 Thomas Risse acknowledged Haas' early thinking about multiple loyalties: 'It is wrong to conceptualise European identity in zero-sum terms, as if an increase in European identity necessarily decreases one's loyalty to national or other communities' (Risse 2005: 295).

actions, which in turn create a further condition and a need for more action and so forth' (Lindberg 1963: 10; Haas 1968: 484).[7] If spillover is to rest on such an assumption, its logic becomes inherently expansive (see Rosamond 2000: 60). In order to maintain progress in a specific sector, the logic requires intervention in another sector.[8] But this measure will, again, create conditions for subsequent actions, and so on and so forth (Burley and Mattli 1993: 55), since 'policies made pursuant to an initial task and grant of power can be made real only if the task itself is expanded, as reflected in the compromises among the states interested in the task' (Haas 1961: 368).

As the progress of sectoral integration becomes visible, citizens become aware of this fact and begin to pay attention to the many ways in which the community affects their daily life, leaving new winners and new losers at the end of the day (Schmitter 2005); thus, some degree of uncertainty about *who* is going to be a winner, and *who* is going to be a loser, is necessary for the union to hold. From the moment actors realise that they are not going to reap any benefit from the process, disintegration might arise (Haas and Schmitter 1964: 708; Schmitter 2005: 268). But, in contrast to benefits that might arise from a mere cooperative reduction of tariffs, the expectations sparked by sectoral integration begin to transit from the nation state to a new and larger entity (Haas and Schmitter 1964: 710). Therefore, such a mechanism entails some agency: economics is not enough to vanquish politics (Haas 1968: xix). This adaptive behaviour of interest groups, as a response to sectoral integration, was identified by Haas as an 'incremental shifting of expectations' and conceptualised as political spillover (Burley and Mattli 1993: 55).

Within the explanation for expansive integration, the notion of the 'upgrading of common interests' is also part of the causal mechanism. When member states experience difficulties in achieving certain common policies, pressure on them to overcome the logic of the minimum common denominator begins to grow, especially because they have acknowledged the necessity of safeguarding other aspects of their interdependence (Burley and Mattli 1993: 56).

---

7 Accordingly, isolating the coal and steel industry from the rest of the economy is artificial; it has a security aim – making war as difficult as possible – but, as the sector tends to develop, its logical boundaries would be reached very soon (Haas 1968: 243; Pentland 1973: 78–9). An early test for the market of coal and steel came with inflationary tendencies in several ECSC countries, and the pressure for harmonising wages and social security prices increased, since member states had been influencing the price structure of the coal and steel industry. Therefore, and following the same logic of tasks expansion, the Council of Ministers became aware of the difficulties of effective policy-making in the coal industry if the Community continued lacking authority over other kind of fuel and its prices (Haas 1968: 105, 106).

8 Accordingly, the establishment of a free trade area will create pressure for the establishment of a customs union, and subsequently for a common market, and finally for a monetary union (Rosamond 2000: 60; Balassa 1962).

Nevertheless, member states face high transaction costs associated with interstate bargaining. Supranational authorities, on the contrary, do not, and can therefore efficiently initiate, mediate, and mobilise interest groups that hinge around the general goals of the framework arrangement. In the case of European integration, the European Commission, the Court, and the Parliament become supranational entrepreneurs, and conspicuous leaders like Jean Monnet or Jacques Delors have used every round of negotiations to set the course in the direction favoured by the European technocracy and increase the efficiency of supranational bargaining (for a different account of the role played by Jean Monnet and Jacques Delors, see Moravcsik 1998).

Early functionalist writers noted that international organisations – entirely dependent at first on national support – gradually establish their competence to perform functional tasks on their own with reference to a global social system (Pentland 1973: 76). Similarly, supranational institutions are 'able to construct patterns of mutual concessions from various policy contexts and in so doing usually manage to upgrade [their] own powers at the expense of the member governments' (Haas 1968: 152). The goal of reaching a common stand is best mediated by supranational institutions because they represent the common interests that motivated the member states to unite (Lindberg 1963: 8–9). Supranational institutions expand the political system by channelling the flow of information and socialising actors to new norms, thus providing a permanent arena for conflict resolution (Pentland 1973: 117).

Often, this action is facilitated by frequent fragmentation of positions among member states' governments. Sometimes, and in certain policy fields, a single government can oppose the expansion of supranational tasks; but, at other times, in a different policy field, that same government might very well favour more supranational action. Sectoral integration becomes difficult. In functionalist terms, these institutions are spawned with the sole purpose of overcoming these difficulties, although there is no blueprint as to how the solutions should look (Pentland 1973: 78). Consequently, a resourceful supranational authority, anxious to accelerate the spillover process, could figure out strategies across different policy fields, availing itself of the fact that government representatives have both short-term and long-term aims and, therefore, never use opposition to further integration as a permanent strategy (Haas 1968: 482). In this way, supranational officials become essential in the advancement of integrationist ideas, with every opportunity that arises to increase their own role (Pentland 1973: 123). Their autonomy helps explain the success because without them interstate bargaining would remain the lowest common denominator (Moravcsik 1998: 54); therefore, it suffices that their discourse stresses 'that the ends already agreed upon cannot be attained without further united steps', compensating eventual opponents to further integration (Haas 1968: 484; Haas and Schmitter 1964: 708).

A supranational court certainly possesses supranational authority, but it is not a mediator that can barter concessions in order to overcome a deadlock, or upgrade the minimal common denominator in a negotiation (Burley and Mattli 1993: 68). Courts have to adjudicate and are not committed to any other outcome but the respect for the law. Nevertheless, European integration has shown that a supranational court can consistently link the interpretation of the law to common objectives and goals, such as the rule of law, economic growth and efficiency (Burley and Mattli 1993: 72) by means of a teleological interpretation of the treaty. Therefore, courts can accentuate the higher interest that a member state is allegedly honouring whenever it has to yield to a ruling enhancing the authority of supranational law. In the case of the ECJ and its case law, such assertions were made through 'concepts such as the customs union, equality of treatment and non-discrimination, freedom of movement, mutual assistance and solidarity, economic interpenetration and finally economic and legal unity as the supreme objective' (Pescatore 1974: 88). These 'formulas', depicting the customs union as one of the 'foundations of the Community', the role of which are essential for integration, were repeatedly used by the ECJ in its case law (Pescatore 1985: 89).

Scope conditions for spillover in legal integration

The magic triangle

Following the logic proposed by neofunctionalism, integration in the legal domain requires conditions for the spillover mechanism to work. Neofunctionalists have suggested three main conditions. These are the doctrines of direct effect, supremacy, and the preliminary ruling procedure – the 'magic triangle' postulated as the story's backbone (Vauchez 2008).

The saga inspired by European legal integration begins with the judicial forging of a set of principles by the European Court of Justice, and the introduction of the doctrines of direct effect and supremacy of European law; the principle of member states' responsibility for breaching EC law; and, lastly, the role as a court of constitutional review. Once these conditions have been established, the Court will not eschew taking a proactive function of driving the Community towards further and deeper integration. The Court acts as a motor of integration just like an engine would propel a vehicle (Hunt and Shaw 2009: 103). Using a creative metaphor inspired in architecture, Mancini and Keeling suggest that:

> If the doctrines of direct effect and supremacy are ... the 'twin pillars of the Community's legal system', the [preliminary ruling] reference procedure ... must surely be the keystone in the edifice; without it the roof would collapse and the two pillars would be left as a desolate ruin, evocative of the temple at Cape Sounion – beautiful but not of much practical utility.
>
> (Mancini and Keeling 1992: 2–3)

The doctrines provide the normative pull that compels states to stick to their promises by including the ordinary citizen as an agent of the clockwork. From the perspective of neofunctionalism, this trait is what distinguishes the Community from an ordinary international organisation (Mancini and Keeling 1992: 183).

The third component of the magic triangle, namely the procedure of preliminary rulings, provides the technical setting where the disputes take place. Contrary to some legal disputes between states or disputes in multilateral forums, where the dispute is settled by arbiters, mediators or even panels, the quarrel between the individual and the member state is mediated by courts: national and supranational. Pre-established procedures dominate the style of argumentation, as well as the language that parties have to use. As member states are parties to these given judicial processes at national level, they see themselves forced to enter the national judicial arena, where the supranational court is widely dominant (Weiler 1994: 519; Alter 1998: 133).

Once the parties converge at the national judicial level, the Court consistently presents itself as acting within a non-politicised environment. This strategy reminds us of the claim that economics and politics were allegedly separate fields; a point made by early neofunctionalists. Here in the legal realm the Court would promote the idea that it had to resolve 'technical' matters. There is allegedly no room for political considerations. It resembles an ideology of political asepticism. But an absolute divide between law and politics is just as impossible as between economics and politics and, therefore, the political impact of judicial decisions can be ameliorated by the initial aura of political neutrality (Burley and Mattli 1993: 69). If politics and law cannot be kept absolutely isolated from one another, then speaking of technical decisions in a political vacuum would boil down to a fiction.

Advocates of this kind of legal integration usually portray court rulings as technical or neutral. Nevertheless, a key for understanding the consequences of such a dynamic is that, although such judicial decisions indeed end up acquiring a political substrate, they are not fully political in nature. Therefore, when criticism arises from a political arena, the 'shield' of law's non-political rationale drives the debate back to the technical arena. The consequence is that political attacks on judicial rulings are forced to counter-argue according to non-political criteria. Burley and Mattli called this sequence a 'battle by proxy' (Burley and Mattli 1993: 72). In this regard, the law acts as a 'mask' that hides the political agenda judges might be trying to advance. The assumption is that those political actors that would supposedly resist activist rulings coming from the ECJ do not fully understand the implications of the day-to-day political process that such highly doctrinal contents could beget. The arcane legal jargon obscures the ramifications of the decisions (Burley and Mattli 1993: 72–3).

Finally, if national courts accept the ruling handed down by the Community's court, there will be hardly any diplomatic means at the government's disposal that might dispute the compliance-pull of the preliminary ruling; as Joseph Weiler puts it, 'the legal arena imposes different rules of discourse' (see Weiler 1994: 519). Hence, according to neofunctionalists, the domestic judiciaries cooperate with the ECJ via article 234 TEC (ex 177) in order to enhance their own power and increase their authority. Through the procedure of preliminary rulings, national judges gradually assume the functions of agents of the Community legal order (Stone Sweet and Brunell 2004: 97).

The role of private litigants

One of the weaknesses of early neofunctionalism was that it neglected the role played by private actors, especially private litigants. Although Haas' neofunctionalism acknowledged the role of interest groups in general, it was merely assumed that they acted upon 'self-interest' (Haas 1964a: 128). But this assumption does not account for many other phenomena where functionality and national identity converge, like public interest litigation (Mattli and Slaughter 1998: 184). The new framework disaggregates the state into several actors, moving beyond the bold assumption that states are unitary actors. Within the states, there is a government, but there are also several governmental branches that often collaborate with the executive, though sometimes they compete; there is also an array of subnational actors that interact with state officials, and it would be wrong and misleading to assume that they all share the same interests of their member states (Mattli and Slaughter 1996, 1998; Burley and Mattli 1993). On the contrary, such states summon a diversity of interests and players – private litigants in particular – that do not necessarily match the interests of their governments (Stone Sweet *et al.* 2001).

In this regard, the working assumption of the neofunctionalism of Slaughter (formerly Burley) and Mattli is that private litigants pursue outcomes that would not normally be feasible by deploying the means available solely at the national level. Since supranational courts sit on the outside of the national process, litigants can resort to the preliminary rulings procedure whenever there is a transnational link in the controversy. However, this does not mean that private litigants have a vested interest in promoting transnational trade; rather, it is an assumption that private litigants will challenge rules they do not like, whether they do or do not bolster the establishment of a common market (Alter 2001: 53).

Moreover, not all litigants have the same strategies when it comes to litigating at supranational level. A first distinction that must be made relates to the frequency of litigation, for there are individuals who go to court only when a certain problem arises, and seek remedy for this matter only. This is a 'one-shooter', who gives priority to winning his or her own case (Mattli and Slaughter 1998: 187–8; Galanter 1974). Conversely, there are litigants who turn to courts on a frequent basis and are, therefore, not constrained by a single judicial outcome; rather they are constrained by an overall set of judicial cycles that allows them to influence policy outcomes – or, in Galanter's words, a 'rule gain'. Put simply, for repeated players it is not about winning a battle, but 'winning the war' (Mattli and Slaughter 1998: 190). By having a consistent litigation strategy over time, interest groups can hold a sustained attack on given policies, like the Sunday trading saga before the ECJ (Mattli and Slaughter 1998: 188; Rawlings 1993), or preparing necessary conditions in order to favour desired policy outcomes. In other words, private actors can further their individual interests by means of a strategic use of preliminary rulings (Stone Sweet and Brunell 2004: 52–5) and exert influence on the policy-making process, with the aim of changing less favourable norms into more favourable ones (Stone Sweet and Brunell 2004: 9, 10).

The individual might have particular policy preferences. However, he or she is not politically biased, and therefore small infringements are just as likely to be brought before the Court as larger violations; and, 'in terms of monitoring, the Community citizen becomes, willy-nilly, a decentralized agent for monitoring compliance by Member States with their Treaty obligations' (Weiler 1991: 2421). It follows from this contention that commitment institutions are more effective if they grant private actors access to the Court (Alter 2006: 25), especially those individuals with the greatest vested interest in advancing integration (Mattli 1999a: 14). Accordingly, individuals act with the conviction that they might reap gains from integration. The expected gains, of course, will be greater if the size of the integrating market is bigger (see Mattli 1999a: 20).

Some scholars have seen private litigation as a driving force within a general framework on judicial governance in Europe. Their starting point is the assumption of demand for integration by transnational entrepreneurs – generally, importers and exporters. As transnational transactions increase in number, so do conflicts between national law and EC law. According to the framework, this will necessarily lead to more transnational litigation. In their study on judicial governance in Europe, Stone Sweet and Brunell stress the correlation between rates of references to the ECJ and rates of transnational economic activity in order to test their hypothesis (Stone Sweet and Brunell 2004).

It follows, according to neofunctionalism, that, if the scope conditions presented above are present, courts will expand supranational law. In order to test the theory and assess an eventual expansive jurisprudence in any comparable case, we must know in advance what will constitute an expansive or activist judicial behaviour for our research. In the next section, I present a framework for judicial activism that is apt for the purpose of testing supranational courts.

Judicial politics and judicial activism

It is not easy to explain why a Court becomes an activist court. Indeed, it is difficult to describe what activism really is (see the interesting rhetoric in Koopmans 1978: 317, 326). There is no unitary understanding of what judicial activism should mean. To start with, this concept should be differentiated from the term of an 'active court'. An active court is one that exercises its ordinary task, as opposed to an inactive court, which is not performing any judicial tasks, be it permanently or temporarily. Judicial activism, as an inflation denoted by the suffix 'ism', points to hyperbolic action. It suggests that a certain action is part of a distinctive doctrine or cause, as opposed to an ordinary course of action.

Some writers take a normative stance regarding judicial activism. In this sense, judicial activism becomes the doctrine of wrongful activity. Accordingly, an activist court acts when it should, instead, abstain; similarly, an activist court typically acts in a manner that is incorrect – or, more specifically, unconstitutional. These views link activism with misuse of judicial power, and denote activity in a manner or opportunity that is not foreseen by the law or is oriented to achieve a predetermined result (Kmiec 2004: 1447). Other writers measure judicial activism with the proxy of exercising judicial review, or striking down legislation enacted by other branches of government. This practice is frequently linked to the protection of rights that have been entrenched within constitutions. It goes hand in hand with the conviction that higher values or higher rights could be in danger if left to the discretion of the legislator.

Such doctrines imply a loss of confidence in the 'wisdom' of parliaments and majoritarian law-makers (Koopmans 1978: 321). The problem with this perspective, however, is that it still needs a normative judgement to determine the threshold of judicial review, beyond which striking down legislation becomes judicial activism (e.g. Ringhand 2007). Setting such a threshold that separates legitimate judicial review from judicial activism is neither easy nor uncontroversial. We might settle on a given number of provoking rulings before a court is officially considered to be an activist court. But then, we would like to know whether there could be degrees of judicial activism. American scholars of constitutional law have, therefore, developed research designs that compare fellow judges within the same court, as well as their behaviour over time (cf. Cross and Lindquist 2007). This means that judicial review can be assessed in relative terms.

Judicial activism can also be understood as a kind of 'exorbitant action'; in other words, behaviour that radically departs from established patterns or bluntly ignores existing precedents (Breyer 2006). In European integration studies, this proxy has proven very useful, as the radical departure of the ECJ from established doctrines of international public law is precisely the puzzle that scholars are trying to solve, and all the relevant theories of European integration concede that a transformation has indeed taken place. Joseph Weiler referred to this behaviour when he characterised judicial expansion as 'the case in which the original legislation of the Community "breaks" jurisdictional limits' (Weiler 1991).

Theories of European integration have made their general assumptions when resorting to more than one paradigm of judicial activism. Judicial review, disregarding precedents, and 'constitutional quarrels' are all elements that are present in their hypothesis. For one thing, neofunctionalism relies on the assumption that judges are permanently interested in practising judicial review, especially if they lack that attribution in regards to the national legal system. Practising judicial review over national executives – in the place of national higher courts – seduces judges 'both on a common-sense psychological level and on an institutional plane as well' (Weiler 1994: 523); this is because they get to rule on matters that are more interesting, and increase their influence vis-à-vis politicians (Alter 2001: 42; Weiler 1991: 2426). Working assumptions on judicial interests is also a cornerstone for explaining the constitutionalisation of the Treaty of Rome. In the specific case of the tandem relationship between the ECJ and national courts, judges are not regarded as an epistemic community, because they do not share a belief, or a set of policies, nor do they promote a particular type of legal decision-making; hence, judges are to be regarded as bureaucrats who are interested in being promoted, gaining independence, influence and authority, and serving the state with their judicial service (Alter 2001: 45–51; Haas 1992).

A court's legitimacy has also been seen as an intervening factor that might shape the boundaries of judicial discretion. Even if we understand law in neofunctionalist terms, we still have to acknowledge that law requires judges to respect minimal legal criteria if they want to keep the non-partisan aura upon the law (Helfer and Slaughter 1997: 356). It must not be forgotten that, although judges have the power to influence the political process, they are under normative constraints that limit their free discretion because every legal solution that is chosen can disrupt the 'internal coherence, consistency and links among the various norms' (Canor 1998: 15, fn. 22). Only in this way can law perform its political function of acting as a mask and as a shield[9] in order to advance its agenda of constructing a community's legal system (Burley and Mattli 1993: 73). Scholars who have observed judicial behaviour from a governance perspective suggest that certain judicial decisions 'lock-in', making judges path-dependent.[10] Alec Stone Sweet claims that sustained litigation can lead adjudication to become a mode of governance and, given that litigation is a continuous process, judges are in a permanent legitimacy crisis. Judicialisation, he argues, constantly requires that judges give reasons for their rulings as well as for *how* the law should be interpreted. This will be impossible for judges that persistently produce 'capricious rulings' (Stone Sweet 2004a: 6, 12).

---

9 See above, p. 23.
10 It must be clarified, however, that this approach contends that judicial path-dependency is contingent upon the social feedback that judges receive for their decisions (Stone Sweet 2004a: 31).

A more formalist argument suggests that judicial rulings are a scientific endeavour, and therefore develop beyond political questions. Sketched in this way, court rulings are allegedly neutral to political claims (Weiler 1994: 525). Moreover, the mere appearance that a court is basing its decision on reasoning that is immune from political pressure already increases the legitimacy of such rulings (Helfer and Slaughter 1997: 353). This is especially the case for 'unpleasant decisions', which people seem to be more inclined to accept when they have the conviction that they have been rigorously deduced from legal principles (Murphy 1964: 17).

The circumstance in which rulings are followed and complied with is also a factor that can shape judicial behaviour. Judges are less likely to be satisfied with a situation where their rulings are disobeyed. On the one hand, it would mean a contravention to general rules of the division of powers that determine the existence of the rule of law in a liberal democracy. This is only possible if there is a shared belief that conflicts will be solved by judges and not by means of self-justice. According to this institutional view, failing to accept a judicial decision means undermining the judicial authority within the political system; this is because the assumption is that judicial power is exerted through authority and, although it is utopian for any legal order to achieve complete obedience, it implies that any case of non-compliance will have negative effects on the judiciary as a whole. Exacerbating this view runs the danger of increasing the fragility of the law and judicial dispute settlement; in other words, if judges are ignored, judicial institutions will be curtailed and, in turn, the broad political system will be affected. This view can be found in many writings on the ECJ, as Stanley Hoffmann states:

> [The] normative order itself, when practice contradicts it blatantly and repeatedly usually ends up collapsing-which means that the law ceases to be taken seriously. A violation is no longer perceived as such, nor are the provisions of the law any longer seen as conferring genuine rights and duties: we are merely in the realm of rhetoric, not of norms ... For any normative order to deserve being called by that name, it must partake both of the realm of 'oughts' and of the empirical one: it must be at least in part a set of some rules of actual behavior; it must not only ask, but actually inspire, some practise. Otherwise it withers away.
> (Hoffmann 1987: 375)[11]

In addition, open defiance of judicial decisions undermines the legitimacy of the individual judge vis-à-vis his or her peers. In this view, the judge is not measured corporatively, but individually against other judges whose rulings are not ignored. Furthermore, when his or her rulings are non-complied with,

---

11 Cf. Alter 2001: 211–12.

it is not judicial institutions that are undermined generally, but an individual career (Alter 2001: 45). This view stresses the bureaucratic character of the judiciary.

It has been suggested that courts, especially constitutional courts, have ample discretion to cast their rulings, as they can fill in incomplete contracting. This assertion is closely connected with principal-agent theory. Treaties, according to the argument, are frameworks that cannot rule every possible situation into the future (Garrett and Weingast 1993: 27–8). Thus, the principal (the framers of the treaty) delegates authority to an agent (the Court) to apply general rules to concrete future situations. Stated in these terms, the general character of a treaty is a virtuous trait: it allows parties to agree on general issues and lets polemic disagreements be solved further ahead in time. To be sure, this comes at the cost of uncertainty about whether the agent will decide the cases in the exact manner as the principal – the framer – would have done it. Alec Stone Sweet uses such a framework as a starting point for his analysis. However, he immediately renounces some of the assumptions of the principal-agent approach, as he intends to capture a judicial mode of governance, where it is the principal who governs the principles, but it is the agent who has the powers to make rules.

> Of course, any state of normative uncertainty constitutes a delegation of discretion to judges. From the point of view of the Member States, generalities and vagueness may have facilitated agreement. But vagueness, by definition, is normative uncertainty, which threatens to undermine rationales for contracting in the first place. For those who are governed by EC law, indeterminacy itself may generate conflict and thereby spur litigation; and litigation provides judges with opportunities to make law real and effective for these same actors. The establishment of the ECJ therefore can be understood as an institutional response to the incomplete contract, that is, as a solution to a set of general commitment problems.
> (Stone Sweet 2004a: 25)

Against the backdrop of such diverse notions of judicial activism, it becomes important, if we want to assess judicial activism, to reflect upon what activism is *not*. One could think of the antonym of activism: passivism. But this does not seem to be very helpful, because it would be an equally relative term, i.e. allowing executives to overstep existing boundaries without ruling on it. Instead, we should be asking about the normal state of judicial action, thereby understanding activism as something extraordinary that can be measured against normality – or, even better, the maintenance of the status quo.[12]

---

12 Which could also be the measurement for judicial passivism. The same applies for an ordinary measurement of temperature, where we enquire how many degrees above the value

The kind of behaviour with which we should compare judicial activism is judicial self-restraint. The model would link judicial action with changes in prevailing law. If such judicial action produces changes in prevailing law, it will be suspicious for incurring in activism. If, notwithstanding pressure for activism, the status quo is maintained because of the action of the courts, it should be considered self-restraint (Canor 1998: 212). Following the logic, the term we just found unhelpful, namely judicial passivism, would entail a court allowing changes in prevailing law precisely because it refuses to act.

In the light of such an uncertain meaning of judicial activism, I will concentrate on two main traits that have been identified by scholarship. The framework becomes manageable for analysing activism in a scheme of legal integration. Therefore, I understand the following:

1 Judicial activism means a substantial departure from precedents or previous traditions that are in place at the time of the ruling.
2 Judicial activism means striking down national legislation, especially those related to 'constitutional quarrels', which seek to reshape domestic law.
3 Judicial activism means expanding the court's own authority.

Why some judicial rulings are accepted and others are not has always been an intriguing question. In addressing this puzzle, scholars of European legal integration have developed a model that aims to offer some explanation regarding supranational jurisprudence. They start from the observation that there is much variation in the levels of acceptance of rulings handed down by comparable courts.

One explanatory model refers to judicial competition. Competition between judges can be either horizontal, mainly between higher courts, or vertical. The competition model has the merit of accounting for the quest for power, since those courts that already exert power or enjoy prestige will not pursue disruptive rulings. Conversely, lower courts striving for power or prestige will, most likely, accept innovating or disruptive rulings (Mattli and Slaughter 1998: 192). But competition presents itself across member states, too. As Weiler suggests:

> Once some of the highest courts of a few of the Member States endorsed the new constitutional construct, their counterparts in other Member States heard more arguments that those courts should do the same, and it became more difficult for national courts to resist the trend with any modicum of credibility.
> (Weiler 1991: 2425)

zero can be read on the thermometer. We do not measure warm temperature against a negative value.

But inter-court competition is not the only criterion that has caught the attention of legal integration scholars. Differences across member states regarding access to the judicial arena, for instance, are also linked to diverging patterns of adaptation, or Europeanisation of national courts (Conant 2001: 105). Accordingly, there is a strong correlation between national substantive law and institutional fit, and this is why Germany allegedly shows a better record in Europeanisation than Great Britain or France. The German Constitutional Court has played an important role performing 'judicial lawmaking' within the domestic realm. Conversely, a French *gouvernement des juges* is very limited (Conant 2001: 103; for a similar argument, see Stone Sweet and Brunell 2004: 104). One could make a similar claim focusing on national constitutional culture. In this regard, it makes a difference if a state already has a means of judicial review in its legal system (Mattli and Slaughter 1998: 196).

Other models suggest that promoting substantive policies is important to courts (Mattli and Slaughter 1998: 191). Yet, how can judges' preferences possibly be identified? Golub has argued that patterns of reference can reveal certain preferences (Golub 1996). If it is true that judicial preferences can be identified and also operationalised, then the analytical framework for judicial politics could be considerably enhanced with new intervening factors, motivations or constraints that determine judicial behaviour. Mattli and Slaughter claim that some of these important judicial constraints include a minimal fidelity of the legal discourse, and a minimal democratic accountability (Mattli and Slaughter 1998: 194).

The neofunctionalist hypothesis

In sum, the hypothesis that can be uncovered from the neofunctionalist approach suggests that legal integration in the Andean Community will be advanced by the Andean Court of Justice through expansive law-making. This should take place even if it contradicts member states' governments.

There are several initial conditions for the hypothesis to work. Some are general and point to regional integration, while some are particular to legal integration. General conditions for regional integration to be successful include measures of sectorial integration. This is to say, integration has to be planned to occur in a field that is governed by technical knowledge producing benefits for certain individuals. Economics and law are such fields, as they distinguish certain experts as having a qualified role. In the case of lawyers and judges, specific qualifying knowledge and, to some extent, even limited admission to exercise the profession, qualifies them as experts in their field.

Furthermore, individuals who might benefit from such integration must have the possibility to organise themselves so that they can be in a position to demand more integration in a particular field. This condition is represented by the existence of minimal levels of pluralism. In the legal field, individuals should be granted access to justice if they are to file their claims in favour of more integration. From the moment individuals are deprived from access to justice, there can be no demand for further integration.

Specific conditions for successful legal integration include the appointment of a supranational body with the authority to make compulsory interpretations of supranational law; this is to say, a supranational court. Furthermore, the institutions of the 'magic triangle' should be established: a procedure of preliminary rulings, the doctrines of direct effect and supremacy of Community law.

The procedure of preliminary ruling is a condition that enables private litigants to reach the supranational courts, thus granting them access through procedures opened at the national level. In addition, preliminary rulings allow the supranational court to hand down its authoritative interpretation of Community law, and trusting its enforcement to the national tribunal that requested them.

The doctrine of direct effect is a necessary condition inasmuch as legal standing is given to private litigants, who would normally be neglected by rules of international public law. In turn, the doctrine of supremacy of Community law is a requirement for direct effect to be effective; this is so, because of the legal principle that states that a law can be derogated by a subsequent law regulating the same matter. This means that the last law derogates the prior law – *lex posteriori derogat*.

If the conditions are present in the Andean Community, the hypothesis foresees that private entrepreneurs in the Andean region will recognise eventual benefits that stem from supranational legislation in contrast to national legislation. These individuals will challenge national legislation before national courts invoking Andean law. The individual will become a private litigant and dispute any interpretation of Community law made by its government, as it is Andean law that offers increasing benefits for him or her.

Once the national court has been activated, it will realise that the interpretation of Andean law is at stake. As a consequence, it will refer the cases to the Andean Court of Justice requesting an interpretation of Andean law. Member states, represented by their governments, are expected to oppose the claim, albeit under the jurisdiction of the national court.

The Andean Court of Justice will interpret the relevant provision of Community law expansively; in other words, in a way that furthers its scope of application. As is the case in all other international treaties, questions regarding new, unforeseen situations will arise, creating a situation of incomplete contracting. The court will be called to fill in the gaps in the law.

The legal logic on which such decisions should be based will be teleological. In other words, the expansion of the scope of Andean law serves the accomplishment of the goals established by the member states in the foundational treaty.

As this expansion entails that Community law penetrates national law, this is making Andean law enforceable at the domestic level against the member states; as a result, governments are expected to oppose the expansive interpretation. However, since the relevant judicial controversies take place within a national judicial process, the arguments are stated in legal terms. In other words, unlike a diplomatic quarrel, the controversy is led here by legal practitioners and judges. Since it is the national judge who will finally enforce Andean law, governments will not be able to stop the expansion of Andean law.

The neofunctionalist hypothesis, then, reads as follows. If the institutional conditions are given this is, a supranational court, a procedure of preliminary ruling, and doctrines of direct effect and supremacy; then, the ACJ's rulings will gradually penetrate the national legal system by means of expansive interpretation. This interpretation will lead to an enhanced enforcement of Community law against member states. As member states cannot disregard their own justice, compliance with Andean law will increase. Increased compliance with Andean law will result in advancement of the overall process of regional integration in the Andean Community.

Intergovernmentalism

States as principal actors

The Single European Act (SEA) provided major institutional reform for the Treaties of Rome in 1987; a theoretical renewal accompanied the new institutional dynamism that was observable within the EC system. The SEA not only established a framework with expanded EC policy competencies, it also laid down a timetable for the completion of the European internal market. This facilitated a broad debate on the future of European integration in general, and the grand theories in particular. Scholars contested federalists' claims and pointed to the fact that the EC never became a super state, or any kind of federation. States, it is suggested, never lost significance in the international system and, even in a sophisticated setting as the EC, they were far from having been cast to the peripheries of political action, as functional theories would predict (Puchala 1972: 273; Rosamond 2000: 130; Hoffmann 1966). In addition, neofunctionalism was contested in that the relations between European states were quite similar to those between states elsewhere (Taylor 1983: 60).

Intergovernmentalism rejects the idea that European integration has been driven by a committed, technocratic bureaucracy that advocated for economic planning, and exploited unintended consequences of previous decisions (Moravcsik 1998: 4). Member states, intergovernmentalism assumes, can be committed to integration and push towards that goal, but the decisive mechanisms for such ends and for solving states' main problems remain intergovernmental arrangements, be they within the Community or with non-members (Dahrendorf 1973). Even conspicuous statesmen like de Gaulle would welcome active problem-solving strategies within the Community – though in terms specific to the member states (Lindberg 1966), and always within the context of significant agreements between governments. In the case of European integration, they argue, the outcome is not a consequence of supranational actors circumventing the will of member states' executives; rather, the outcome is decisively shaped by the relative power of member states and, therefore, reflects the will of member states as they are the source of the authority that drives European integration, be it as a product of inter-state bargains, pooling of sovereignty, or delegation of competences (Moravcsik 1998: 7).[13] It follows that even the existence of an eventual network that can

---

13 With the benefit of hindsight, it seems that Haas failed to give a neofunctionalist account of the 'empty-chair' crisis (Hoffmann 1966), for he suggests that the driving force pushing charismatic leaders to constantly oppose the strengthening of supranational institutions is not more than a candid vanity, a certain *Grosspolitik*, that claims for leadership in Europe, and for the case of France, an imagery that praises more importance to resist the involvement of supranational technocrats in national affairs than to negotiate better conditions for their nationals (Haas 1968: xxii). Given this alleged anti-functionalist interest that drives some leaders, Haas tried to incorporate it into neofunctionalism. Hence, he pointed to the pragmatism of its logic and its immanent weakness. In turn, Haas grounded this weakness in the argument that there was no 'deep ideological or philosophical commitment', resulting in extremely ephemeral interests. The process that was articulated by those ephemeral interests was, therefore, frail and susceptible to reversal or disintegration (Haas 1968: xiii). The gradualism of European integration can be understood as an idea that is opposed to the energy and vigour of personalities like Bismarck or Charles de Gaulle. Those personalities were able to summon and enchant *many*, to use Haas' words; but, if big and masterful steps were to be taken by actors that lacked the talents and competences to mobilise people, then *many* would oppose integration. It is precisely that kind of charismatic leader that Europe did not have in 1948, or the 1950s (Haas 1968: xxiii).

It is, however, difficult to prove such a contention wrong, since it would require proving that there was indeed a strong leadership that failed in the attempt to bring integration to a halt. Haas' position could easily escape such critique by arguing that eventual candidates were simply not heroic enough; because, if they had been dramatic or heroic enough, they would have succeeded like Charles de Gaulle did. Such a debate brings the argument no further, and instead begs for an explanation of when an actor can be labelled as heroic enough. Unless we accept a tautology, a definition of heroic statesmanship cannot rest on whether he or she succeeds to stop incrementalism. Therefore, we should preferably ask under what conditions a single actor could stop integration and test a hypothesis in a different case, or why interests change so as to accept the costs of stagnation.

Finally, Haas' new approach was severely criticised due to the fact that it relied on the big crisis to explain the relative success of integration. A theory that is able to explain a solely humble progress of integration, or incomplete integration, loses much of its plausibility to its rival. Accordingly, systemic approaches suggest that a crisis should be approached with a frame of systems' survival, where conflict is a source of persistent tension. *Grosspolitik* and the crisis derived from it do not inhibit, but rather 'add to our understanding of the dynamics of the system and the various kinds of stress to which it is subject' (Lindberg 1966:

be described as 'supranational' in nature, will necessarily rest on a set of intergovernmental bargains. The reinvigoration of Community institutions by means of the Single European Act, and the introduction of qualified majority voting in the field of the internal market, testifies to a decision-making style that is 'supranationality without supranational institutions' (Keohane and Hoffmann 1991: 4, 16).

Following the above-mentioned logic, states can also set limits on the pace of integration and movement of regional centralisation of decision-making. Furthermore, during the 1970s, 'the challenges to sovereignty were successfully resisted and the central institutions failed to obtain the qualities of supranationalism' (Taylor 1983: 56; Keohane and Hoffmann 1991).

Power as articulator of supranational action

Realist intergovernmentalism focuses on state interest within structures of international power, claiming that states are the central actors in international politics and act in a context of anarchy (Schimmelfennig 2004: 76; Moravcsik 1991: 27). International integration is considered 'a pattern of international relations and not as something above, beyond or aside from politics among nations' (Puchala 1972: 274). Interaction among states and the collision of interests and power relations leaves a trail of 'nodal history-making moments' (Wincott 1995c: 602, cited by Rosamond 2000: 146; Haltern 2004) that is of central interest for the intergovernmentalists; at the same time, the big 'constitutive, constitutional, history-making, or grand bargains' (Moravcsik 1998: 1) reveal much about developments in the international system. In the case of the EC, each nodal moment determines the relations among member states for almost a decade, suggesting the theological analogy that it has evolved in a 'sequence of irregular big bangs' (Katzenstein 1989: 296).

234–5; Easton 1965a: 82, 8; 1965b). Leon Lindberg suggested that the empty-chair crisis confirmed the validity of spillover, in that Charles de Gaulle was clearly aware of it, and did not attempt 'to undo integration but to turn it to his own purposes' (Lindberg 1966: 240). He was able to do so, Lindberg argues, because while the other members of the Community were trapped by the logic of spillover and the web of relationships, France was not 'engaged' by the process, 'because de Gaulle is not as subject as his colleagues in the other member countries to internal political controls on his freedom of action' (Lindberg 1966: 240). However, despite Lindberg's efforts to keep the force of the spillover argument alive, his account still maintains the logic of integration contingent upon choices of individual statesmen or stateswomen, who can use it or abuse it depending on national circumstances. In such a frame, spillover becomes an auxiliary theory, at best, that unveils its explanatory force only when political leaders decide to engage in interdependencies or rationally use the logic of spillover to advance integration. Overall, if we have to resort to domestic power politics to explain the voluntary use or abuse of the logic, the theory is not helpful for explaining regional integration.

In its traditional realist reading, intergovernmentalism's focus on state interest relies on clear assumptions of power structures, a strand to which Stanley Hoffmann belongs, and which made a noted critique of neofunctionalism especially in the light of de Gaulle's influence on the pace of integration (Hoffmann 1966). This approach stresses the barrier that separates 'low politics' technocracy from 'high politics' power topics. This approach has been used very often to explain the outcome of European integration, linking it to individual states' power in order to impose their preferences (Moravcsik 1998: 60). Sovereignty and national interest issues are typical topics among those preferences, rendering them non-negotiable (Rosamond 2005: 248). National leaders are, therefore, regarded as autonomous vis-à-vis supranational institutions, especially in matters that concern power resources (Moravcsik 1991: 27).

The typical outcome in bargains that involve national interests is the lowest common denominator; furthermore, this outcome reflects the relative power of states in the international system (Keohane 1984: 61–4; Moravcsik 1991: 25). Smaller states can be bought off with side payments by states that are larger in relative terms. These larger states, however, will not yield to fundamental changes in the system and will be prone to use whatever veto mechanism is at their disposal. Following this logic, the expected outcome will converge towards the lowest common denominator of large state interests (Moravcsik 1991: 25–6).

International regimes shape interstate politics by providing a common framework that reduces transactional costs and uncertainties associated with a setting of power relations (Moravcsik 1991: 27). But, even in such key bargains, member states are constrained not by an inherent integration dynamic, nor by a domestic constellation of interest groups, but by the state conceived as a unitary actor. Furthermore, within the international system, states face stimulus from other states and shape their decisions accordingly. It has also been argued by intergovernmentalists that the French support to a monetary union in the early 1970s came about thanks to foreign policy reasons, as France 'wished Europe to establish her own monetary personality in opposition to the USA' (although Taylor recognises that intergovernmentalism shows a changing pattern during the 1970s; see Taylor 1983: 65).

As power relations and their changing patterns are at the forefront of this kind of intergovernmentalism – 'modified structural realism', according to Robert Keohane (Keohane 1984: 61–4; 1986: 192–5; Moravcsik 1991: 27) – internal patterns of change and domestic constellation of interests become less important and states appear as 'black boxes' (Moravcsik 1991: 27). Critiquing in the same direction, Keohane notes that there is a difference between taking a state-centric approach for explaining the outcomes of European integration, and explanations that limit themselves to governmental actions just because they are the only things we see. The research, according to Keohane and Hoffmann, should 'go beyond these interstate bargains to the domestic political processes of the member states, on the one hand, and to the constraints of international institutions, on the other' (Keohane and Hoffmann 1991: 17).

National interest as determinant of supranational action

A prominent attempt to explain European integration within a framework of two-level games (Putnam 1988) is Andrew Moravcsik's 'liberal intergovernmentalism' (LI), which offers an account that is grounded on a liberal notion of national preference formation, and intergovernmental traits regarding the bargain process at the international level (Moravcsik 1991, 1997b, 1998). The liberal dimension is conspicuous in LI writings, primarily because it assumes actors to be rational, self-interested and risk-averse (Rosamond 2000: 142). At the national level, the issue-specific preferences of domestic interest groups are fundamental for LI, since national governments find their constituencies in these interest groups, and are therefore responsible to them (Schimmelfennig 2004: 80; Moravcsik 1991: 27). Member states' executives are rational actors that identify the most relevant and powerful interests within the domestic realm and align their choices at the international and European level primarily in accordance with them, and secondarily with their own governmental economic preferences.

As for the international level, LI maintains the realist assumption that states behave rationally. But contrary to realism, LI argues that national interests have been shaped by domestic politics, and patterns of both conflict and cooperation at the international system are a manifestation of state interests (Rosamond 2000: 142). In Moravcsik's words:

> The primary interest of governments is to maintain themselves in office ... this requires the support of a coalition of domestic voters, parties, interest groups and bureaucracies whose views are transmitted, directly or indirectly, through domestic institutions and practices of political representation. Through this process emerges the set of national interests or goals that states bring to international negotiations.
> (Moravcsik 1993: 483)

In the history of the establishment of the EC, it is the commercial interests that have determined bargains and its outcome, rather than sheer power politics. This assertion stems from the fact that states have entered the negotiation arena voluntarily, and reached the most prominent 'history-making' agreements under conditions of unanimity (Rosamond 2000: 137–8). Even for spillover to take place, 'a prior programmatic agreement among governments, expressed in an intergovernmental bargain', is a requirement (Keohane and Hoffmann 1991: 17).

There is a noted example of how state interest shaped European integration outcomes in the negotiations around the Single European Act of 1986, as shown by Andrew Moravcsik (Moravcsik 1998, 1991). Starting from the underlying preferences of the biggest three member states, namely Germany, France and Britain, Moravcsik traces the credible threat of exclusion and includes it as a constraint: a two-tier Europe, or a *Europe à deux vitesses* (cf. Grabitz 1984 for the concept of *abgestufte Integration*). The French government repeatedly invoked this possibility so as to circumvent an eventual British veto. Although the British Prime Minister, Margaret Thatcher, favoured increased market liberalisation, the Common Agricultural Policy appeared as a Franco-German bargain forged prior to British membership of the EC (Moravcsik 1991: 32). The outcome is an example of political craftsmanship; there is neither an endogenous dynamic nor an upgrading of common interests favoured by supranational institutions, but an acceptance of the lowest common denominator, backed by the threat of exclusion (Moravcsik 1991: 47–8).

Evidently, an understanding like that of the liberal intergovernmentalists is in sharp opposition with notions of European integration being the ultimate victory over nationalism, or the reaffirmation of a federalist ideology. But, at the same time, LI does not endorse the convergence of post-war 'low politics' of foreign economic policy and the geopolitical 'high politics' (Moravcsik 1998: 4). Even high-profile impasses that have been traditionally explained on the ground of geopolitics and security concerns are challenged by LI, which argues that economic interests tend to trump geopolitical ideologies. Accordingly, General de Gaulle's staunch opposition to British membership to the EC was not the consequence of an alleged self-image of French magnificence, but rather the result of concerns about the price of French wheat (Moravcsik 1998: 7).

Furthermore, liberal intergovernmentalism relies on international interdependence as a condition of durable international cooperation, even if the maintenance of such cooperation demands further integration or delegation to supranational organisations against the short-term interests of governments. In such cases, international interdependence can be a catalyst of demand for integration, albeit not transnational, as neofunctionalists would say (Schimmelfennig 2004: 80). It follows, then, that contrary to the view of neofunctionalists and supranational institutionalists, member states are not weakened by progressive transference of sovereignty in certain fields; in fact, the states' executives increase their institutional and informational resources that empower them against parliamentary control and against powerful domestic interest groups. In other words, the process actually strengthens national governments' domestic autonomy (Schimmelfennig 2004: 80; Moravcsik 1994). Interestingly, Leon Lindberg argues that this is precisely the logic of circumventing political resistance that neofunctionalism had posited before (see Lindberg 1994; also Rosamond 2000: 145).

Legal integration

Intergovernmentalism strongly disagrees with neofunctionalism about the process of European integration, but it has been neglected during the debate in which both agreed on theorising European integration from the domestic bottom up, and shared a 'soft rationalist ontology' (Risse 2005: 294–5). Such an account contends that, even in cases of judicial enforcement of EC law, it is national interests that account for increasing compliance. Even though European officials forged strategies in order to advance integration, mechanisms of judicially enforcing treaty provisions did not enjoy the Commission's first priority when compared to other attributions. The reluctance to pursue defection can be explained by the Commission's fragile relationship with member states. In this view, enforcement action is seen as inherently defiant by whoever performs this function, as even member states shy away from bringing other fellow states before the ECJ (Stein 1981: 6).

Similar to many agreements in international law, the Treaty of Rome included enforcement mechanisms that were rather weak (Kuper 1998: 4). Although the Commission could take action against recalcitrant states, the 'situation where the Commission is constantly suing the governments of the member states, or they are suing each other, is unlikely to be one which encourages constructive cooperation in other areas' (Kuper 1998: 4). Sanctioning powers were only (re)established in 1993, long after the European legal system had proven its effectiveness, despite having been included in the ECSC. What accounts for this reincorporation into the treaty is the fact that the most law-abiding states exerted pressure for the 'worst cheaters' to raise their rates of compliance, as the former were being held accountable by their own domestic courts (Alter 2001: 11). However, the fact that these mechanisms were at one point excluded from the Common Market has been interpreted by scholars as the intention of the drafters to be protective of national sovereignty, and achieve integration through diplomacy and political will (Alter 2001: 16).

The role of courts

Among political science theories, realism has dwelt on the role of the ECJ but asserted the importance of sovereign member states. From a realist's point of view, the Court plays, at best, an essentially 'technical servant role' (Weiler 1982). In the forefront stands national politics and sovereignty, and, if community law was to threaten either of them, national legislatures would be in the position to nullify treaty provisions, or make them ineffectual (Burley and Mattli 1993: 49). Stuart Scheingold emphasised that it is the political process of decision-making that is decisive, not the legal process, which, though it might have showed some federalising features, would be confined to the role of validating policies agreed by states. Therefore, according to Scheingold, the impact of the ECJ on the integration process would be indirect at best (Scheingold 1971).

Another branch introduced by political scientists is neorationalism, which provided an important corrective to legalist approaches, in its argument that political factors had the potential to shape judicial behaviour (Garrett 1995;

Garrett and Weingast 1993). Geoffrey Garrett and Barry Weingast explicitly focused on the ECJ in their studies, starting from the assumption that the Court, indeed, has the power to influence national politics. However, its power to do so does not stem from an inherent power, but from the alignment with member states' interests. Judges' interests mirror national interests, because the former are concerned about the latter's political response following each ruling. Garrett and Weingast's argument starts from the explicit assumption that the complexity of EC politics gives member states a huge incentive to defect from their commitments, and therefore the ECJ provides the means for monitoring compliance with the obligations agreed upon in the treaty. Member states benefit from an umpire that resolves disputes regarding mutual agreements, as this prevents retaliation and trade wars (Weiler 1994: 526).

For this task to be properly performed, member states have to delegate necessary powers to the Court. In this way, 'the logic of retaliation and reputation in iterated games' is facilitated (Garrett 1995: 27). However, the authority comes from the states, according to Garrett, and therefore they have the power to overrule the Court whenever their interests are in opposition with the Court's rulings.

> Embedding a legal system in a broader political structure places direct constraints on the discretion of a court, even one with as much constitutional independence as the United States Supreme Court. This conclusion holds even if the constitution makes no explicit provisions for altering a court's role. The reason is that political actors have a range of avenues through which they may alter or limit the role of courts. Sometimes such changes require amendment of the constitutions, but usually the appropriate alterations may be accomplished more directly through statute, as by alteration of the court's jurisdiction in a way that makes it clear that continued undesired behaviour will result in more radical changes.
> (Garrett and Weingast 1993: 200–1)

Furthermore, the Court is a rational player and has no interest in losing authority that has been delegated to it; hence, it will avoid taking steps against the member states' interest. From this assumption, it can be inferred that, if states have not overturned the Court powers for adjudication, it means that, whatever the content of such judicial decisions, they have stood in harmony with states' interests. This contention, however, is strongly criticised by Burley and Mattli, who argue that such a framework deduces interest-compatibility from compliance with court rulings. However, compliance with the rulings of the ECJ is precisely the puzzle to be solved. This critique is underpinned by the fact that, according to Burley and Mattli, in several landmark cases that suggest disrupting adjudication against member states' interest, they have consistently and fiercely opposed that ruling's content within each judicial stage (Burley and Mattli 1993: 51). The fact that states comply with such rulings in the aftermath 'is precisely [what] needs to be explained' (Burley and Mattli 1993: 51). Neorationalism cements the link between national judiciaries and their governments with the assumption that judges will never deviate from national interests without giving strong evidence of this logic. It therefore begets the fallacy of *petitio principi*, as it is very tempting to 'come up with a post hoc definition of national interest to justify any legal decision' (Alter 2001: 40).

Nevertheless, the Treaty of Maastricht posed an interesting challenge to neofunctionalist assumptions, since the areas left out of any kind of harmonisation have still not been affected by spillover. This would suggest prima facie that member states' control is, in fact, determines the pace of integration. Burley and Mattli admit that Maastricht rendered some neorationalist explanations plausible, in the sense that states could, indeed, effectively set a direct check on spillover by means of extreme measures crafted in the Court's own legal terms (Burley and Mattli 1993: 74). However, from the point of view of the logic of integration, Burley and Mattli claim that Maastricht only confirms that there is a spillover that member states fear: they scrutinise Garrett and Weingast's assumptions and argue that if it was true that the Court followed the member states' agenda, it would not make sense to have excluded harmonisation from sensible political fields. As they state, if it were so, 'then, why worry?' The answer is that only exclusion provides certainty, which is opposed to neorationalist accounts because it is based on an assumption of autonomy of the legal-judicial realm that can only be curtailed through explicit counter-measures. This autonomy allows the Court to advance its political agenda and, thereby, favour integration (Burley and Mattli 1993: 74).

Control mechanisms in the case of courts are difficult to operationalise, since we will never know the exact impact of them. The principal control mechanism of delegators over the courts is the power to amend the relevant statute or legislation. This is so to the extent that legislators with the capacity of rapidly enacting legislation will have a bigger impact on courts than legislators with low or no capacity to pass amending statutes (to illustrate this point, Shapiro makes a comparison between the US Congress with its multi-road-block law-making process and the UK's draconian Cabinet control over parliamentary law-making; Shapiro 2002b: 186).

The intergovernmental hypothesis

Intergovernmentalists have offered several accounts of the outcome of European integration. In contrast to neofunctionalists, the focus has been on explanations rather than on a testable hypothesis (Rosamond 2000: 146). One of the sharpest critiques in regard to LI's submission to scrutiny (Moravcsik, 1995) is that liberal intergovernmentalism should be thought of as an 'approach' rather than a 'theory' (Wincott 1995c). This is because liberal intergovernmentalism, as laid down by Moravcsik, does not lay out the circumstances on which it could be empirically refuted. Because of this, it is impossible to treat the clear intergovernmental bases of liberal intergovernmentalism as working assumptions. Moravcsik is not inferring his claims from a set of carefully selected assumptions. He is rather performing an act of closure upon certain potential sources of explanation (Rosamond 2000: 146).

Nevertheless, from the assumptions that have been laid out in this chapter, it is possible to draw a general research hypothesis. Since the most prominent claims of intergovernmentalists and neorationalists came as a reaction to neofunctionalism, the hypothesis that I present uses most of the initial conditions that were deemed necessary by neofunctionalists.

A necessary condition for integration is interdependence, which sparks demand for integration. The key enabling condition is an intergovernmental bargain that allows member states to overcome coordination problems. As international agreements entail the lowest common denominator and recurrent defection, the incentives for delegating authority to a supranational dispute settlement body increase. The powers and competences of delegated bodies (the agent) stem from the member states (the principal). As a consequence, the action of the agent depends on the terms established by the principal. From the moment that the agent acts in ways that contradict the terms of the original act of delegation, the principal is in the position to correct the course and bring the agent's action into acquiescence. When the agent is a court of justice, the most effective means for correcting activism is amending the statutes that govern the court. In this way, the court's behaviour will mirror the member states' interests.

This last circumstance, namely that court rulings mirror national interests, has been assumed by some intergovernmentalists in their writings, as they assert it as an explanation rather than testable propositions. In order to operationalize their research questions, intergovernmentalism assumes that the member states' strategies in regard to the court are an indicator of their interests, even when a two-level game approach is taken. The logic of this test follows the hoop test. Passing the test would give it some support, but flunking the test would kill the explanation.

If the judicial rulings match or are reasonably compatible with states' strategies, then it is highly probable that the court's behaviour is mirroring member states' interests. If court action overtly contradicts member states' strategies, it cannot be plausibly argued that the rulings mirror member states' interests. The intergovernmentalists' explanations forcefully demand corrective actions in order not to flunk the test.

Thus, the hypothesis reads as follows. If the necessary conditions of interdependence, an intergovernmental bargain, and judicial delegation are present, then the rulings of the ACJ will mirror the interests of member states. Eventual activism will result in measures of correction by the member states, as long as it contradicts their interests. Conversely, member states will refrain from corrective measures against an activist ACJ, as long as the rulings mirror states' interests.

Chapter 3

The saga of European legal integration

The court and its case law

Since 1995, when Anne-Marie Slaughter and Walter Mattli presented the revival of neofunctionalism, there have been abundant accounts, additions and variations to the narrative of the European Court of Justice and legal integration. It is, therefore, not my intention either to repeat the story or to add new details that earlier commentators might have left out of their narratives. What I consider most surprising is that despite the numerous studies and analysis of the ECJ, there is an impressive gap regarding the research of the impact that the European case law had in other regions. Apparently, law and legal institutions can travel and we can see them proliferating in foreign settings. Not surprisingly, the ECJ enjoys a high reputation among its peers. For judges around the world, knowing European case law and learning from it can represent a huge epistemic advantage because it problematises legal disputes from the point of view of a successful legal system. Judges talk to each other, and they certainly learn from each other; and still, we seem to know too little about what happens when legal institutions migrate from one context to another.

This chapter aims to recapitulate the narrative of the judicial construction of the European legal system with the explicit intention of reconstructing the archetype that was transplanted to the Andean Community. If Chapter 2 explored the theoretical framework that underpinned the emergence of the ECJ as a model, I present here the concrete legal procedure and doctrines that were acknowledged as the 'magic triangle' that appeared to advance legal integration. It is very important to recall the context in which they emerged, and the functions that the institutions were expected to fulfil within the European legal order. Specifying the conditions under which they were drafted, and the expectations tied to them, will be crucial for understanding the difference between the European and the Andean stories.

Forging the European judicial archetype

The implications of the ECJ's activity within the legal framework of the European Community, especially for member states' sovereignty, has been closely studied by legal scholars since the 1980s. Eric Stein drew attention to the inconspicuous, albeit laborious, caseload forged by the Court.

> Tucked away in the fairyland Duchy of Luxembourg and blessed, until recently, with benign neglect by the powers that be and the mass media, the Court of Justice of the European Communities has fashioned a constitutional framework for a federal-type Europe.
>
> (Stein 1981: 1)

Legal scholars started to give new readings to the rulings. If law had previously been the object of integration (Hunt and Shaw 2009: 93), as from the 1980s and 1990s it began to be assessed as an agent of integration (Dehousse and Weiler 1990: 243). From the point of view of legal scholars and lawyers, law is the prime element and object of research, and therefore it is not surprising that the transformative power of law was promptly addressed in major research projects, highlighting law as the agent par excellence (Hunt and Shaw 2009) of European integration: the result was the notion of 'integration through law' (Cappelletti *et al*. 1985).

The constitutional language of EC law, which developed from the case law, had considerable political implications. However, legal scholars have most likely been concerned with the question of what this process is, and to what extent the ideas of law, the protection of individual rights, and the overall legal order are reflected in the ongoing integrative process, in which '"constitutionalisation" is used as a short-hand for "rendering the EU more state-like"' (Hunt and Shaw 2009).

This image of law and its potential to create and shape realities, as the incarnation of what is just or right, has left political scientists persistently unsatisfied, for it did not explain one major puzzle: the reasons that drive a member state to accept that its own sovereignty can be permeated (Conant 2007: 45). Progressively, new questions arose, dwelling on the broader implications of the politics of the ECJ, identifying new actors that appeared to be relevant, new networks that became visible, and the interests that were driving those actors. Overall, new narratives emerged on the establishment of the EC's legal and political order, and it became clearer that the 'heroic' vision of the Court and the integrative process could be challenged; not everyone subscribed to the 'fairy tale of Luxembourg' (Hunt and Shaw 2009).

It has been suggested that the founders of the treaty intended the ECJ to primarily interact with other Community organs and member states (Burley and Mattli 1993: 58), especially as a check on the Council and the Commission. Its establishment had found inspiration in the French Conseil d'Etat (Haas 1958: 44), and its primary goal was to protect member states and private firms from abuses by the High Authority. This task was also taken on by the ECJ by virtue of the Treaty of Rome since the institutional structure was generally taken from the ECSC, providing the 'blueprint' for the EC (Alter 2001: 6).

A central role of the ECJ is that of deciding on obscure points of EC law, ruling on questions that relate to the interpretation of European law. National policies and national laws are, therefore, out of the scope of the interpretative powers of the ECJ. Private litigants cannot challenge their domestic legislation by motivating referrals to the ECJ. As Mancini states:

> under Article 177 national judges can only request the Court of Justice to interpret a Community measure. The Court never told [national courts] they were entitled to overstep that bound: in fact, whenever they did so – for example, whenever they asked if national rule A is in violation of Community Regulation B or Directive C – the Court answered that its only power is to explain what B or C actually mean.
> (Mancini 1989: 606)

Similar to many agreements in international law, the Treaty of Rome included enforcement mechanisms that were rather weak (Kuper 1998: 4). Although the Commission could take action against recalcitrant states, the 'situation where the Commission is constantly suing the governments of the member states, or they are suing each other, is unlikely to be one which encourages constructive cooperation in other areas' (Kuper 1998: 4).

Sanctionary powers were only (re)established in 1993, long after the European legal system had proven its effectiveness, despite having been included in the ECSC. What accounts for this reincorporation into the treaty is the fact that the most law-abiding states exerted pressure on the 'worst cheaters' in order to push them to raise their rates of compliance, as the former were being held accountable by their own domestic courts (Alter 2001: 11). However, the fact that these mechanisms were at one point excluded from the Common Market has been interpreted by scholars as the intention of the drafters to be protective of national sovereignty, and achieve integration through diplomacy and political will (Alter 2001: 16).

As for the strategies of European officials to advance integration, scholars have suggested that the Commission was not inclined to make use of treaty enforcement mechanisms compared to other available attributions. Eric Stein argues that the reluctance to pursue defection can be explained by the Commission's fragile relationship with member states. In this view, enforcement action is interpreted as inherently defiant by whoever performs this function, as even member states shy away from bringing other fellow states before the ECJ (Stein 1981: 6). On the contrary, some other actions are seen as inherently fostering integration and, if executed by the Commission, they can provide other actors – as the ECJ itself – with valuable information about the possible controversies in the conflicting relationship with member states (Helfer and Slaughter 1997: 303).

From the point of view of the Commission, persuading the Council to adopt drafted legislation might be more effective in attaining integration rather than taking judicial actions before the Court. Consistent with this institutionalist view, the increasing numbers of cases brought before the ECJ by the Commission between 1985 and 1993 are not the result of a change of strategy of the latter, but rather a consequence of more authoritative decisions of the ECJ, which increased the expectation of success in using the infringement proceedings. In other words, the increasing numbers in infringement proceedings are not the catalyst for transformation, since they 'came well after the transformation of the European legal system' (Alter 2001: 14). Alec Stone Sweet, on the other hand, suggests that the reason behind more litigation is increased transnational commercial activity, thus creating pressure to challenge national legislation (Stone Sweet 2004b, 2004a).

Integration and international public law

The implication of the doctrines pronounced by the ECJ cannot be fully grasped without reference to the legal environment in which they were created. In the 1950s, the main doctrinal cleavage that divided jurists and scholars in regard to the effectiveness of international public law within the national order was the monism–dualism divide. Legal scholars understand through monism the idea of a unitarian legal order, in which both national and international legal orders are integrated into one single system, hence not requiring any act of incorporation whatsoever. The question that follows from this assumption is what this single legal system is an instance of. That is to say, is this single system predominantly international public law, or national law? Depending on the answer to this question, there can be different appreciations of the essence of legal monism (for a theory that stresses the international order, see Kelsen 1928; for an approach that looks at the international system as deriving from national law, see Pohl 1929). A noted example for a monist tradition that gives primacy to international law is the Dutch legal system (Claes and De Witte 1996), which is also the system where the judicial saga on the doctrines of the ECJ began.

Dualism, on the other hand, stands for the existence of two separate legal orders, the national and the international. Under such an assumption, it has been debated whether both systems can mutually influence each other. The strict version of dualism, as upheld by Heinrich Triepel (Triepel 1958 [1899]), argues that both systems are inevitably separated, and the best that lawyers can do is to mediate between the systems so as to avoid conflicts. Milder versions of dualism – which seem to take a higher position in current legal scholarship – argue that international law can be effective within the national realm, as long as it is previously incorporated by a national legislative act into national law in order to become enforceable. According to the German legal scholar Georg Jellinek, it is the sovereignty of states that allows them to bind themselves within the international system. Sovereignty is precisely their attribute that allows state self-engagement (Jellinek 1914: 481–2). All the norms that regulate this relationship of mild dualism pertain to national law; international public law does not ordinarily contain rules on this relationship, except for the principle contained in article 27 of the Vienna Convention,[1] which provides that no state can avoid the compliance with its international obligation on the grounds of its domestic law (Hobe and Kimminich 2004: 226).

Preliminary rulings originated the most noted doctrines of the ECJ on the relationship between European law and national law. Specifically, the doctrines of direct effect[2] and supremacy[3] ignited the European legal system's substantial transformation. The source for this interpretation was the general spirit of the treaty, which had been established by its founders for the realisation of the Common Market. It is the goals of the treaty that drive the interpretation of law, and law serves those general objectives. This is the teleological method of interpretation (Lecourt 1976: 305).

As for the moment when the doctrines were handed down, the Treaty of the ECSC and the Treaty of Rome were regarded in the traditional fashion of mild dualism. Even in the case of individual rights created by international treaties, the transposition of international law was, at that time, the ordinary way for it to be applicable within national systems, as the incumbent obligations had been created *by* states and *between* states (Weiler 1991; Alter 2001).

The transformation of the preliminary ruling procedure: the case law

There is much scholarship on the significance of the case law of the ECJ for European integration. Although there are different approaches, almost everybody agrees that there were key developments that determined the transformation of the European legal system: specifically, the system of preliminary rulings, and the doctrines of direct effect plus supremacy are worthy of close examination. Differences among scholars arise when it comes to explaining the origins, causes, interpretations and implications for the integration process of this transformation.

Legalistic accounts stress the importance of the ECJ's articulation of the doctrines, as they stand for compelling legal reasoning. According to such views, 'law matters', and consequently, not only is law capable of producing change, but the implementation of the law already *is* the right change (Vauchez 2008; Mancini and Keeling 1992: 2–3).

---

1 Convention on the Law of Treaties, 'Article 27: Internal law and observance of treaties. A party may not invoke the provisions of its internal law as justification for its failure to perform a treaty.'
2 *Van Gend en Loos v. Nederlandse Administratie der Belastingen*, ECJ Case 26/62, [1963] ECR 1.
3 *Costa v. Ente Nazionale per l'Energia Elettrica (ENEL)*, ECJ Case 6/64 [1964].

Institutionalist accounts generally focus on the evolution of EU institutions and their effects on European political processes; although there are numerous variations and nuances among institutionalists, the idea of 'institutions matter' seems to effectively bring them under one roof (Schmitter 2003: 48). In 2001, Alter argued that the 'design of the legal system' contributes to whether states are pulled into the rule of law. It follows, then, that such a design should be suitable to being exported, especially to those arrangements that show a manifest weakness concerning the subjugation to the rule of law (Alter 2001). Others suggest that 'structural changes' make it possible for legal systems to overcome vicious circles that are so often seen in institutional settings governed by international law (Weiler 1991).

Following much of neofunctionalist reasoning, Stone Sweet and Brunell argue that it is not so much the institutional design that constructed the constitutional polity, as the laborious work of the ECJ fostering constitutional dialogues with national courts. For this purpose, the Court 'worked assiduously to develop what is now a robust and taken-for-granted set of practices associated with precedents' (Stone Sweet and Brunell 2004: 97).

The preliminary ruling system was conceived by the signing member states as a means to challenge EC law, rather than as a vehicle for challenging national law (Alter 2001). Few scholars, especially legal scholars, would disagree that the EC legal order has become something akin to a constitutional order (Dehousse 1998; for some exceptions, see Schilling 1996: 389; Hartley 2001: 225). In connection with the doctrines of direct effect and supremacy, the European polity decisively moved from an international system to a supranational order.

The doctrine of direct effect

The doctrine of direct effect provides that Community norms that are clear, precise and self-sufficient are to be regarded within the sphere of competencies of the Community – as the law of the land (Weiler 1991: 2413). It follows that, if the Community has to be regarded as the law of the land, 'breach by a government of Community law becomes a breach of its own law with remedies lying before its national courts' (Weiler 1982: 46). Under that mandate, and provided that individuals have a standing to go to court, European Community law is creating rights that are enforceable by private persons.

From the point of view of classical international law, this is a dramatic change, since international provisions could traditionally be enforced by individuals only if the state had previously incorporated that particular international rule into the domestic legal order.

The Court handed down its famous doctrine of direct effect in 1963. The strong opposition of the member states testifies to the importance that this issue already had at that time. The idea that individuals could directly enforce supranational provisions in national courts clashed with the traditional notion of the national state mediating rights between the law and the citizen. The ruling invokes the text of the treaty, but the main argument stems directly from the idea of what the Community should become: the teleological method in action. Therefore, the Community is not to be understood as a traditional compact of states, but rather as an order, where individuals were also taken into consideration (Craig and de Búrca 2008: 274).

In the ruling of *Van Gend en Loos*, the Court declared that:

> the Community constitutes a new legal order of international law for the benefit of which the states have limited their sovereign rights, albeit within limited fields, and the subject of which comprise not only Member States, but also their nationals. Independent of the legislation of Member States, Community law therefore not only imposes obligations on individuals but is also intended to confer upon them rights which become part of their legal heritage.[4]

It has been noted that this change is not only conceptual; it has considerable empirical implications because member states that were breaching their community obligations would have to face their own courts under the rules of their domestic legal orders. They could not shift the 'locus of dispute to the interstate or Community plane'. Individuals became protagonists of Community law enforcement, guarding its integrity 'similar to the way that individuals in the United States have been the principal actors in ensuring the vindication of the Bill of Rights and other federal law'. (Weiler 1991: 2414)

Supremacy

Supremacy was the logical consequence of the doctrine of direct effect, in that member states were inhibited from ignoring the *Van Gend en Loos* ruling and simply passing new legislation that would contradict and replace European law. The Court declared European law superior to national law. National law was not to be understood as abrogated, but rather as 'set aside', as became clear with the *Costa* ruling:

> By contrast with ordinary international treaties, the EEC Treaty has created its own legal system which, on the entry into force of the treaty, became an integral part of the legal systems of the member states and which their courts are bound to apply ...
>
> The integration into the laws of each member state of provisions which derive from the Community, and more generally the terms and the spirit of the Treaty, make it impossible for the states, as a corollary, to accord

---

4 *Van Gend en Loos v. Nederlandse Administratie der Belastingen*, ECJ Case 26/62, [1963] ECR 1.

precedence to a unilateral and subsequent measure over a legal system accepted by them on a basis of reciprocity. Such a measure cannot therefore be inconsistent with that legal system. The executive force of community law cannot vary from one state to another in deference to subsequent domestic laws, without jeopardizing the attainment of the objectives of the treaty set out in article 5 (2) and giving rise to the discrimination prohibited by article 7.

(Case 6/64 *Costa v. ENEL*)

The ruling leaves no doubt that from that moment member states would not be able to pass new laws that could nullify Community law. These were the first steps of the process of constitutionalisation of a treaty. The measures seem to be simple; a legal scholar would say that it is about establishing legal hierarchy. But the influence of this new course of action in the political process has further reaches.

The doctrine broke with the principle of international public law *lex posteriori derogat legi apriori*, according to which the latest legislation would abrogate earlier legislation in case of conflict between two pieces of legislation of a similar kind. The political implication of this departure is that democratically elected law-makers were inhibited from legislating in those matters that had been resolved by the ECJ. Furthermore, this hindrance was originated not by a judicial organ with ordinary competencies of national judicial review – as would be the case of a national constitutional court – but by the referral of a national lower court (Alter 2001: 24).

The critical phenomenon behind the process of constitutionalisation is that some issues like fundamental rights, the institutional framework and organisation of the state, are taken out from the political process of decision-making, so that they remain immutable in time (Weiler 2002, 1994). One of the ideas behind this measure is to shield it from eventual attacks during certain time points, when support for institutions may decline, for any possible reason. The stability of these institutions is regarded as a goal in itself, and therefore they have to be immune to spontaneous measures that might well be driven, for instance, by a charismatic leadership or a *caudillo* whose support could rest on the claim for structural changes.

When analysing the ruling from a political angle, we distinguish the first traits of constitutionalisation of the treaty, and hence Community law (Kuper 1998: 3–18; Pernice 2001). Member states would no longer be able to amend the content of the treaty, save the possibility of unanimity among all of them. So, the treaty being an agreement on the establishment of a common market, all provisions that regulate this issue were taken out of the domestic political process, shielding them against certain national pressure that could have resisted this attainment. What seems to be a remarkable idea is not the practice itself of shielding some political areas from everyday politics, but rather the fact that the content of the *hijacked* statutes (Weiler 2002: 570) hardly resemble those fundamental principles that, traditionally, prevent society from living in tyranny or, worse, in anarchy. From now on, completion of a common market had to be regarded as one of those higher principles that merits being taken out of the regular political process and placed in a higher position in the hierarchy that causes them to be immune to subsequent national regulations.

But it was in 1977 that the ECJ seems to have forced national courts to yield to the treaty's authority and its supremacy over national constitutions, as in the case *Italian Minister for Finance v. Simmenthal*:

> Furthermore, in accordance with the principle of the precedence of Community law, the relationship between provisions of the Treaty and directly applicable measures of the institutions on the one hand and the national law of the member states on the other is such that those provisions and measures not only by their entry into force render automatically inapplicable any conflicting provision of current national law but – in so far as they are an integral part of, and take precedence in, the legal order applicable in the territory of each of the member states – also preclude the valid adoption of new national legislative measures to the extent to which they would be incompatible with community provisions.
> (Case 106/77 *Italian Minister for Finance v. Simmenthal*, par. 17)

It follows from the foregoing that every national court must, in a case within its jurisdiction, apply Community law in its entirety and protect rights of individuals, and must accordingly set aside any provision of national law that may conflict with it, whether prior or subsequent to the Community rule.[5]

If we rely exclusively on the text of the rulings, the path towards a constitutionalisation of the treaty seems to be one of no return. The treaty in the light of the rulings seems to be almighty. Not even national constitutions or national parliaments are in a position to challenge it. Beyond the text, there is a possibility of amending the treaty which is, in Mark Pollack's words, the 'nuclear option' because it requires unanimity among member states (Pollack 1997). Naturally, there will still be the option of passing new secondary legislation, but that has not yet proven to be superior to the objectives of the treaty, in the particular view of the ECJ. Up to this point, the ECJ had implicitly hinted at the constitutional dimension of the Community, but had not acknowledged it explicitly. The formal investiture as the Basic Constitutional Charter took place in the case known as *'Les Verts'*:

> It must first be emphasized in this regard that the European Economic Community is a community based on the Rule of Law, inasmuch as neither its member states nor its institutions can avoid a review of the

---

[5] *Administrazione delle Finanze dello Statu v. Simmenthal SpA* (II), ECJ Case 106/77, (1978) ECR 629.

question whether the measures adopted by them are in conformity with the Basic Constitutional Charter, the Treaty.[6]

If we consider that it took more than 20 years to finally declare the treaty as the Basic Constitutional Charter, we could well say that the path towards constitutionalisation was a very progressive one, where the Court laid down one milestone after another.

In his article 'The Transformation of Europe', Joseph Weiler suggests that it is the supremacy doctrine that gives the direct effect doctrine the distinctive constitutional architecture, since EC law would now become not only the 'Law of the Land', but also the 'Higher Law of the Land'. Furthermore, the forging of a supremacy clause – which was not included in the treaty itself by its drafters – constructed an edifice that resembled national constitutional orders of federal states, as they explicitly include supremacy in their constitutional texts (Weiler 1991: 2414–15). He further makes an argument from a historical-institutional point of view, according to which member states had particular difficulties accepting the doctrine of supremacy, as it did not offer any guarantee that minimal standards of human rights protection would be granted and protected at European level (Weiler 1991: 2418).

The doctrine of pre-emption

The pre-emption doctrine is closely linked to the idea that EC law must claim to have *effet utile*. According to this doctrine, once the Community has been entrusted with the authority to make law in a given field, member states cease to be able to regulate it. In other words, the existence of a Community policy precludes member states regulating in that specific area. This means, in fact, that the Community enjoys exclusivity in a policy area: 'Exclusivity means that the competence has been completely transferred by the Member States to the Community and that there is no concurrent Member State competence' (Craig and de Búrca 2008: 176).

In the case known as *ERTA*, the Court stated that, once the Community lays down common rules, member states have no concurrent powers to undertake obligations with third parties. The reasoning behind this ruling is that the Community needs to conduct coordinated actions if it is to attain the objectives of the treaty because, if member states were to act unilaterally, it would threaten uniform application of Community law (Craig and de Búrca 2008: 177). The Court stated:

> In particular, each time the Community, with a view to implementing a common policy envisaged by the Treaty, adopts provisions laying down

---

6 *Parti Écologiste 'Les Verts' v. European Parliament*, case 294/83 ECJ [1986] par. 23.

common rules, whatever form these may take, the Member States no longer have the right, acting individually or even collectively, to undertake obligations with third countries which affect those rules ... These Community powers exclude the possibility of concurrent powers on the part of Member States, since any steps taken outside the framework of the Community institutions would be incompatible with the unity of the Common Market and the uniform application of Community law.[7]

In the case of *Commission v. UK*,[8] the Court went further, as it 'held that member states were no longer at liberty to enact conservation laws, even though no Community measures had been taken' (Mancini 1989: 602). The 1994 Opinion on WTO Agreements GATS and TRIPS underpinned the widening of community competences, even if there was no explicit provision authorising community action. The Court stated that the Community has exclusive external competence when an explicit provision delegates such competence. In addition:

The same applies in any event, even in the absence of any express provision authorizing its institutions to negotiate with non-member countries, where the Community has achieved complete harmonization of the rules governing access to a self-employed activity, because the common rules thus adopted could be affected within the meaning of the AETR judgement if the Member States retained freedom to negotiate with non-member countries.[9]

This notion of implied powers corresponds to a 'classic form' of the preemption doctrine (Cremona 1999), from which the Court has moved 'a considerable distance' away, towards one of shared powers between member states and Community (Craig and de Búrca 2008: 177).

Protecting fundamental rights

When the Community was launched, the approach was economically sectorial and thereby limited to a 'common market'. Cognate fields were not included in the process – at least, not explicitly. The early Community was far from the notion of broad rights that would underpin the whole Community. Although the Common Market was based on the ideas of economic freedoms and the prohibition of discrimination based on nationality, it lacked a catalogue that would list the most important rights and the mechanism that would make

---

7 *Commission v. Council (AETR/ERTA)*, case 22/70 [1971] ECR 263, par. 17, 31.
8 *Commission v. UK*, case 804/79 [1981] ECR 1045, par. 17, 18.
9 Opinion 1/94 on the WTO Agreements (GATS and TRIPS) [1994] ECR I-5267, par. 96.

them available to individuals. The judicial enforcement mechanism suggested that the drafters of the treaty were more deferential to the sovereignty of member states, to whom they left the protection of fundamental rights (Weiler 1986).

In terms of protecting fundamental rights, the Court's initial stance was timid, as it was probably concerned with the preservation of the autonomy of the nascent Community law (Dehousse 1998: 62). For instance, in the 1959 case of *Stork*, the Court separated the interpretation of European law from any duty to 'ensure the protection of rules of domestic law, be they of constitutional rank'.[10] A similar elusive interpretation was handed down in *Geitling*[11] and *Sgarlata*.[12]

The introduction of the doctrines of supremacy, direct effect and preemption, however, motivated a deep change in the way the Court saw its role within the Community. The importance of the constitutional course of action adopted by the Court is not limited to the legal-textual implications of portraying the ECJ as a constitutional court. It also has wide implications for the relationship with the domestic orders of the member states. As the case law transformed the legal system and constitutionalised the Treaty of Rome (Maduro 2002; Mancini 1989; Mancini and Keeling 1992; Hunt and Shaw 2009), frictions between the supranational and the domestic systems began to emerge. The acceptance of the doctrine of supremacy raised many questions in regard to the penetration of European provisions into the domestic order. Whether the constitutionalisation of the treaties imply a hierarchy between national and European law is still a question that admits as many possible answers as there are views (see, for instance, MacCormick 1999; Kirchhof 1999; Kumm 1999). Beyond that thorny issue, however, the prerogative to protect the individuals became the focus of new disputes between the Court and the member states.

As the ECJ's rulings demanded subordination of domestic law to Community law, including national constitutions, questions regarding the protection of human rights and fundamental rights began to be raised. The Court had established that, in those matters that fell within the competences of the treaty, the member states had ceded sovereignty to the Community (*Van Gend en Loos*). However, the Court also stated that this cession was limited and national constitutions were not to be considered abolished; the treaty only renders them inapplicable in regard to the establishment of the Common Market.

Yet, from the end of World War II, member states began protecting several rights of their citizens and it was in the national constitutions where these

---

10 Case 1/58 *Stork v. High Authority* [1959] ECR 17.
11 Cases 36, 37, 38, and 40/59 *Geitling v. High Authority* [1960] ECR 423.
12 Case 40/64 *Sgarlata and others v. Commission* [1965] ECR 215.

catalogues of rights were enshrined.[13] States had learned the lessons from the dark episodes of pre-war history. Therefore, these fundamental rights were conceived to protect individuals from possible abuses coming from their own states.

Disputes related to the Common Market fall into the jurisdiction of the ECJ. If, however, such disputes extend to matters of fundamental rights, the clash can hardly be avoided. The issue was first raised in the case of *Stauder*,[14] where the Court declared that 'fundamental human rights were enshrined in the general principles of Community law and protected by the Court' (for a discussion of *Stauder* in the light of a comprehensive collection of the ECJ's case law, see Craig and de Búrca 2008). However, the empirical implications of this declaration were initially modest, as the Court was refusing to strike down EC legislation. National law was not at stake.

Nonetheless, the clash between legal systems proved to be unavoidable as nationals of different states would start demanding that European law should grant them the same level of protection as the national law (Dehousse 1998: 62).

At this point, a bold interpretation of supremacy would entail that national constitutions and their regulation on fundamental rights would have to yield to European law. The reason for such an interpretation lies in the necessity to procure a uniform application of European law within the domestic legal order.

In part, this is what the Court did. It stated in the case *Internationale Handelsgesellschaft* that the Treaty of Rome would not fulfil its purpose if national laws could inhibit its action:

> Recourse to the legal rules or concepts of national law in order to judge the validity of measures adopted by the institutions of the Community would have an adverse effect on the uniformity and efficacy of Community law ... Therefore the validity of a Community instrument or its effect within a member state cannot be affected by allegations that it strikes at either the fundamental rights as formulated in that State's constitutions or the principle of a national constitutional structure.[15]

Nevertheless, in the same ruling, the Court provided a solution that would not leave fundamental rights unprotected. It asserted that fundamental rights

---

13 Legal scholars have suggested that it is almost impossible to give a univocal and universal definition of fundamental rights (Rengeling 1992). A fair listing, sufficient for this research, would certainly include the right to judicial defence, and to be heard in court, the right to legal certainty, equality, and proportionality, among others (Cappelletti 1989).
14 Case *Stauder v. City of Ulm* [1969] ECR 419.
15 Case 11/70 *Internationale Handelsgesellschaft GMBH v. Einfuhr- und Vorratsstelle für Getreide und Futtermittel* [1970] ECR 1125. See also case 25/70 *Einfuhr- und Vorratsstelle* [1970] ECR 1161 (cf. Rengeling 1992; Pernice 1979).

protected by member states would also be protected by the Community. It declared that fundamental rights were part of the new order, and had to find protection within the supranational order. This was another gradual, expansive step towards centralisation of authority; at the same time, the Court offered a solution to the main problem of protection of rights:

> In fact, respect for fundamental rights forms an integral part of the general principles of Community law protected by the Court of Justice. The protection of such rights, whilst inspired by the constitutional traditions common to the Member States, must be ensured within the framework of the structure and objectives of the Community.[16]

It must be recalled that there was no bill of rights to which the Court could resort.[17] As a consequence, in the case of *Nold* of 1974, the Court clarified that protection for fundamental rights was to find its inspiration not only in the common national constitutional traditions, but in international treaties such as the European Convention for the Protection of Human Rights and Fundamental Freedoms and the European Social Charter (Craig and de Búrca 2008: 383–5; Kuper 1998: 10).

The widening of the scope of European law by means of expansive interpretation provoked a considerable reaction. In particular, domestic higher courts engaged the ECJ in a dispute over the role of protector of fundamental rights. The same year *Nold* had been decided, the German Constitutional Court declared that as long as the EC did not have a catalogue of fundamental rights, the compatibility of European law with German Basic Law could be proved by that Court.[18]

The ECJ's continuing concern about the protection of fundamental rights,[19] and the constitutional dialogue it held with the German Constitutional Court, led to the *Solange II* ruling,[20] whereby the German court declared that it was no longer necessary to control the acts of the Community, as long as the ECJ assumed that responsibility.

The fact that the ECJ exercises the control of fundamental rights has crucial political implications in regard to the Common Market. As EC legislation grows in content and scope, the task of the ECJ becomes expansive. Moreover,

---

16 Case 11/70 *Internationale Handelsgesellschaft*.
17 Up to today there is still no such catalogue.
18 Case 2 BvL 52/71, *Internationale Handelsgesellschaft*, 29.05.1974, known as the *Solange* ruling.
19 Legal scholars have suggested that the ECJ has developed its own principled method of interpretation of fundamental rights. See *Grundrechtsdogmatik* (Rengeling 1992: 229; Beutler 1991: n. 32, 108; Streinz: 1989: 399).
20 Case 2 BvR 197/83 *Wünsche Handelsgesellschaft*, 22.10.1986.

constant expansion entails constant transfer of prerogative to oversee fundamental rights from the member states to the Community (Rengeling 1992: 4). This is especially true considering that the ECJ tied the protection of fundamental rights to the structure and goals of the Community (Nicolaysen 1991: 61).

The concept of fundamental freedom has frequently been associated to fundamental rights. Although they share many properties, they are not the same. At national level, fundamental rights protect the individual against the action of the states. In the same sense, fundamental rights protected at the European level are directed against Community organs in order to protect the individual. However, fundamental freedoms that protect the individual at Community level are basically directed against the state, and enforced by the ECJ (Pernice 1979; Streinz 1989: 73,444). The purpose of fundamental freedoms is to ensure the establishment of the Common Market, keeping a check on the hindering action of member states (Rengeling 1992: 172; Beutler 1991: n. 42).

Because of the doctrines of direct effect, and because of the link established by the ECJ, individuals can invoke their fundamental freedoms against their states as if they were fundamental rights; this triad has been called the 'interests triangle' ('*Interessendreieck*', in Pernice 1990: 2413).

Chapter 4

The politics of judicial design
Professionals and legal experts

It is no secret that most legal reforms have borrowed much from other legal systems. Migration of legal concepts, transfer of institutions and legal transplants are almost as old as humankind itself. It is a mystery, though, how these processes have come about. In other words, we do not know *who* gets to decide *what* solution, and from *where* it should be taken. The case of the Andean Community and the transplantation of the European Court of Justice, together with its whole procedural system, raises these kinds of questions. In this chapter, I complement the literature on diffusion of European ideas, as well as scholarship, by working on the idea of legal transplants.

The reader will notice that the chapter incorporates a distinctive theoretical framework, composed of two theoretical levels. At a higher theoretical level, I resort to neofunctionalism, as explained in Chapter 2, as an overall strategy for legal development that can be used as a model for other regions. At a lower level of abstraction, the chapter introduces network analysis.

I argue that a network approach can offer a nuanced explanation of important legal transformation. Whenever legal change is on the agenda, the search for a suitable model is determined not only by legitimacy but by personal linkages within a network and the professional background of its members. In addition, professional networks tend to frame problems as technically as possible in order to further their policy agenda. However, the mere existence of networks is not sufficient for provoking legal-institutional change. As the case of the European-Andean networks shows, there must be enabling conditions that allow networks to accommodate existing preferences by proposing technical solutions that satisfy governments' needs, as well as their own professional agenda.

This chapter begins by establishing its theoretical framework and points to three puzzles that drive the research on the agents of legal change. After this the empirical data found in the history of the establishment of the Andean Court of Justice is revealed. The focus is on the mechanism found in the process of legal transformation and on the role of professional legal networks. The chapter traces the efforts of a selected group of legal experts who assisted the Andean Junta in the task of drafting a report on the need for a dispute settlement body first, and subsequently making a concrete proposal on the institutional design for an Andean Court of Justice. In order to trace the activities of this professional network, the background of the participants is explored. This reveals the policy core that linked them to scholars of European integration.

The action of this network can be portrayed as a two-level game: a first level of persuasion, followed by a second level of incorporation exploiting a window of opportunity. The final section gives an account of the expansion of these networks and the impact this had on the actual case law handed down by the Court. It suggests that the legal network also significantly influenced the early production of case law. Thus, contrary to the traditional strategies used by international financial organisations, the politics of judicial design of the ACJ suggest that persuasion is a mechanism far more effective than conditionality. It would be advisable to consider this fact in times of global uncertainties.

Brief notes on the transplant approach: aims and limitations

The term 'legal transplant' has been with us for some time and has spurred interesting conversations.[1] We still do not know what it means exactly, and it seems clear that legal scholars have divergent understandings of what a legal transplant is. The most prominent literature on legal transplants stresses the diffusion of law, principles and societal beliefs from one legal system to another (Watson 1993; Horwitz 2009). Such transfers of law can be observed throughout human history, especially in times of imperial expansion, colonialism, and enlightenment. From Roman Law to Napoleon's Civil Code, from the Swiss Civil Code to the Fundamental Rights of the German Basic Law, the number of transplanted laws is considerable. Nonetheless, despite the numerous cases that can be observed, the transplant approach has still very limited explanatory capacities.

Scholars using this approach are largely unable to explain why similar transplants do not produce a similar result or why legal transplants tend to change over time. There are, nevertheless, some valuable attempts. Some scholars have suggested that certain legal traditions – or legal families – have immanent qualities that determine or predict adaptation in a new environment; many contend that transplanting Common Law systems produces higher levels of legality in the host system than transplanting norms from

---

1 For instance, the July 2009 issue of *Theoretical Inquiries in Law* is 'made up of studies of histories of legal transplantations'. In addition, a long-lasting debate about the theoretical robustness of the legal transplant approach has not been settled yet (see Legrand 1997; cf. Watson 2000).

Civil Law systems (e.g. La Porta *et al.* 1998; Mahoney 2001). In addition, recent literature links the performance of legal transplants with the ability of the recipient legal community to internalise the rules, principles, and values of the donor system (Berkowitz *et al.* 2003: 179). It is often assumed, therefore, that successful internalisation of new norms depends on the inherent abilities of either the donor – also called origin – or the recipient legal order. Moreover, these theories share the assumption that the only interaction that takes place occurs among legal systems.

However, this strand of the literature does not acknowledge certain important circumstances regarding the transplant approach. First, the transplant approach is not a theory – at least, not yet. Writers have yet to come up with any system of causal links, analytical explanations or knowledge accumulation. It is not a normative theory either because it lacks a core of value that could be regarded as the genesis of a principled discourse. Second, the transplant approach is not a method. Scholars have failed to analyse legal transplants according to any consensual proceeding that would allow the establishment of hypotheses. Until this happens, it will be very difficult to falsify any claim on legal transplants, or to make any meaningful operationalisation.

Therefore, I use this concept in a more abstract way, as a heuristic device that should inspire more than problematise. When I talk about legal transplants, I refer to an approach based on a metaphor (Nelken and Feest 2001). Using the idea of a physical transplant helps us to think about diffusion of law in creative ways. It is very useful to depict the process of legal transformation in terms of a donor and a recipient. As a metaphor, legal transplants provide a heuristic frame, an umbrella under which scholars can use a wide range of analytical toolkits. Conducting interdisciplinary research is just one possible way of combining the transplant metaphor with middle-range theories (Saldías 2010).

Political scientists are increasingly including the study of legal transplants in their research agendas, especially as a dimension of policy transfer and norm diffusion (see, for instance, Börzel and Risse 2009). The central question is how the process of transplantation comes about. Law can obviously not transport itself. There are mechanisms and actors that are responsible for the process of diffusion. Following these questions of how law is able to travel, some writers focus on the agency that the phenomenon of transplantation is associated with. According to them, legal experts are frequently agents of transplantation in that they advocate for the transplantation of well-functioning legal systems, and introduce to developing countries a swarm of constitutions, codes, statutes and regulations (Berkowitz *et al.* 2003: 164; also called 'entrepreneurial transplants' by Likhovski 2009: 621).

So far, there has not been a clear explanation about who these experts are and how the mechanisms for the diffusion of legal institutions work. In what follows, I focus on the actors that make these legal transfers – transplants, if you may – possible. I also ask under what conditions such networked action can be effective. The answer, I hope, will underpin my claim that the choice for certain legal institutions, as well as the material content of the statutes that are imported, is neither coincidence nor the immediate result of a true deliberative legislative process. It is a consistent and comprehensive set of actions set out by networks of professionals that share some core beliefs.

Three Andean puzzles around the establishment of the Andean Court of Justice

Chapter 1 chronicled some relevant phases in South American integration. In the late 1970s and early 1980s, the process of regional integration in South America was reinvigorated. MERCOSUR, the southern common market, saw the light, and the Andean Pact underwent significant transformations. Specifically, in 1979 the Andean main intergovernmental and legislative body, the Commission, approved a proposal for the establishment of a supranational Court of Justice in the image of the ECJ. This meant that EC law and EC judicial remedies were to be transplanted into the Andean Pact, in one of the most striking actions of legal diffusion in the history of South American republics.

The usual narrative about the establishment of the Andean Court of Justice begins with the approval of its founding document. The Treaty on the Establishment of the Court of Justice of the Cartagena Agreement had been signed in 1979, and approved in 1984. It is precisely at this point that literature on the Andean Court of Justice begins to be produced.[2] The establishment of the Court is often presented in the literature as a *fait accompli* that does not need further inquiry about the process of legal reform. However, the fact that a rather controversial judicial institution like the ECJ could be transplanted with so few mutations is utterly intriguing and deserves a deeper analysis. Scholars of regional integration have failed to notice that such phenomena are not necessarily natural to international organisations. Why this is so remains unclear. Maybe the political and economic convictions of the 1970s and 1980s repressed such questions; or perhaps the collective expectations about economic development were so high that it provoked much wishful thinking. Or perhaps it is just a blind faith in transplanted institutions because they have performed so well in industrialised countries.

Be that as it may, a first look at the history of the establishment of the ACJ reveals some interesting facts that have, so far, not been acknowledged by the leading literature on this topic. Consider for instance, that already in 1972 the Andean Commission – the organisation's major decision-making body[3] – had

---

2 Just as an example of noted work on the subject: Andueza 1986; da Cruz Vilaça and Sobrino 1996; Ekmekdjian 1994; Sáchica 1985a; Suárez Mejías 2001; Tangarife 2001a.
3 See Chapter 5 for a description of the Andean Community's main bodies and institutions.

manifested the necessity of creating a dispute settlement body. During one of its summits, it instructed the Junta, to a great extent the Andean executive organ, to present a report (henceforward 'the report') with a concrete recommendation on the matter of an Andean dispute resolution body.[4] For the reader who might usually focus on institutions rather than on contextual variables or factors, this may not be too impressive a fact. After all, all institutions have a genesis. For a pure kind of institutional theory, a really interesting question would be *whether* institutions matter, and *how* they influence the world. The dominant Latin American literature on Andean integrations tends to adopt such a perspective. Almost every noted author begins his or her narrative with the treaty establishing the Court of Justice of the Andean Community (Saldías 2008). Conversely, for scholars adopting alternative perspectives, the establishment of the ACJ can be utterly puzzling. This is especially true for approaches that seek to explain particular institutional outcomes across time, such as historical institutionalism; also, for those who focus on the dissemination of ideas and institutions, the emergence of the Andean Court of Justice is not self-evident either.

An example of such historical inconsistencies will suffice as an initial puzzle for now: the Commission charged the Junta with the task of reporting on a possible dispute settlement scheme only three years after the establishment of the Cartagena Agreement. How is it possible that a judicial body was needed after only three years of Andean integration? If such incorporation followed in such a short time, why was the Cartagena Agreement adopted without a court in the first place? The literature does not offer a conclusive answer for historical institutionalists. The most recurrent explanations point to functional requirements, as mentioned above, namely the search for a solution to endemic non-compliance with Andean laws. In general, this contention is plausible. However, it fails to address some questions in regard to its historical context. Three puzzles strike me as helpful for guiding the enquiry on the Andean Court of Justice.

First, how could the Commission come to the conclusion that there was a compliance problem serious enough to justify a judicial body, after only three years of Andean integration? Consider that the Cartagena Agreement already included the possibility of using the dispute settlement system of the Latin American Free Trade Association (Zelada Castedo 1985: 126). What explains the possible dissatisfaction with a system that had not been used even once?

Second, Latin American states have a strong tradition in respecting national sovereignty, even if it violates mutual agreements. Conflicts have traditionally been solved through discrete negotiations between the parties, and the prevailing style for international coordination has been the consensus at the highest political level. In Latin American jargon, this is described as *Concertación*

---

4 Sexto Período de Sesiones Extraordinarias, Acta Final; Lima, 9–18 December 1971.

(Emmes and Mols 1993: 69; also Paolillo and Ons-Indart 1971; Salazar Santos 1973: 5). Moreover, when it comes to economic processes, there is a known resistance to including lawyers and judges. It is assumed that these professionals frequently lead such dynamic developments to a paralysis.[5] What could have driven the member states to break with this tradition, only three years after the Cartagena Agreement was negotiated?

Third, why did the Andean Group establish a court so similar to the European Court of Justice, a court widely known for its pro-integrationist case law? This puzzle is even more intriguing considering the dominance of the principles of *Concertación* and sovereignty in Latin America.

I suggest that the Andean governments faced serious resistance when they tried to incorporate the founding treaty, the Cartagena Agreement, into the national orders. The cases of the Chilean Parliament and the Colombian Supreme Court show how these actors challenged their governments and contested their powers to control the process of regional integration. Although the governments could finally accomplish their task, it came at a very high cost: the political and legal control of the process had to be shared with other supranational actors. This scenario of legal contestation from the domestic level laid the conditions for the action of professional networks, as member states' governments were willing to cede some sovereignty to a court as long as it would mitigate the growing domestic demand for control. The network, in turn, had a record advocating for the establishment of a judicial organ in the integration process and used the opportunity to frame the problems of the organisation as a strict technical-legal matter. Moreover, the network was heavily biased towards Europe, which suggests that those drafting the final report used mainly European informational resources to look for a solution and to shape their proposal.

Epistemic communities and advocacy coalitions: an overview

It is a truism to say that the emergence and diffusion of laws depend on factors that sometimes transcend pure normative criteria. Nevertheless, the traditional literature of comparative law overwhelmingly tends to focus more on legal institutions than on the social implications of law (see, for example, Zweigert and Kötz 1996). The underlying juridical assumption in the traditional comparatist literature is that law – and law alone – shapes reality. As a consequence, the processes that change these institutions, or the actors that shape them, remain under-researched topics. This is unfortunate because actors, as well as conglomerates of actors, can explain much of the outcome of

---

5 Although there is no study that offers conclusive evidence, there seems to be a consensus among scholars that this is true. See Padilla 1979: 91 and Orrego Vicuña 1973: 135; 1974: 31.

legal reform and legal transformations. Approaching law through actors can sometimes prove useful when it comes to explaining the spread or emergence of certain types of law.

One possibility for adopting such an actor-centred perspective is to focus on networks. Such an analysis can contribute to the understanding of legal reforms generally and of legal transplants specifically. Exploring the actors involved implies that we look for interests and logics of behaviour that drive them. If we are thorough enough, we will be able to make general causal claims about legal transformations. We will also be in a position to drop many working assumptions about the proliferation of legal institutions. In other words, the existence, incorporation and performance of legal norms depend not only on the law itself, but also on a variety of actors that participate in the legal process at different stages. These actors are interested in the outcomes of legal transformations and legal transplants. Therefore, they interact in complex patterns that can be better grasped if we abandon the assumption that law alone shapes reality.

The literature on networks offers some frameworks that are very helpful when gauging the actors that are relevant in the process of a legal transplant. For instance, the Advocacy Coalition Framework (Jenkins-Smith and Sabatier 1994; Zafonte and Sabatier 1998) portrays the process of institutional change brought about by groups of actors that share a policy interest and have common beliefs about norms and institutions. This constitutes their common policy core and is a 'glue' that holds them together. In the case of professionals, the common academic background and socialisation can bring them together into networks and spur coordinated action that will lead them to achieve specific policy goals. This framework introduces new insights into the process of legal change because it includes a wider number of institutions participating in the decision-making process in the analysis; it also acknowledges that there are converging as well as diverging interests that interact in the pursuit of specific goals within the law-making process.[6] This focus deviates from traditional institutionalism in that it focuses on the legal profession as it tries to channel certain preferences regarding the design of legal institutions, instead of merely focusing on the institutions themselves. By paraphrasing two noted scholars: it is the members of the profession who act as 'rationalisers' and push for change (DiMaggio and Powell 1983).[7]

Parallel to the Advocacy Coalition Framework, some scholars focus on epistemic communities and their role in international policy coordination. Peter Haas defined them as 'networks of knowledge-based experts' and assumed that their members were primarily interested in knowledge and in understanding

---

6 Originally, Zafonte and Sabatier focused on policy-making instead of law-making and also on different institutions within the government.

7 DiMaggio and Powell made this claim when they referred to the process of homogenisation within an epistemic field (see DiMaggio and Powell 1983: 147).

the world according to analytic or scientific methods. The procedures for acquiring this knowledge would validate their output and distinguish them from an ordinary interest group. For this literature, the relevance of epistemic communities lies in their ability to understand problems of high complexity and give advice to decision-makers. Sometimes their output can even help states identify their interests. This means that the ways in which states and organisations identify their problems and try to solve them result from how problems are understood by the policy-makers themselves, or by whom they turn for advice. The logic of epistemic policy coordination, then, begins to reveal itself due to an initial uncertainty on how to solve problems; this uncertainty is likely to become more salient as the complexity of issues rises (Haas 1992: 3, 12).[8] Therefore, epistemic communities can influence policy-making by identifying relevant problems and proposing solutions. Nonetheless, epistemic communities are strongly committed to the same episteme that unites them. This means that, unlike other interest groups, they would withdraw from the policy debate after consistent evidence proved their causal beliefs to be wrong.

On a closely related strand, organisation theorists have examined the role that uncertainty plays in the processes of diffusion. They suggest that organisations 'tend to model themselves after similar organisations in their field that they perceive to be more legitimate or successful' (DiMaggio and Powell 1983: 152). Therefore, members of epistemic networks will most probably advocate for the implementation of solutions found in successful organisations primarily because there is more information available; there are more resources, and it provides increased legitimacy. According to DiMaggio and Powell, the uncertainty that characterises our world only exacerbates such pressure; hence, their hypothesis reads: 'the more uncertain the relationship between means and ends, the greater the extent to which an organization will model itself after organizations it perceives to be successful' (DiMaggio and Powell 1983: 154; Zucker 1987: 443). The modelling after other organisations, or the copycat process that takes place, begins with the emulation of formal structures and institutions.

Lawyers do not escape that logic. Lawyers and legal scholars are experts in a field, produce legal knowledge, and seek to promote and expand what they have to offer, namely laws, regulations and legal institutions (Dezalay and Garth 2002). The quality of the product these experts offer is difficult to assess: difficult, but not impossible. To start with, the performance of certain legal institutions in their home setting is a strong indicator. In addition, the prestige of the legal experts is important too. A well-known reputation increases when an international organisation or academic institution endorses the skills of the legal expert. Lastly, the attractiveness of certain legal institutions can be

---

8 'Poorly understood conditions may create enough turbulence that established operating procedures may break down, making institutions unworkable. Neither power nor institutional cues to behavior will be available, and new patterns of action may ensue' (Haas 1992: 14).

enhanced by rewards offered to the 'buyers'. This means that the adoption of certain foreign laws by a state (frequently a developing state) can be rewarded. This is positive conditionality.

Of course, if a state refuses to adopt certain laws, it could also face negative conditionality measures, meaning sanctions. International financial institutions show a long record of applying conditionality measures as a means of incentives. Especially during the 1980s and the 1990s, the World Bank and the International Monetary Fund made loans to developing countries contingent upon legal and economic reforms. The access to money, together with a respectable reputation of their experts made it very difficult to resist the economic and legal requirements imposed by these organisations. This is how US-friendly ideas of the Washington Consensus permeated the economies of several developing countries and prompted market-oriented judicial reforms (Faundez 2010). Interestingly, there is much truth in the assertion that there is a competition between European and US approaches for dominance in legal fields (Dezalay and Garth 1996, 2002). The case of the judicial reform in the Andean Community confirms that thesis.

The findings that follow are interpreted in this light. The assumptions and causal mechanism are certainly not identical in the different network approaches described above. Sometimes they are even incompatible. However, these approaches are useful tools in the process of understanding the process of judicial reform in the Andean Community. The Andean narrative on the establishment of its court of justice shows that focusing on networks across institutions offers a plausible account of the reasons that led Andean decision-makers to transplant an entire court of justice. At some points, however, when applied to the Andean case, the different frameworks tend to overlap and it becomes unclear whether the observable networks are epistemic communities, advocacy coalitions, or just organisations mimicking other organisations.

The Andean network analysed below features many traits of epistemic communities, although its behaviour seems to be more consistent with the logic of legal advocacy coalitions. Similarly, the documentation analysed here suggests that the European Court of Justice has always been a highly regarded institution. Yet, there are strong reasons to believe that this is not a case of sheer mimicry or copycat action. The claim is that the process of judicial transformation of Andean integration was the result of rational bargaining between professional legal networks and national governments under very special enabling conditions of domestic political contestation.

The Andean-European network

Crafting a policy core for the network

The Andean Junta conducted its research on a possible judicial reform with significant assistance from the Institute for the Integration of Latin America and the Caribbean (INTAL), established by the Inter-American Development Bank in 1965. INTAL's headquarters are located in Buenos Aires and its mission is 'to promote and consolidate Latin American and Caribbean integration at the sub-regional, regional, inter-regional, hemispheric and international levels'.[9] Among other tools, the institute achieves this goal by means of technical assistance and capacity-building activities for the formulation and enforcement of integration policies. INTAL is also an agent for dissemination of knowledge in the field of regional integration, with an explicit focus on European integration. During the 1960s and 1970s, this task was undertaken by means of several periodicals that were published and financed by the institute, notably *Revista Integración Latinoamericana*, *Derecho de la Integración*, *Revista de la Integración*, and the *Serie Publicaciones INTAL*.[10] During the time between the discussion and establishment of the Andean Court of Justice, the work of distinguished international scholars was translated and published in INTAL's periodicals, including Ernst Haas (1972), Bela Balassa (1972), Joseph Nye (1969), Philippe Schmitter (1969a), Maurice Lagrange (1968), and Pierre Pescatore (1967). Although the institution sees itself as an academic research centre, it might very well be regarded as a policy-oriented institution, with a clear mandate that is not questioned or scrutinised by its members. In other words, it has a clear bias towards regional integration.

Following the Commission's mandate, the Junta set up a working group ('the working group') that would meet several times within a short period of time. Contrary to what would be suggested by a bold institutionalist approach, which is that institutions are all that matter, the convictions and backgrounds of the participants of that group were very relevant to the outcome of the deliberations on the ACJ. The members constituted an active network of scholars and officials capable of influencing the ongoing conversations about the future of the Andean integration process. Felix Peña, for instance, was at that time a senior consultant at INTAL and directed by the institute's department for legal studies.[11]

Peña's academic background is strongly tied to European studies and European legal integration. Born in Argentina, he earned a degree in European law in Leuven, writing his dissertation at the Law School of the University

---

9 Taken from its mission statement available at <http://www.iadb.org/intal/detalle_articulo.asp?idioma=ENG&aid=490&cid=206&nivel=>.
10 All of them have ceased to be published. *Revista Integracion Latinoamericana* was published 1976–95, *Derecho de la Integracion* 1967–78, *Revista de la Integracion* 1967–75, *Serie Publicaciones INTAL* 1964–96. They were replaced by other periodicals that are equally devoted to the topic of regional integration, for instance *Revista Integracion & Comercio*, established in 1996.
11 Two years later he would become Director of INTAL and vice-manager (subgerente) of Integration at the Inter-American Development Bank.

of Madrid. In regard to European integration theorists, it is worthy to note that he worked under the supervision of Ernst Haas, the neofunctionalist theorist, at the University of Berkeley in 1973.[12] Between 1966 and 1975 he directed the department of legal studies of INTAL. Some evidence shows that comparative ideas about the ECJ and an eventual Andean Court were discussed by Peña and some collaborators as early as 1971.

In March of that year, Peña and Francisco Orrego Vicuña, a Chilean law professor and one of the consultants to INTAL, participated in a colloquium on the 'Legal Aspects of Economic Integration' organised by The Hague Academy of International Law. Vicuña had the task of presenting the Latin American experience with integration. This event gave both of them the opportunity to meet their European colleagues, especially those concerned with the role of the European Court of Justice. Among the participants in that colloquium was ECJ Judge Roberto Monaco, as well as Eric Stein, a noted EC scholar from the University of Michigan. The event had a strong comparative perspective and, accordingly, several reports were presented for the cases of the European Community, Eastern Europe, and Africa.

Vicuña's report focused on the necessity of dispute settlement bodies that could strengthen the different processes of integration in Latin America, especially in light of the ambitious goals. The edited volume that resulted incorporates the oral intervention of the participants. One telling contribution during the conference belonged to Eric Stein, who made a comparison between the regions, delicately suggesting that existing integration schemes can be understood as belonging to a common type of organisation. They only differ in their degree of intimacy between national law and 'integration law', which can be measured against a continuum (Rideau 1973: 465f.). This seems to be one of the earliest comparisons that mentions the term 'integration law', a term that would influence a strand of Latin American legal scholars studying *derecho de la integración*.[13] In this continuum, Stein locates the Andean Pact far away from the European Community, mainly because of the deciding role that the ECJ played in Europe through the Article 177 of the Treaty of the European Community. It is fair to note that Stein undertakes this exercise rather reluctantly in an academic environment, admitting that he is not an expert in fields other than European Law. Nevertheless, this experience indicates that the INTAL network was familiar with the ECJ as early

---

12 All information is taken from his CV, available online at <http://www.felixpena.com.ar/index.php?contenido=trayectoria> consulted 18 August 2010.
13 It is interesting to note that in Latin America *derecho de la integración* is a widely accepted term that refers to a discipline, as well as a university course that studies all integration schemes. In contrast, there is no equivalent notion among EU scholars, who would study it under the intellectual umbrella of 'EU law', 'European integration', or 'comparative regionalism'. See Saldías (2008).

as 1971.[14] Soon after this event, the INTAL periodical *Derecho de la Integración* published and translated articles of Maurice Lagrange[15] and Pierre Pescatore.[16] Furthermore, one of the editorials in 1971,[17] although not signed by Peña, sets the foundations for the document that would be incorporated into the Junta's final report for the Commission.

In regard to the report that was being drafted, the Junta commissioned INTAL consultants to deliver opinions on specific issues related to Andean law and regional integration. Felix Peña himself delivered an opinion on alternatives for a dispute settlement system within an integration scheme. The second issue, penned by Francisco Kramer Villagrán, covered the alleged need for some control of legality for Andean administrative acts. Villagrán was also part of the INTAL team; prior to the assignment, he had written in *Derecho de la Integración* about the legal instrument of Central American integration.[18] The third INTAL consultant was Felipe Paolillo, a scholar from the University of Montevideo, who had an equal presence in the journal.[19] Furthermore, several national specialists from each member state briefed the Junta about the validity of rulings and awards of international tribunals within their national legal traditions. These national experts would play an important role in diffusing the outcomes of these deliberations. Among them were Jacobo Schaulson from Chile and Jaime Vidal Perdomo from Colombia.[20]

Having collected the written material, the Junta called for an experts' meeting on 23 June 1972, bringing together all the authors mentioned above. In addition, two European officials were invited to that summit, in order to provide insights from the European experience, namely the European Commission's acting director of the Legal Service, Gerard Olivier, and ECJ

---

14 Interestingly, Felix Peña attempts an argument that stresses the trait of *concertación* within the judicial function. Although acknowledging the control function of the judiciary, his tone is rather sceptical of radical jurisdiction in Latin America: a line of thought that would markedly change after this event (see his opinion in the report).

15 'La interpretación unitaria del derecho de las Comunidades Europeas: aspectos de la interpretación prejudicial', *Derecho de la Integración* No. 3 (October 1968), 59–80.

16 'Distribución de competencias y de poderes entre los Estados miembros de las Comunidades Europeas: estudio de las relaciones entre las Comunidades y los Estados miembros', *Revista Derecho de la Integración* No. 1 (October 1967). This was the same year Pescatore received his appointment as a judge to the European Court of Justice.

17 'La idea de conflicto y el ordenamiento jurídico e institucional de la integración económica', *Revista de la Integración* No. 8 (April 1971), 5f.

18 'Los instrumentos legales de la integración economica centroamericana', *Derecho de la Integración* No. 3 (October 1968), 36–58.

19 'Reparticion de competencies y poderes entre la ALALC y los Estados miembros', *Derecho de la Integración* No. 2 (April 1968), 20–49.

20 Also attending that particular meeting were Renato Crespo (Bolivia), Ramiro Borja y Borja (Ecuador), and Hector Cornejo Chavez (Peru).

Judge Pierre Pescatore, together with the scholars that had delivered the opinions and the briefings.

An examination of all the above-mentioned contributions suggests that it was not intended by the working group to design a new dispute settlement mechanism from scratch. It was, rather, a preliminary introduction of five dispute resolution prototypes that appeared as possible candidates, namely that of the Latin American Free Trade Association (LAFTA), the Central American Common Market (CACM), the European Community (EC), the Economic Community of West African States (ECOWAS), and the General Agreement on Tariffs and Trade (GATT). Yet, the report is strongly biased in favour of the European Court of Justice. INTAL consultants make constant references to the European experience and most of them are laudatory remarks.[21] Conversely, references to the system of LAFTA are tainted with a rather sceptical tone,[22] probably because it was the model that was being questioned.

Therefore, the outcome of the report is not a surprise. The Junta presents a blueprint for a court based on the design of the ECJ, armoured with procedures of nullification, non-compliance, and preliminary rulings, all three procedures flanked by the doctrine of supremacy of supranational law (JUNAC 1973: 139, 49f.).[23] The Commission formally approved the report in December 1972, and the main meeting's protocol recorded a brief passage referring to a 'wide exchange of opinions' that supposedly took place, followed by the expression of 'satisfaction on how the Junta has been conducting its work'. It instructed the Junta to further develop the content of this report, and make a concrete proposal on how to materialise these ideas.[24] The Junta agreed to present a final proposal and to assist member states in the task of diffusing and explaining the meaning of its newly approved institutional agenda.

Diffusing the network's policy programme

The fact that the INTAL-Junta network was very aware of the importance of diffusion can be inferred from its regional activities. After the working

---

21 See, for example, INTAL 1972: 123, 6; also JUNAC 1973: 139, 40, 41, 46.
22 'El sistema de solucion de controversias establecido en la ALALC no satisface los requisitos que acabamos de apuntar' (JUNAC 1973: 144).
23 See Chapter 2 for an overview of the European Court of Justice and its main case law.
24 Com/XE- acta final, 1972, p. 3: 'La presentación del informe dio lugar a un amplio intercambio de opiniones de carácter preliminar, que permitió a la Junta dar explicaciones adicionales sobre el proyecto de bases de tratado que ha elaborado y escuchar las reacciones iniciales de las Representaciones en torno a este tema.

'Las Representaciones reiteraron la importancia de contra en la Subregión con un instrumento de esta naturaleza *y su conformidad con la manera en que la Junta viene desarrollando estos trabajos*' (emphasis added).

sessions in different cities, like Lima and Ciudad de Guatemala, the network hosted several meetings with Andean key actors in order to diffuse the content of the report. In October 1972, at the occasion of the Lawyers' Congress of the Andean Group, Felipe Salazar Santos, coordinator of the Junta and one of the drafters of the report, was in charge of presenting the draft and reaffirming the need for an Andean judicial organ before the legal community (Salazar Santos 1973). The congress focused on issues related to law and integration, the role of lawyers in the integration process and, of course, the establishment of a jurisdictional organ for the Cartagena Agreement (INTAL 1973b: 179). Only few weeks later (20–24 November), INTAL sponsored a seminar at a Colombian university, the Colegio Mayor de Nuestra Señora del Rosario. The topic hinged around 'legal aspects of economic integration' and the presentations focused on the new Andean legal system and the European experience with its Court of Justice. Among the Andean presenters were, again, noted participants of the working group: Felipe Salazar Santos and Gustavo Fernandez Saavedra, both Junta officials; Felix Peña and Francisco Villagran from INTAL; Jacobo Schaulson and Jaime Vidal Perdomo, who had represented Chile and Colombia in the initial meeting; and finally, presenting the European experience, Jean Victor Louis, professor for European law at Brussels University, and Michel Gaudet, former director of the EC's Legal Service (INTAL 1973a: 178).

Between 1973 and 1979, INTAL consistently used its periodicals for the diffusion of the ACJ project and the convenience of legal integration. This was made particularly through the journal *Derecho de la Integración*[25] and penned by the members of the network, notably Pierre Pescatore,[26] Francisco Orrego Vicuña,[27] Felipe Salazar,[28] and Felix Peña[29]. In addition, the journal

---

25 Editorial, 'El aporte del derecho económico al derecho de la integración', *Derecho de la Integración* No. 18–19 (March/July 1975), 5–7.
26 'Nuevo fenómeno en las relaciones internacionales', *Derecho de la Integración* (1973); 'La importancia del derecho en un proceso de integración económica', *Derecho de la Integración* No. 15 (March 1974), 11–21. Also 'Las exigencias de la democracia y la legitimidad de la Comunidad Europea', *Derecho de la Integración* No. 17 (November 1974), 45–54; 'El ejecutivo comunitario: justificación del cuatripartismo instituido por los tratados de Paris y Roma', *Derecho de la Integración* No. 25–26 (November 1977), 53–62.
27 'La creación de un tribunal de justicia en el Grupo Andino', *Derecho de la Integración* No. 15 (March 1974), 31–46; 'La adaptación de lo pactado a los cambios contextuales que inciden en un proceso de integración', *Derecho de la Integración* No. 20 (November 1975), 37–46; 'Los presupuestos juridicos de un proceso de integración económica efectivo', *Derecho de la Integración* No. 24 (March 1977), 11–20.
28 'Solución de conflictos en organizaciones interestatales para la integración económica y otras formas de cooperación económica', *Derecho de la Integración* No. 28–29 (November 1978), 11–34.
29 'La experiencia institucional de la integración económica de América Latina', *Integración Latinoamericana* 6(64) (1979), 27–32.

began a series containing relevant rulings of the ECJ.[30] This effort of diffusion does not have many parallels in the history of international organisations in the region.

Conditions for the action of networks: using windows of opportunity

In 1979, the Andean Junta finally presented the proposal for legal reform to be adopted by the Andean Commission during that year's summit. It is difficult to gauge what exactly happened in the meetings where the proposal for a court was debated, as written accounts are rare. Of the few chronicles, most of them portray profuse deliberations. They suggest that the proposal prompted rounds of deep discussion, followed by hard bargaining and deliberation.[31]

As a matter of fact, the final proposal approved by the Commission included all the features that the European Court of Justice became noted for: an annulment procedure, a non-compliance procedure, a procedure of preliminary rulings, and the principle of direct applicability of Andean law. In other words, the final outcome is consistent with the work of the INTAL-Junta network, and there is no significant change that could bolster the claim of an approval based on deliberation. Rather, it seems to be that the final proposal's approval in 1979 followed a similar path of the preliminary report that asserted the need for a judicial body in 1972: a swift confirmation of what had been done

---

30 Corte Europea de Justicia: 'CEE: sentencias de la Corte de Justicia', *Derecho de la Integración* No. 21 (March 1976), 190–222. Also 'CEC: sentencias de la Corte de Justicia (II parte)', *Derecho de la Integración* No. 22–23 (July–November 1976), 120–53; 'Sentencias de la Corte (IV parte)', *Derecho de la Integración* No. 25–26 (November 1977), 143–50; 'Sentencias de la Corte (V parte)', *Derecho de la Integración* No. 27 (March 1978), 189–212; 'Sentencias de la Corte VI parte)', *Derecho de la Integración* No. 28–29 (November 1978), 162–8.
31 For instance, Andean judge Carlos Sáchica. He describes the negotiation as follows:

> 'The negotiation was slow. Many meetings of experts coming from member states tweaked the original proposal, and along lengthy debates it acquired the tenets that distinguish the Courts from its undeniable model: the Court of Justice of the European Communities' (Sáchica 1985a: 13). Zelada Castedo provides another account consistent with a deliberative approach. He suggests that the reason why it took so long to approve the ACJ's statutes (eight years in total) lies in the fact that preliminary work, as well as intergovernmental negotiations that concluded with the Commission's approval, were especially profound and the agreement was the consequence not of improvisation, but of much reflection and consideration. In a later passage, however, Zelada Castedo admits that there had been a quick consensus about the organization and competencies of the Court. Apparently, any eventual changes incorporated into the report's proposal – especially those motivated by the member states – were not substantial, calling into question whether the outcome was the product of such hard deliberation.
>
> (Zelada Castedo 1985: 131)

by the Junta, with lip service being paid to an image of hard negotiations and confrontation between national representatives. The intellectual substance of the proposal belongs overwhelmingly to the joint work done by INTAL consultants and the Junta. The institutional outcome can be better explained by the conviction of these legal experts than by a process of public, intergovernmental deliberation.

The evidence that upholds such claims is offered in the following section. It is based on reports published in the same years by the Institute for the Integration of Latin America and the Caribbean, INTAL. Also explored are the conditions under which a grand judicial reform like the establishment of the ACJ can be advanced and promoted by a legal network.

Contesting the governments' control over the integration process

The case of the Chilean parliament

The Cartagena Agreement is an international treaty. Certainly, it is a very special one considering its supranational content; but it is still an international treaty. Therefore, it is interesting to note that it was implemented within the domestic order by means of executive decrees only; that is, with no participation of parliaments or any other control organs (Orrego Vicuña 1970: 48). The historical doctrinal justification for this novelty has been so far that the Cartagena Agreement derives from LAFTA's Treaty of Montevideo and, considering the fact that member states had already transferred the necessary powers to this framework treaty (*tratado marco*), they had implied powers to accelerate the process through subnational agreements (Villagrán Kramer 1973).

At the time of the signature and approval of the Cartagena Agreement in the early 1970s, the Chilean parliament was challenging the government's powers to control the integration process. The Andean Group had envisioned a multilateral financial mechanism that would foster common investment projects in the region. The Corporación Andina de Fomento (CAF) was shaped as an international corporation, whose main shareholder would be the member states, along with some minor participation of private investors. All of them united within a shareholders' assembly. Its initial capital entailed over US$100 million. Despite the active support of the signing governments, the CAF, and its statutes, were formally forged outside the Cartagena Agreement. This circumstance did not remain unnoticed by the Chilean Senate. That same year, in 1969, the statutes of the CAF were being discussed in the Chilean parliament – specifically, in its upper chamber, the Senate – as an ordinary international treaty. Some senators were sceptical of the neutrality of the CAF and severely questioned a rule that allowed the shareholders' assembly to change the organisation's very statutes that were being discussed. Incredulous of the assembly's impartiality, these members of congress contended that granting the governments such steering power over the CAF's financial instruments would render the parliamentary discussion futile. Moreover, the underlying fear was that the governments would sell their share in CAF to private investors, eroding national control over the new multilateral financial mechanism.

Alerted by the Chilean government about these growing difficulties in parliament (Orrego Vicuña 1970: 59), the Andean Commission tried to issue a statement reassuring the government that member states would only sell some of their shares in CAF to private actors if the Andean governments agreed unanimously.[32] This declaration addressed all the concerns and points raised by the Chilean Senate. But it did not ease the Senate's worries. On the contrary, it exacerbated the desire for further parliamentary involvement in regional affairs. The Senate now demanded that the government include a further 'declaration'[33] in the statutes of the CAF, through which any decision taken by the organs of CAF that touched these sensitive points required the approval of the Chilean parliament. In addition, all decisions taken by CAF organs had to comply with Chilean law. Although it was highly unlikely that any organ of CAF would issue any decisions as provocative as suggested, the Senate had managed to contest the government's control over the integration process.

Colombia and its Supreme Court

The Colombian Supreme Court was a main protagonist in a short saga that challenged its government's authority to control the pace of regional integration. In 1971, a Colombian citizen presented an action of unconstitutionality before the Supreme Court. The argument was that the incorporation of the Cartagena Agreement by the Colombian government into national law had circumvented parliament, and therefore the relevant executive decree should be invalidated.[34] In its ruling, the Supreme Court initially endorsed the challenger's view in that it assumed that the Cartagena Agreement was an ordinary international treaty, and not a derivative of the Treaty of Montevideo. Therefore, it stated that the Colombian government had indeed violated the regular proceeding for incorporating international law into the domestic order.[35] However, in the same ruling the Court refused to annul the executive decree, based on the

---

32 Segundo Período de Sesiones Ordinarias, Lima, 9–13 March 1970. Also Primera Asamblea de la Corporación Andina de Fomento, Caracas, 8–9 June 1970.
33 Approved 23 June 1970. Its text was disclosed in the newspaper *El Mercurio*, 27 June 1970, p. 15.
34 Executive Decree No. 1245, of 8 August 1969.
35 Corte Suprema de Colombia, ruling of 26 July 1971, reproduced in *Derecho de la Integración* No. 10 (April 1972), 160 ff.

Colombian legal tradition that gives precedence to international commitments whenever the government has given its formal agreement. The Court explained that, even if the Colombian government infringed national rules by avoiding national control by the legislator, it could not break its international commitments. As a consequence, the action was rejected and the Cartagena Agreement was regarded as valid. Nevertheless, the flip-side of this ruling was that this legal tradition did not apply to decisions made by Andean organs, which were not regarded as international treaties. Therefore, the Court left the door open for Andean secondary law to be subjected to parliamentary approval if it was to be valid in Colombia (Orrego Vicuña 1972: 52).

If one reads the Junta's first report of 1972 against the backdrop of these challenges that took place during the debate in the Chilean Senate and the Colombian Supreme Courts, the swift procedure for approving the proposal makes sense. Consequently, a new control mechanism necessary to check the activities of community organs finds its way into the report, namely the annulment procedure (JUNAC 1972, Chapter 5). The supposedly urgent need to have an Andean Court of Justice did not figure at all in the preparatory work; neither did it in the profuse literature of INTAL or in any other integration scheme, even though its authors had a persistent pro-integrationist point of view. The call appears as perfectly plausible, however, if we remember that governments were having severe difficulties with their domestic control organs. As the evidence shows, the Chilean Senate and the Colombian Supreme Court doubted that Andean organs would exercise self-restraint and used the argument to assume the control of legality of secondary community law. Therefore, the creation of a court with powers to control the legality of Andean acts and nullify them if necessary would terminate the exhausting debates that were raging at national level, and shift the oversight function to the supranational level. In addition, the Junta adapted its language and incorporated functional and technical vocabulary like 'further harmonization, stage of progress, uniform interpretation'. This strategy might have served the purpose of capping an eventual politicisation of the report and the proposal of a court. In fact, observers of that episode note that, at the end, the establishment of the court was 'regarded as just one among many proposals' (Ferris 1979: 99).

It remains unclear who came up with this instrumental strategy: the governments representatives' themselves, the Junta, or maybe the INTAL network. According to the evidence found, the first time this idea appears in writing is a brief passage in the final protocol of a summit of the Commission in 1971. Based on this isolated fact, one could easily assume that it was the national governments that initiated this project. However, it can be inferred from consistent work of the European-Andean network that this group of legal scholars and professionals was the pioneering force. The fact that the proposal included not only control mechanisms needed by the governments, but all the procedures of the ECJ, suggests that the project was conceived to go much further than envisioned by the member states. The network needed only a window of opportunity in order for its legal agenda to materialise. As a consequence, a treaty establishing the Andean Court of Justice was signed in 1979 and ratified by the last member states in 1983.[36]

Assessing the efficacy of legal networks: a counterfactual inference

All the written material produced by the INTAL network during the process of creation of the Andean Court of Justice is consistent with the final institutional outcome. In other words, there is a strong correlation between the legal and policy core advocated by the network, and the institutional decisions made ultimately by the member states. However, it is fair to ask whether the evidence is sufficient to affirm that the legal scholars that worked for INTAL were a necessary factor to transplant the ECJ. It is a fair question, because correlation does not necessarily imply causality. Is it possible that the member states, gathered in the Andean Commission, took an autonomous decision to transplant the ECJ, together with the complete procedural scheme, into the Andean Community? Such a contention would imply that the joint Junta-INTAL report was only accessory, or that it merely confirmed a decision that member states might have taken earlier. Moreover, it is plausible to contest that the Andean Junta is responsible for all the intellectual content of the reports. This could suggest that the institutions of the organisation are far more relevant than external experts. Maybe the experts of INTAL provided only some minor legitimacy to the proposals. It would follow, then, that regional integration schemes have an inherent potential for emulating, copying, or transplanting other institutions. This sounds improbable, but not impossible.

In order to address the relevance of the legal network, one research strategy is to make a counterfactual inference.[37] In other words, would the member states have adopted the institutional design of the ECJ if there were no INTAL support? Moreover, would the Junta have made a similar report without the involvement of INTAL consultants? The challenge of inferring the causal weight of each actor involved in the process of transplanting the ECJ into the Andean pact requires that we resolve what would have happened had one of the agents been missing. This would tell us whether the missing agent was a necessary condition for the outcome of the transplant. We can attain this by

---

36 That it took so long for this treaty to be ratified by the member states is convincingly explained by Marwege, based on the objection, at national level, of the Venezuelan Constitutional Court (Marwege 1995).

37 I am indebted to Karen Alter, Thomas Gehring and Paul Turner for drawing my attention to this point.

controlling the results with a comparable case that resembles the establishment of the ACJ.[38]

The case of the Central American Economic and Social Community presents a good opportunity to make this comparison. It resembles the case of the ACJ in every respect but one: there is no Junta equivalent. It has the same INTAL network, it features member states willing to adopt a court, it involves the ECJ scheme with supranational powers, but its secretariat did not participate in the drafting.

The Central American Common Market (CACM) is one of the many integration arrangements in Latin America. It was created in 1960 and aimed at securing a common market, as well as a customs union.[39] After a decade of promising growth due to favourable conditions in international markets, the process of integration stagnated before accomplishing a common market. Prices of commodities fell during the 1970s, hitting the region's economies. In addition, war broke out in 1969 between two of its members: Honduras and El Salvador.[40] Against this backdrop, member states called for a reinvigoration of regional integration, and the CACM's Permanent Secretariat (SIECA), appointed INTAL (the same organisation that worked in the Andean Community) to draft a proposal and present it to the member states.[41] The latter established an intergovernmental committee in 1973, comprising ministerial representatives who would evaluate and adopt the proposal.[42] INTAL appointed the same network that had drafted the Andean proposal.[43]

---

38 On comparative research see Lijphart 1975; George and Bennett 2004.

39 Tratado General de Integración Económica Centroamericana, signed by Guatemala, El Salvador, Honduras and Nicaragua on 13 December 1960, in Managua, Nicaragua. Costa Rica joined in 1963. F. de Paula Gutiérrez, 'América Central 1978–1984: una región en crisis', *Integración Latinoamericana* 101 (1985), 3–16, at 4.

40 R. Mayorga Quiros, 'Aspectos institucionales de la integración centroamericana durante 1980', *Integración Latinoamericana* 59 (1981), 25–30; A. E. Villalta Vizcarra, 'La integración centroamericana, el comercio y el desarrollo', *Anuario Hispano-Luso-Americano de derecho internacional* (2007), 541–65.

41 INTAL, 'Asistencia técnica al Grupo Andino y al Mercado Común Centroamericano', *Derecho de la Integración* 8 (1971), 68; R. Mayorga Quiros, 'El crecimiento desigual en Centroamérica', *Serie Publicaciones Intal* No. 147 (1982), 133, at 84.

42 See the First Declaration of the 'Comité de Alto Nivel para el Perfeccionamiento y la Reestructuración del Mercado Común Centroamerican', reproduced in INTAL, 'Comité de Alto Nivel para el Perfeccionamiento y la Reestructuración del Mercado Común Centroamericano', *Derecho de la Integración* 14 (1973), 242–3; R. Mayorga Quiros, 'Perspectivas socioeconómicas de Centroamerica en el decenio de 1980', *Integración Latinoamericana* 51 (1980), 3–17, at 10.

43 Among the participants who drafted the proposal on the ATJ were Félix Peña, Francisco Villagrán Kramer, Felipe Paolillo, Felipe Salazar from INTAL; and Walter Müch and Maurice Lagrange from the EC. All of them converged in an official meeting in Guatemala,

The consultants worked on a comprehensive reform of the CACM, which included a court of justice. The result was the project on a Central American Economic and Social Community (CAESC).[44] The project was formally adopted by member states in March 1976[45] and cleared for approval and implementation in domestic orders. The CAESC provided an ambitious institutional framework very similar to the EC.[46] It envisioned an intergovernmental council, an executive commission, and a Court of Justice that would adjudicate in matters related to the treaty. Similar to the ECJ and the ACJ, it envisioned procedures of nullification, non-compliance, and preliminary rulings.[47]

Unfortunately, the controlled comparison can be made to the point of formal adoption only, because the CAESC was never implemented. Member states delayed its incorporation into national law first,[48] followed by declining enthusiasm as the region began suffering the effects of the economic crisis and armed conflicts. Scholars of Central American integration suggest that CAESC ultimately failed due to the hostilities between Honduras and El Salvador[49] and the regional economic crisis of the late 1970s.[50]

Nonetheless, the comparison underpins the claim that, in the Andean case, it is the INTAL network, with its legal consultants, that are necessary for a

---

April 1972. See INTAL, 'Asistencia técnica al MCCA, *Derecho de la Integración* 10 (1972), 99; INTAL, 'Asistencia técnica al MCCA', *Derecho de la Integración* 11 (1972), 117–18.

44 P. Solares Flores, *La integración como instrumento clave para el desarrollo y la modernización de Centroamérica en el proceo de inserción internacional de la región*. University of San Carlos de Guatemala (2005), at 34.

45 ECLAC, E.C.F.L.A.A.T.C., 'Reflexiones sobre la situación actual y las perspectivas del proceso de integración centroamericana'. *Integración Latinoamericana* 65 (1982), 21–6.

46 M. Colom Argueta, 'Comunidad económico social o consorcio administrativo de Centro América? Implicaciones del esquema institucional del proyecto de creación de la comunidad económica social centroamericana', *Anuario de Estudios Centroamericanos* No. 4 (1978), 11–21, at 11.

47 See SIECA, S.F.T.C.A.E.I., 'Tratado que crea la Comunidad Económica y Social Centroamericana'. *Derecho de la Integración* (March–July 1975), 87–123.

48 INTAL, 1976. Editorial, *Integración Latinoamericana* 9 (1976), 1–5, at 3; H. Dada Hirezi, 'Evaluación de la integración centroamericana', *Integración Latinoamericana* 86 (1983), 23–37, at 29; R. Mayorga Quiros, 'Aspectos institucionales de la integración centroamericana durante 1980', *Integración Latinoamericana* 59 (1980), 25–30, at 30; A. E. Villalta Vizcarra, 'La integración centroamericana, el comercio y el desarrollo', *Anuario Hispano-Luso-Americano de derecho internacional* (2007), 541–65, at 546.

49 INTAL, 'El proceso de integración en América Latina en 1979', *Integración Latinoamericana* 54 (1981), 20–3, at 29.

50 SIECA, S.F.T.C.A.E.I., 'El proceso de integración económica centroamericana: evaluación crítica de algunas experiencias', *Integración Latinoamericana* 65 (1982), 4–13; INTAL, Editorial, *Integración Latinoamericana* 55 (1985), 68–9.

The politics of judicial design 79

transplant to be adopted – formally, at least. Unlike the Andean case, it was the SIECA secretariat that initially sought external technical assistance and not the member states; and, unlike the Junta, SIECA did not participate in the process of drafting the project. The consultants were present in every stage of the process until its formal adoption, and provide the intellectual content. Contrary to a bold institutionalist view, it is not the institutions of the organisation that are willing to adopt foreign legal solutions, but external experts. And contrary to a bold intergovernmental perspective, it is not the member states that suggest the emulation of European institutions, but a coordinated transnational legal network.

Expanding the Andean network: bringing the judges in

Scholars have recently suggested that, once established, the judges of the Andean Court of Justice began explicitly resorting to the case law of the ECJ in their own rulings, as they incorporated doctrines of direct effect and supremacy of Andean law, by means of a procedure of preliminary rulings. All these were institutions and concepts modelled on the European Court of Justice, European case law, and the European procedure of preliminary rulings.[51] The European legal vocabulary was adopted, with the result of an isomorphic technical jargon that is almost identical to that of the EC.[52]

There have been few attempts to explain why a court would be so open to cross-fertilisation. The Latin American literature contends that these types of rulings are a natural legal development when supranational courts begin their work. This nomothetic perspective implies that every supranational court would tend to hand down similar rulings because it is standard practice for supranational courts to follow the compelling nature of community law.[53] Some scholars add further possibilities. Karen Alter suggests that it was the personal engagement of a few judges that actively pursued a case law open to European doctrines. She mentions one in particular, Judge Galo Pico Mantilla, who was the president of the Court when the doctrines of supremacy and direct effect were incorporated (Alter 2008: 26). Arguing at a global level, Anne-Marie Slaughter views the processes of judicial cross-fertilisation as the product of judicial globalisation. In her view, judges talk to each other in a

---

51 By the time the Andean Court took on its activities, milestones of European case law were already in place, e.g. case 3/62 *Commission v. Luxembourg* [1963] ECR 445; case 26/62 *Van Gend en Loos* [1963] ECR 1; case 6/64 *Costa v. ENEL* [1964] ECR 585; case 6/72 *Continental Can* [1973] ECR 215; case 8/74 *Dassonville* [1974] ECR 837.
52 See Chapter 5.
53 For a critique of such arguments, see Saldías 2008.

process of intellectual exchange and mutual learning that leads to courts using the ideas of their peers (Slaughter 2000b, 2003, 1998).

I claim that professional networks can explain much of the jurisprudential outcome. The incorporation of the ECJ's core repertoire into Andean case law can be traced back to the same network that procured its transplantation. The initial cadre of Andean judges was appointed in January 1984, in a meeting that took place in Quito. The new magistrates included Luis Carlos Sáchica, José Guillermo Andueza, Estuardo Hurtado Larrea, and the Court Secretary Iván Gabaldón Márquez. The following year, in 1985, the four of them were reunited by INTAL and, under the lead of Alberto Zelada Castedo, the institute's head of the legal department, the first comprehensive monograph on the Andean Court of Justice was penned (BID-INTAL 1985). This coordinated work had the potential of massively influencing future case law, since it was published between the date of enactment of the treaty establishing the Court (19 May 1983) and the first ruling in 1987.

In the introductory part of the monograph, INTAL's director Juan Vacchino acknowledges the importance of diffusing 'the competencies, the organization, and functioning of this organ', as well as the close collaboration between the institute and the Junta in the 1970s (Vacchino 1985: 3). In the light of network analysis, there are two striking aspects in regard to this work.

First, all articles explicitly address key aspects of Andean law that had been discussed in the Junta's final report. These community-enhancing features were precisely the doctrines of direct effect, supremacy, and the procedure of preliminary rulings.[54] The content substantially reflects the ideas of the working group that prepared the final report back in 1979.

Second, key European authors, who were part of the working group, monopolise the European scholarly influence. For the newly sworn in Andean judges, they seem to represent the main point of reference in matters of European community law. The names of Pierre Pescatore, Jean Victor Louis, Maurice Lagrange and Michel Gaudet are invoked whenever the ECJ is used as an object of comparison.[55]

Following the publication of this monograph, Andean judges continued diffusing the ideas on supranational law and the newly established ACJ (e.g. Andueza 1986). There was plenty of time for this preparatory phase, since it took the ACJ four years to hand down its first rulings, allegedly due to an initial lack of cases.[56] Although the number of articles or books published by

---

54 See Sáchica 1985a: 8, 13, 24; Andueza 1985a: 33, 41; Hurtado Larrea 1985: 70; Andueza 1985b: 97; Zelada Castedo 1985: 139.
55 See especially Andueza 1985a: 42, 5; Sáchica 1985b: 52; Andueza 1985b: 109; Zelada Castedo 1985: 148, 56, 59.
56 Karen Alter suggests that member states refused to authorise the Andean legal secretariat to proceed with cases (Alter 2008: 24).

the judges was modest in comparison to the European workload, it was fully consistent with the project that occupied the working group that assisted the Junta. A comparison between the final report, and the work described so far, shows a striking similarity. It was just a matter of time before European case law found its way into Andean law. The first ECJ doctrines appeared in ruling 1-IP-87, when the Court was presided over by the Ecuadorian judge Galo Pico Mantilla. Karen Alter rightly suggests that it might have been Mantilla who penned that ruling. His commitment to Andean integration is closely related to his involvement in the process of establishment of the Court. As Alter puts it elegantly:

> A gentleman-lawyer who was once Secretary of the Minister of Industry and Ambassador to Venezuela, Mantilla sought to emulate the European legal integration strategy. Mantilla was committed to Andean integration as an end in itself, *having been a participant in negotiations involving Andean integration and in the negotiations that led to the founding of the Andean Court.*
> (Alter 2008: 26, emphasis added)

Newcomers to the court, like Nicolás de Piérola, were socialised into the doctrinal lines of the Court and continued the process of diffusion (see de Piérola 1987). In fact, de Piérola presided over the Court when a noted ruling was handed down, reaffirming the doctrines of supremacy in May 1988 (2-IP-88).[57] Yet, although the contributions of judges like Pico Mantilla or Nicolás de Piérola can be regarded as a doctrinal milestone, the foundations for the judicial reception of European case law can be found earlier, namely in the working group on the establishment of the ACJ. The Court does not acknowledge this explicitly, but in both rulings mentioned above one can find in the preliminary considerations cross-references to EC law when it comes to introducing the issue of supremacy and direct effect,[58] as well as the method of teleological interpretation within the procedure of preliminary rulings.[59]

---

57 ACJ Case 2-IP-88.
58 'El Tribunal de Justicia de las Comunidades Europeas, en las sentencias antes citadas, ha afirmado la preeminencia absoluta del derecho comunitario sobre el interno, tesis que resulta ser tambien applicable en el ordenamiento juridico de la integracion andina conforme antes se indico' (ruling 2-IP-88, p. 3).
59 'En cuanto a los metodos de interpretacion que debe utilizar el Tribunal, ha de tenerse presente la realidad y caracteristica esenciales del Nuevo Derecho de la Integracion y la importante contribucion que en esta material tiene ya acumulada la experiencia europea, sobre todo por el aporte de la jurisprudencia de la Corte de Justicia, Tribunal unico de las Comunidades Europeas en la aplicacion de este derecho, que se esta haciendo constantemente en beneficio de la construccion comuntaira, sin perder de vista el fin permanente de la norma. Por estas consideraciones corresponde el empleo preferente de los metodos de

In sum, the network that worked on the transplantation of the ECJ into the Andean region was more relevant than the literature has assumed so far. It is a small, dense web of relations that was able to use certain conditions in order to achieve their goal of establishing a supranational court of justice. However, their influence does not stop there. As this research has shown, the action of professional networks can shape the content of the initial case law of the court they were advocating for. The observable pattern is not one of cross-judicial dialogues. Rather, it corresponds to a two-level process. The first level comprises the convictions of the INTAL consultants about particular mechanisms for achieving economic and legal integration through community law. The evidence that I have offered suggests that these professional beliefs began to blossom as the experts gained exposure in European academics, such as the conference at The Hague Academy.

Once the exchange with European grand professors took place, the INTAL scholars internalised much of the doctrines and principles of European law and slightly adapted it for a Latin American context. They published these ideas and restated part of the European theories in their own words; but it was not a simple translation. It was a public intellectual and professional endorsement. In other words, they had been persuaded to transplant the European Court of Justice. This is a significant claim for a region that is usually the target of policies that are based on conditionality. The consequence of rooted beliefs is that it allows persuaded actors to wait for a window of opportunity. In addition, the beliefs and convictions can be shared with newcomers, who can be socialised into existing doctrines. The narrative of the INTAL network and the beginnings of the Andean Court of Justice testifies to the importance of exchange and principled persuasion.

This pattern shows greater efficacy than strategies based on conditionality. First, the supporters of legal transformations are local experts that can use domestic venues for their actions. Second, these experts are not replaced on a regular basis, in contrast to democratic governments. Therefore, they can hold their action until a window of opportunity arises to submit their proposals to the democratic decision-making process. This is precisely what the INTAL network did. Using the favourable conditions of domestic contestation, a 'window of opportunity', the network aligned itself with member state governments along with a technical discourse, positioning themselves as their agents. Once accepted as agents, they used their epistemic resources to accommodate governments' preferences and convince them to break with established doctrines of state sovereignty. The incorporation of the annulment procedure at supranational level corresponds to this strategy. At the same time, the new agent incorporates its own policy agenda; for the INTAL

interpretacion llamados "funcionales", como los metodos sistemativos y de interpretacion teleological ...' (ruling 1-IP-87, p. 5).

network, this was a full-blown court inspired in the ECJ. To be sure, it is difficult to label the INTAL network as a pure epistemic community or an advocacy coalition. In the narrative above we recognise features of both ideal types. This ratifies the fact that theories on those kinds of communities are ideal tools that help us understand the world, and do not necessarily mirror reality.

At a more abstract level, there are significant implications for theories of European integration and diffusion. First, the establishment of new institutions and the shift of decisional powers to the centre of the organisation were provoked by a concerted advocacy coalition with the complicity of member states against national actors that had emerged as alternative gatekeepers of Andean integration. In Europe, neofunctionalist theorists observed how self-interested private actors challenged their governments and shifted their loyalties towards the Community.[60] To be sure, if this chapter of Andean integration should become a challenge to neofunctionalist assumption, it will certainly need more evidence. Nevertheless, it is interesting to note that the technical discourse used by the network takes much inspiration from neofunctionalist thinking. Second, it took much agency in order to successfully transplant the ECJ into the Andean region. Functional requirements and automatic mechanisms of the common market, as espoused by some scholars of European integration, were not enough. This speaks against arguments of automaticity in regional integration.

In regard to network theories, the Andean case allows us to make some further claims; for example, it is much more decisive for policy and legal outcomes to determine who gets to give the relevant advice. Once the adviser has been chosen, the content will largely depend on the actors' background and socialisation. Moreover, some professional advocacy coalitions use their special knowledge in order to accommodate the preferences of important stakeholders, like governments. Once the networks become an agent, they can use their epistemic resources to propose solutions that are consistent with both the stakeholder's needs and their own policy agenda. In the Andean case, the INTAL network framed the problems as 'legal matters' and proposed a strong functional pro-integrationist policy agenda. Consistent with network theories, technical knowledge can be presented as neutral and subject to scientific scrutiny only.

---

60 See Chapter 2.

Chapter 5

The Andean Court of Justice
Charting the course for its case law

This chapter delves into the institutional dimension of the Andean Court of Justice. It consists of two main sections. First, there is a description of the institutions, organs, procedures and functions of the Court; this is followed by an analytical insight into its case law. Both sections are inherently comparative because they follow the approach outlined in Chapter 2; this means that I use the functionalist lens for assessing the process of integration through judicial law-making. When analysing the case law of the Andean Court of Justice, the chapter places the emphasis on the procedure of preliminary ruling, as well as the doctrines of direct effect and supremacy of Community law. In the eyes of neofunctionalism, these were precisely the traits that allowed the European Court of Justice to permeate national law, and begin the process of constitutionalisation of European law.

The origins of the Andean Group

The inception of the Andean Pact can be found in the Latin American Free Trade Association (LAFTA; in Spanish ALALC – Asociación Latinoamericana de Libre Comercio). This free trade arrangement was signed in 1960 in Montevideo, and embraced all South American countries, including Mexico.

It has been argued that the model of the Treaty of Montevideo had the disadvantage in that the most influential states, like Brazil and Argentina, saw in it a mere commercial tool, whereas less influential states, like the Andean states, put more value on the potential for economic development (Marwege 1995: 22–3; Hufbauer and Kotschwar 1998). Be that as it may, scholars have emphasised the diverging size and lack of complementarity of the involved economies, as well as the variable of 'political will' that inhibited multilateralism as a possible cause for the failure of the ALALC (Emmes and Mols 1993: 60).

In 1966, representatives of Chile, Colombia, Ecuador, Peru and Venezuela signed the *Declaración de Bogotá*, in which those states agreed a common stance within the frame of the ALALC, with a view to achieve a proportional treatment by the rest of the member states. This cleavage resulted in a common statement in 1967, the *Declaración de los Presidentes de América*, in Punta del Este, Uruguay, which framed an understanding that would allow less developed countries to follow a stronger strategy for economic development within the general framework of the Treaty of Montevideo.

On 26 May 1969, the Andean states of Bolivia, Chile, Colombia, Ecuador and Peru signed the treaty entitled *Acuerdo de Integración Subregional*, which was subsequently labelled as *Acuerdo de Cartagena* by means of its first regulatory act: Decision 1 of the Commission. The name Andean Pact, on the other hand, was never officially recognised (Marwege 1995: 25).

Member states changed during the 1970s. For example, Chile withdrew on 30 October 1976 (on the reasons that led Chile to exit the Agreement, see Emmes and Mols 1993). On 13 February 1973, Venezuela joined the Agreement. Although that state had participated in the negotiations, the reason given for the delay was an alleged inability to compete in a free trade scheme. However, some scholars have argued that the real reason behind it is to be found in the interests of some national business, as well as the influence of the United States (Marwege 1995: 26).

The subsidiarity character of the subnational Cartagena Agreement (CA) is underscored by the fact that, according to its Article 110 I, it had to be declared compatible with the Treaty of Montevideo if it was to come into force. The declaration of compatibility was to be cast by the permanent executive committee of ALALC (Marwege 1995: 27). This institutional requirement testifies to the embeddedness of the Andean Pact into the general frame of ALALC (Villagrán Kramer 1989).

The close link between the Treaty of Montevideo and the CA is also evident, as the latter explicitly grants the right to the rest of the member states of ALALC to join the subnational scheme.[1] Moreover, in case of disputes between member states, the Commission was to get involved as a mediator. If no agreement was reached in this phase, the Cartagena Agreement provided for the ALALC mechanism of dispute settlement to be applied. This is to say, the controversies had to be brought before the arbitral tribunal set for in the *Protocolo para la Solución de Controversias* signed on 2 September 1967 (Zelada Castedo 1985: 126).

Therefore, consistent with the action of splitting from the ALALC, the first and highest goal of the CA was economic development. Formally, these objectives were laid down in the first articles of the Treaty. Hence, the first article of the CA already contains the goal of harmonic and balanced economic development of the member states. The strategy behind Article 1 was to transform ALALC into a common market; the Andean Common Market was foreseen to be completed by 1995 (Andueza 1985a: 28; 1985b: 88; Keener 1987: 39).

The second goal of the CA related to the living conditions of the Andean population, which were to be improved, along with the levels of employment

---

1 Article 109 I, Cartagena Agreement; also Villagrán Kramer 1989: 12–13.

(Art. 1 CA). For Uribe Restrepo, this objective is a leitmotiv of any integration process (Uribe Restrepo 1990: 22). Moreover, it became clear to many others, too, that achieving this particular goal depended upon complying with the general obligations stemming from the CA. The conviction that general welfare can be attained only through complying with the commitments endures to this day, despite the disappointing results of regional integration in the Andean region. Andean judges were very aware of this. In 1987, for instance, while commenting on the new system that was shaped with the creation of the Andean Court of Justice, Nicolás de Piérola, a former Attorney General of Peru and President of the ACJ, publicly restated that the Court would play an important role in the process of economic integration: 'and in doing so hope to upgrade the standard of living in the community' (de Piérola 1987: 37; Andueza 1985a: 40).

The third goal, the principle of solidarity, was established, whereby the benefits resulting from economic integration were to reach the member states so as to diminish their differences in economic development (Art. 2 CA). The redistribution that would take place was thought to be contingent upon the creation of a new export industry and regional growth, and regulation of foreign investment, as benefits were to be shared according to the particular need of each member state (Helfer *et al.* 2009: 6).

A fourth goal was bolstering the Andean states' position in international negotiations (Art. 1 CA). Scholars have seen the increasing influence of European trade policies as a cause for the inclusion of this norm. This becomes especially clear in the light of the critical stance in regard to the 'Banana policy' of the EC (Keener 1987: 40). Lastly, the development of infrastructure is a fifth goal of the Cartagena Agreement in its original version (Art. 25).

Economic development, then, would be achieved when developing states could manage to cut free from their dependence upon more industrialised regions and, therefore, the development of a local industry and technologies was thought to be the appropriate means for this. This pursuit of development and the persistent attempt to cut loose from an alleged dominance of the industrialised world is consistent with tendencies of critical theories, and is described by Waldemar Hummer as an 'ideology of integration' (Hummer 1979: 219; Díaz Barrado 1999: 23, fn. 1). Carlos Sáchica, who would become the first judge of the Andean Court of Justice, embodied much of this conviction in his writings. He regarded critical narratives to be an 'authentic mythology' that draws its resources from the utopia of a united Latin America: the 'bolivarian' dream; one that could subsume market-oriented strategies and critical theories on development (Sáchica 1985a: 7, 9).[2] Similarly, Andueza

---

2 'La definición de lo regional, como perfil resultante de la combinación de lo comunitario proyectado y lo vario y plural preexistente al proceso, ya sea como un proyecto histórico necesario, o como una política pragmática y racionalista, pero hábilmente motivada por una

laments over the lack of union, which he describes as the 'disunited states of America', and draws on historical symbols and heroes while calling for a more vigorous integration:

> From the same moment in which the process of emancipation of the new Hispano-American States takes place, certain disintegrative forces arise against the movements of Latin American unity. The efforts of Simón Bolivar and Pedro Gual — the Chancellor of the *Gran Colombia* — in order to maintain this unity, are rendered worthless. Whilst in the North, the thirteen colonies decided to form the United States of America, in the South the twenty Hispano-American republics decided to establish the disunited states of América.
>
> (Andueza 1985a: 28)[3]

In practical terms, however, there are concrete mechanisms that were established to spur development. Striving for an economic, monetary and political union was considered as the means for development, as well as the ultimate goal to achieve.

The mechanisms for the attainment of the goals declared by the Cartagena Agreement, were:

1. The liberalisation of trade by means of dismantling of tariffs between the member states.
2. The introduction of a common external tariff (Arts 3c, d; 34e; 41–68, 104, 105).
3. Planification of the industrial sector in the Andean region (Art. 3b).
4. Regulation of foreign investment and foreign technology (Arts 3f; 27).
5. Expansion of programmes for the development of the agricultural sector (Arts 3e; 69–74).
6. Development of programmes aimed at the integration of infrastructure (Arts 3g; 86–88).

---

mitologia auténtica, capaz de suscitar adhesiones, afectos, elevación de miras, esto es, con una justificación ideológica que legitime el proceso y genere, junto al interés económico, creencias e ideas vívidas, y que promueva valores humanos superiores a los domésticos tradicionales. El Pacto Andino dispone, a estos efectos, de la inagotable cantera el pensamiento bolivariano' (Sáchica 1985a: 7).

3 'Desde el momento mismo en que se produce el proceso de emancipacieon de los nuevos Estados hispanoamericanos se hacen presents las fuerzas dsintegradoras del movimiento de unidad de América Latina. De nada valieron los esfuerzos de Simón Bolivar y de Pedro Gual – el Canciller de la Gran Colombia – por mantener esa unidad Cuando en el Norte las trece antiguas colonias inglesas deciden formar los Estados Unidos de América, en el Sur las veinte repúblicas hispanoamericanas decidieron constituir los Estados desunidos de América' (Andueza 1985a: 28) (my own translation).

The Andean institutional setting: an overview

On 10 March 1996, Andean member states approved the Trujillo Protocol. With this agreement, the Andean Pact's import-substitution policy took a twist towards a free trade scheme based on a common market, namely 'open regionalism'. This was mainly as a consequence of international organisations pressing for deregulatory reforms (Helfer and Alter 2009: 8). Organs were to be linked through a system – the Andean Integration System (SAI) – so as to reinforce effective implementation of supranational norms (Comunidad Andina 2006: 15), and the whole scheme was 'rechristened' as the Andean Community (Helfer et al. 2009: 10). This reform procured the strengthening of the Council of Foreign Affairs Ministers (CAMRE – Consejo Andino de Ministros de Relaciones Exteriores) as an intergovernmental political organ, and converted the Junta into a General Secretariat (GS) (da Cruz Vilaça and Sobrino 1998: 26) with an increase in both size and budget, and with the explicit goal of promoting regional integration.[4]

Consistent with these major reforms, the member states amended their national constitutions in order to adapt them to the process of regional integration. With the exception of Bolivia, the topic of Latin American integration, as well as Andean integration, was incorporated into the constitutions of Colombia (1991), Peru (1993), Ecuador (1997), and Venezuela (1999) (Tangarife 2001a: 124).

Before the reform of the Andean Integration System in 1996, the Andean Commission was, according to Article 6 of the Cartagena Agreement, the highest organ of the Andean Community. The semantic similitude with the European Commission could induce the error in thinking that they perform in a similar way. They do not. Rather, it resembles the Council of the EU more than the European Commission, since it is the law-making organ of the Andean Community, and it ordinarily gathers the ministers of integration of the Andean member states (de Piérola 1987: 12; Marwege 1995). It is the truly intergovernmental organ of the system, in that it is constituted by the representatives of the member states. Thus, national interests become predominant (Andueza 1985a: 29). Nicolás de Piérola characterises it as a 'political organ', made up of member states' representatives that act in accordance with the instructions received from their governments (de Piérola 1987: 12). Nevertheless, this intergovernmental dimension is mitigated by the fact that the Andean Commission's Decisions are taken by the vote of two-thirds of its members (Andueza 1985a: 30). Its main task is to set the general policies of the Andean Community and to adopt the necessary measures in order to meet the goals of integration (Art. 7a).

---

4 Helfer et al. report on the appointment of a 'new cadre of young lawyers eager to use the Secretariat's enhanced resources to promote regional integration' (Helfer et al. 2009: 10).

The Commission has legislative, administrative and controlling attributions. The means for performing its legislative functions are the adoption of *Decisiones* (Art. 6 II). Its administrative tasks include, for example, the appointment of the members of the General Secretariat, and the approval of the budget of the Andean Court of Justice (Art. 16 TACJ) and the General Secretariat (Art. 7h; Art 5c, Decision 6).

Before the establishment of the Andean Court of Justice, the Commission was entrusted with the responsibility of overseeing member states' compliance with the obligations that derived from the CA (Art. 7, lit g; and Art. 1 Decision 218).

In terms of the executive function, the General Secretariat inherited in 1997 most of the competences of the Junta.[5] The Junta was the 'technical organ' of the Cartagena Agreement (Art. 131). Scholars have compared the executive character of the GS with that of the European Commission, in that both act in the interests of the Community (Frischhut 2003: 237; Marwege 1995: 46–7; de Piérola 1987: 13; Andueza 1985a: 31). Although, at its inception, the CA avoided the explicit term of 'supranationality', the Junta was conceived as an autonomous organ. For this purpose, it was foreseen that its members were not appointed by the member states, but by the Andean Commission – that is, a Community organ. Moreover, Junta officials did not forcefully have to be citizens of an Andean state, but of any Latin American state (Art. 14; and Art. 2 Decision 9).

The tasks of the Junta were strikingly similar to those of the European Commission. These included:

1 The implementation of the tasks delegated by the Commission (Arts 15h; 7(8) Decision 9).
2 The elaboration of the proposals that were to be presented to the Commission in order to be legislated upon (Arts 15c, d; 7(3), (4) Decision 9).
3 The oversight of the compliance with the provisions of the Cartagena Agreement, as well as the Decisions adopted by the Commission (Arts 15a; 7(1) Decision 9).

The treaty that established the Andean Parliament on 25 October 1979 did not declare it a main organ of the Andean Pact. This characterisation only came by means of Article 5(I) of the new version of the CA. This led the Andean literature to debate on the actual nature of the parliament (Marwege 1995: 49). It has, nevertheless, its own juridical personality, which not even the Andean Pact had as such. This contrasts with the EC, which established its nature of juridical subject of international public law in Articles 210 and 211 CEE.

---

5 On the particular relevance of the former Junta, see Chapter 3.

Among the reasons for its establishment, scholars have mentioned the goal of reaching legitimacy (Marwege 1995: 51). It is mainly an advisory organ that represents the peoples of the Andean region. The representatives would be elected in direct elections; however, until this is implemented, it will be a 'parliament of parliaments' (Sáchica 1985b: 74).

The actual relevance of this organ lies in the fact that it can evaluate the course of integration through issuing *Recomendaciones*. Thereby, it strongly deviates from the current attributions of its European counterpart, the European Parliament. Some scholars have suggested that the Andean Parliament's attributions for democratically controlling political institutions are non-existent (da Cruz Vilaça and Sobrino 1998: 43). Its functions have been described as 'declaratory' or advising (Frischhut 2003: 242; Marwege 1995: 51). Nevertheless, others suggest that despite the lack of formal coercion, its *Recomendaciones* might have an influence on the legal order by shaping Andean statutes (Sáchica 1985a: 11–12).

The Andean Court of Justice

The Andean Court of Justice (ACJ) was established on 28 May 1979,[6] by virtue of the Treaty of Creation of the Court of Justice of the CA, and began its work on 5 January 1984, after a long process of national ratifications.[7] The ACJ was deliberately modelled after the ECJ, together with its system of judicial remedies, in an attempt to emulate the European success (Helfer and Alter 2009: 3). The creation of a supranational court of justice was heralded by many as an impulse to facilitate the integration process (JUNAC 1979: 15, 84), the consolidation of what was considered to be the most important integration scheme among developing countries (Bondia García 1999: 111). Others saw in the ACJ the missing element that was essential to any regional enterprise (da Cruz Vilaça and Sobrino 1996: 92; Díaz Barrado 1999: 62), or the vehicle towards building a judicial discipline like that of the European Community (Weiler 1993: 421). This was particularly so considering that to some Latin American scholars the CA appeared to be the constitutional charter of a community of law, just like its European counterpart (Montaño Galarza 2004: 969; Sáchica 1985a: 10; Andueza 1985a: 29).

If the newly created Andean Court was already exhibiting a striking resemblance to the court in Luxembourg, it was procedural law that would have the most European influence. The treaty establishing the Court of Justice of the Andean Community (TCACJ) contains a non-compliance procedure, a nullifying procedure, a recourse of inaction or omission, and preliminary rulings. Also, from 1996 onwards, the Court has been granted competencies on

---

6 See Chapter 3.
7 On the process of ratification, and particularly the Venezuelan position, see Marwege 1995: 104.

arbitration and labour jurisdiction (Sánchez Chacón 2001: 41–3). The ECJ had provided assistance to the Andean Community for the formulation of the statutes of the ACJ (da Cruz Vilaça and Sobrino 1998: fn. 11). The final draft for those statutes that would establish the ACJ was presented to the Andean Commission on 11 December 1972. The final approval, however, was delayed for several years due to ongoing governmental remarks and meetings (Marwege 1995: 73; de Piérola 1987: 15). Only on 28 May 1979 did representatives of the member states sign the treaty establishing the Andean Court of Justice, which came into force on 23 May 1983.

The goal of the founders of the TCACJ was to give the Court tools equivalent to its European counterpart (Frischhut 2003: 274)[8] and thus achieve the dynamism that was deemed necessary for the Andean Group to succeed in its endeavour. The Court was expected to be independent from member states and the rest of the Andean institutions, and shape Andean Community law by providing authoritative interpretations (de Piérola 1987: 16; Márquez 1985: 115–16).

Before the creation of the Court, member states usually responded to non-compliance with retaliatory action in the form of reciprocity or suspensions (Marwege 1995: 69). Additionally, the European judicial saga that had led to the establishment of the Community legal system (Mattli and Slaughter 1996) was well known by the member states, as were the doctrines of direct effect (case 26/62 *Van Gend en Loos*) and of supremacy of Community law (case 6/64 *Costa v. ENEL*). In the EC, those doctrines had been established through the mechanism of preliminary rulings and, despite initial opposition from the member states, were incorporated into the *acquis communautaire*, labelling the Court the 'engine of integration' (Schroeder 2004: 186). Furthermore, what had rendered the European doctrines so effective was precisely the system of judicial remedies (Weiler 1994: 514), so it could be assumed that one important condition for advancing legal integration – if not the most important – was met.

However, implementation of this judicial mechanism within the Andean region has been far from successful; 34 years after its foundation, the Andean Community has not been able to achieve its main goal of establishing a common market. Indeed, what exists currently is an imperfect customs union (*unión aduanera imperfecta*, see Taccone and Nogueira 2005: 51). Some scholars suggest that 'the participation of the social players in the process is meagre; and finally, the integrationist consciousness, is not, in fact, sufficient' (da Cruz Vilaça and Sobrino 1998: 24). The literature is consistent in that the process of Andean integration is usually dismissed as a failure (Helfer *et al.* 2009: 2; Mattli 1999b: 12, 42).

---

8 See below in this chapter, p. 97.

Andean law and national law

Before the establishment of the Andean Court of Justice, the Andean Group's judicial system was not systematically regulated, as it relied heavily on the dispute settlement scheme of ALALC (de Piérola 1987: 15). The Treaty of Montevideo, however, did not contain specific rules in regard to any particular procedure for the peaceful settlement of controversies between its member states (Marwege 1995: 57). It was not until 1967, several years after its inception, that ALALC states agreed on a permanent mechanism for dispute settlement. This procedure envisaged negotiations between the involved parties, with the involvement of its executive organ, the Comité Ejecutivo Permanente, if the parties could not reach an agreement on their own. If no agreement was possible despite the executive committee's mediation, the parties had to resort to an arbitral procedure (Andueza 1985b: 94). However, this arbitration procedure had several limitations, as it was enforceable only for matters specifically listed by the Consejo de Ministros de Relaciones Exteriores of the ALALC, or in those cases where the parties had convened the jurisdiction of the arbiter (Marwege 1995: 58; Hummer 1980: 534).

The Cartagena Agreement, in contrast, included a dispute settlement procedure prior to the creation of the ACJ. These rules of procedure established that, in the case of controversies, it was for the Commission to get involved and mediate. If there was no agreement despite the Commission's efforts, the parties would be entitled to use the procedure contained in the ALALC protocol (Art. 23 II).

After ten years of the Andean Pact, the TCACJ not only created the ACJ, but also explicitly systemised the Andean legal system, clarifying the underlying categories of legal norms.[9] According to Article 1, Andean law comprises: (a) the Cartagena Agreement, and its protocols and additional instruments; (b) the TCACJ and its protocols; (c) Decisions of the Andean Council of Foreign Affairs, and those of the Andean Commission; (d) Resolutions of the Andean General Secretariat; (e) the Industrial Complementary Agreements, and any such other agreements as the member countries may adopt among themselves within the context of the Andean subregional integration process.

According to Uribe Restrepo, the inclusion of Article 1 on the Andean legal system into the TCACJ was an attempt to bring order to the regulation of secondary law, a rather unsystematic and chaotic set of norms (Uribe Restrepo 1990: 88). Consistent with this view, Sáchica suggests that by systematising the Andean legal system the TCACJ crystallised an autonomous

---

9 Prior to the TCACJ, the validity and hierarchy of Andean law was vaguely regulated in Decisions 6 and 9, leaving many questions unanswered: for instance, the precise moment in which Andean secondary law became binding for member states (Marwege 1995: 87–8).

legal order that could break with the previous scheme provided by ALALC for the settlement of disputes (Sáchica 1985a: 8). However, the TCACJ also took on the task of regulating the relationship between Andean law and national law.

Scholars have underlined the difference with the systematisation of the European legal system, highlighting the fact that Andean Decisions and Resolutions are not mentioned by the founding treaty, the CA (Sáchica 1985c: 52–4). In addition, Andean Decisions and Resolutions show subtle but significant differences from the European regulations and directives (Art. 249 EC). Marwege draws a difference in the scope of both European regulations and directives vis-à-vis Andean Decisions and Resolutions. While EC regulations carry a substantial content that has to be applied by European member states, Decisions are used for a variety of tasks that are not always intended for Andean member states to implement within the national domain. Thus, Decisions sometimes regulate matters related to the common market; however, at other times, Decisions are used for internal administrative issues, like the yearly budget, or administrative delegation of competencies by the Commission to the General Secretariat (Marwege 1995: 84). One Andean scholar referred to this vagueness of Decisions as 'having varying content', and these contents might contain 'legal norms, administrative or financial decisions' (Andueza 1985a: 30; Tangarife 2001b: 161).

The same can be said with regard to Resolutions, which makes it more difficult to compare Andean law to European law (da Cruz Vilaça and Sobrino 1998: 33). Comparatists should be cautious when assuming an identity between both legal systems. Sáchica suggests, for instance, that Resolutions were also to be weighted according to content. If they responded to the original competencies of the General Secretariat, they would be fulfilling a mere technical task; but if a Resolution was the consequence of a delegated attribution by the Commission, it would have to be regarded – according to Sáchica – as a norm-creating act (Sáchica 1985b: 103–5).

It becomes clear that, if the Andean Commission can dictate only one type of legal act, namely Decisions, it will be more difficult to distinguish general laws that are mandatory for the member states from those that are mere administrative acts. The same applies *mutatis mutandis* to the General Secretariat's Resolutions. This vagueness of the legal nature, and the proper scope of Decisions and Resolutions, were not solved by the Andean literature either, giving birth to what has sometimes been referred to as the 'secondary law problem' (Orellana Ayora 1989: 116).

Before the adoption of the TCACJ, the Junta had already expressed its concerns regarding the incorporation of Andean law into national law and its direct applicability within the national domain (de Piérola 1987: 17). Requiring incorporation of international law into the national legal system means embracing the dualist conception of traditional international law (see Chapter 2). The Junta acknowledged this position and explicitly asserted that such an approach to Andean law was in direct opposition to the principles of Andean law (JUNTA integr. Lat. 47, 1980, p. 99). An act of incorporation should not be understood as any sort of legitimation or ratification of Andean law, but rather as a mere execution or implementation. This view contrasted, however, with the practice of the member states (Marwege 1995: 94). Especially noted was the position of the Venezuelan General Attorney, who doubted that the Venezuelan legal system would permit that the interpretations of the ACJ would bind the Supreme Court. Of course, Andean pro-integration scholars firmly criticised such interpretations as being an 'unacceptable dualist conception' (Andueza 1985b: 91).

Perhaps the most sensitive issue is the relationship between Andean law and national law in terms of an eventual hierarchy, especially in the light of a traditional cautious stance of Latin American states. From its inception, scholars – especially those who held positions in the Court – made efforts not to force this new legal order into the traditional categories and hierarchies of international public law. Nicolás de Piérola suggested:

> Communitarian law is different from both domestic internal law and international law. In effect, internal law emanates from the domestic authorities in each state. In contrast, Andean communitarian law originates from the Cartagena Agreement. It can also be distinguished from public international law, which arises directly from agreements between the authorities of sovereign states, either in the form of express agreements or treaties, or in the form of implied agreements or customary law. In contrast, communitarian law is international administrative law in that it emanates from supranational organs.
>
> (de Piérola 1987: 18)

Similarly, and considerably bold in his assertion, Sáchica argues that:

> [Andean law] has immediate validity and is, almost always, directly applicable within the five member states, this is to say, it is not conditioned by any special procedure of approval, reception or incorporation into national legal order that may affect its validity or limit its efficacy, for it is a common law that automatically inserts itself into those orders, with pre-eminence over legislation particular to that countries.[10]

It follows that if the member states created the ACJ, they necessarily ceded competencies in a fashion similar to a 'federal union of states', whereby the

---

10 'El conjunto normativo andino tiene vigencia inmediata y es, casi siempre, de aplicación directa en los cinco países miembros, es decir que no está condicionada a procedimientos especiales de aprobación, recepción o incorporación en los ordenamientos jurídicos

pooled sovereignty is exerted collectively so as to be able to constrain national will (Sáchica 1985a). Similarly, Guillermo Andueza argues that this agreement entails the germ of a federal system, which is the reason why Andean law trumps national law (Andueza 1985b: 86–7). He points to the ECJ *Simmenthal* ruling, stressing that European law has been declared supreme over national law. However, when addressing the Andean case, he makes a value-driven assertion regarding integration, in that Andean community law is superior to national law, 'because the protected interest, which is economic integration aiming at promoting balanced and harmonic development of member states and raising the standards of living of the inhabitants of the sub-region, is above national interests' (Andueza 1985a: 40).[11]

Following a more radical stance, Manuel Medina views international integration as a continuum, whereby the process that states follow culminates with a political union that entails a complete vanishing of the original units (Medina 1989: 6–10). The latter idea is fiercely opposed by Manfred Mols, who believes that Latin American states' participation in international organisations does not lead to any loss of influence; rather, every integration scheme, Mols argues, requires active governmental participation (Mols 1993: 7).

Considerably more cautious, Jorge Luis Suárez Mejías argues that supranationality does not imply that member states make cession or transfer of sovereignty to the organisations of such kind; what in fact happens is that competencies are redistributed among member states and the supranational organisation. However, Suárez Mejías argues, the ultimate sovereignty remains in the domain of intergovernmentalism, for supranationalism does not entail an entity with 'life of its own' (Suárez Mejías 2001: 4). Following a similar strand, Víctor Frontaura prefers to speak of 'conjunction of sovereign capacities' instead of cession of sovereignty (Rico Frontaura 2001: 74).

The first mandate of the TCACJ is that Andean law is binding for member states (Art. 2 TCACJ). Such a mandate can be understood from several angles; it could be argued, for instance, that this is binding traditional international public law. That view was represented by the Colombian Supreme Court when it ruled on the binding nature of the Cartagena Agreement, also drawing to the Colombian constitution and the principle of sovereignty that allowed the state to bind itself in the international setting, even against conflicting national provisions. But, it could also be argued that the binding

---

nacionales que puedan afectar su validez o limitar su eficacia, ya que es un derecho común que se inserta automáticamente en aquellos ordenamientos, con preeminencia sobre la legislación particular de tales países' (Sáchica 1985a: 8) (my own translation).
11 'Si el derecho comunitario andino es superior al derecho interno es porque el interés protegido, que es la integración económica para promover el desarrollo equilibrado y armónico de los países miembros y la elevación del nivel de vida de los habitantes de la subregión, está por encima de los intereses nacionales' (Andueza 1985a: 40) (my own translation).

nature of Andean law derives not from traditional international law but from the spirit of the CA (see, for instance, Garcia Amador 1977). As I will argue, the exact relationship of Andean law to international public law, and the nature of the commitment of member states, strongly determined the course of the ACJ's case law.

More problematic was Article 3 of the TCACJ, as it established that Decisions as well as Resolutions were directly applicable within the member states. It remains unclear how this direct applicability of Andean law should be understood. Before the TCACJ, the Junta had suggested that 'aplicación directa' should be understood in conformity with EC law; that is, Article 189 II CEE (JUNTA Integr. Lat Nr. 47, 1980, p. 99). Related to this point, María Alejandra Rodríguez Lemmo suggests that while direct applicability has been accepted and internalised in the European Union, in the Andean Community the doctrine 'has historically been honoured more in the breach than in practice in the Andean context' (Rodriguez Lemmo 2002: fn. 489). Renate Marwege suggests that the direct applicability in the same terms as the European regulations is impossible, for this would forcefully need an act of disclosure that would give the Decision proper publicity. Holding Decisions directly applicable with regard to the individual would be highly problematic, as it is an unknown statute to the people (Marwege 1995: 90). It is, therefore, not surprising that, prior to the establishment of Article 2 TCACJ, the member states' practices of incorporation of Andean law into national law was very heterogeneous and inconsistent.

In terms of the relation between Andean law and international public law, the debate has not been so fierce compared to the discussion on the Andean law–national law dichotomy. It remains, nevertheless, an equally vague and unsettled debate.

As shown in Chapter 4, the first scholarly legal writings that deal in scholarly terms with the Andean law–international law dichotomy were penned by the jurists who became the first magistrates of the ACJ. It is therefore not surprising that they insist on the normative autonomy of Andean law; in other words, Andean law does not receive its validity from any prior agreement. Andean Community law enjoys a standing of its own and can, therefore, fill the lacunae with its own principles and 'within its own historical-political context' (Sáchica 1985a: 8, 14). According to such a view, the Cartagena Agreement must be regarded as foundational, and it is not bound to foreign law; the comparative method of interpretation is thus reduced to an auxiliary tool.

Most of these judge-scholars use examples of European case law to bolster the doctrines that begin to arise progressively, even though the reasoning is not always consistent with European jurisprudence. Estuardo Hurtado, also an Andean judge and former member of the Ecuadorian Supreme Court, notes that the autonomy of the Cartagena Agreement allows Andean law to be directly applicable within domestic law, based on the *Simmenthal* ruling of the ECJ (Hurtado Larrea 1985: 70).

Former Andean judge Andueza makes an analogy of the ECJ resorting to constitutional principles of member states and also to fundamental rights, with the possibility of the ACJ simultaneously applying principles of international public law and principles of domestic law (Andueza 1985a: 34). His argument relies on the mandatory character of the principle of *pacta sunt servanda*, rather than on a constitutional act of the Community. Allegedly following Hans Kelsen, he suggests that direct applicability of Andean primary law proceeds in those cases where the obligation is clearly defined in its material dimension (*what*), as well as its personal dimension (*who*) (Andueza 1985a: 36). Andean secondary laws, on the other hand, are foundational or constitutional. They are directly applicable because they stem from an organ with autonomous regulatory powers. Thus, they are not foreign laws, nor international treaties (Andueza 1985a: 39; 1985b: 84, 5).

The organisation of the Court

Five justices comprised the Andean Court of Justice at its inception. Today there are only four, after the withdrawal of Venezuela from the Andean Community (for an account of the Venezuelan withdrawal that takes the ACJ into consideration, see Helfer *et al*. 2009; Comunidad Andina 2006: 15). The judges have to be citizens of one of the member states and enjoy a high moral reputation. They must be eligible in their home countries for the highest judicial positions or be a distinguished practitioner (Art. 6 TCACJ). ACJ judges may not undertake any professional activity other than educational positions (de Piérola 1987: 18). Andueza suggests that the judges' roles representing the interests of the Community are reaffirmed by the fact that they are elected not directly by the member states but by a summit of plenipotentiaries (Andueza 1985a: 33).

Judges are appointed for a period of six years, staggered so as to allow for elections every three years, and with the possibility of being re-elected only once (Art. 8). In addition, the TCACJ allows for the future creation of the position of a General Advocate (Art. 6 par. 3) which, according to Carlos Sáchica, should be provided with competencies similar to the General Advocate of the EC (Sáchica 1985a: 16).

Latin American literature on the ACJ, especially legal scholarship, has persistently stressed the efforts of providing ACJ judges with the essential independence from member states. Article 13 of the TCACJ stipulates that member states provide the necessary means so that the court can fulfil its duties with independence. However, Sáchica bemoans the fact that the court lacks a budgetary autonomy, which makes it dependent on the yearly budget that is paid by the member states (Sáchica 1985a: 18; de Piérola 1987: 16).

The procedure of nullification

This procedure aims at striking down Andean law, namely Decisions enacted by the Commission, or Resolutions enacted by the General Secretariat, when they have been adopted in violation of the Cartagena Agreement (TCACJ II). Its ultimate goal has been described as the 'defense of legality' (Sáchica 1985a: 19). This procedure can be initiated by any member state, the Commission, the Secretariat Generals, as well as individuals (Arts 17–20 TCACJ). The latter have standing whenever Decisions or Resolutions are applicable to them and affect their individual rights or legitimate interests (Art. 19). The original wording of the TCACJ was more specific, because it allowed individuals to file a lawsuit only if Andean provisions were applicable to them and 'caused them harm' (de Piérola 1987: 26; Sáchica 1985a: 19–20).

According to Latin American scholarship this procedure can be understood in the light of traditional doctrines on national constitutional law and separation of powers (Sáchica 1985a: 19). Thus, it is applicable in those cases where organs have enacted statutes without having sufficient powers. This situation is known in legal constitutional theory as *ultra vires*.[12] In addition, situations of 'deviation of power' are also situations that justify the procedure of nullification (Art. 17) (Sáchica 1985a: 19). Interestingly, Guillermo Andueza stresses that the intergovernmental character of the Andean Commission might carry some representatives of member states, when deciding on a proposal made by the Junta (today, General Secretariat), to put national interests above Community interests. Such a possibility would testify to the member states lacking the 'political will' to advance integration, although it might very well be controlled by the ACJ by way of the procedure of nullification (Andueza 1985a: 31).

The final ruling that annuls a Decision or a Resolution must explicitly address the temporal implications that the ruling shall have; this is to say, how far it reaches into the past (Art. 22) (Sáchica 1985a: 21).

The non-compliance procedure

This procedure may be initiated by the General Secretariat or by a member state when it considers that another member state is not complying with the provisions of Andean law (Arts 23–24). However, member states are required to file a complaint before the General Secretariat prior to commencement of proceedings before the Court. The same requirement is applied to individuals if they want to file a non-compliance action, provided the alleged non-compliance is affecting their rights (Art. 25).

The procedure is divided into two parts. The first is the administrative phase, where the GS plays an active role in mediating; the second part involves the judgement of the ACJ.

Sáchica stresses the non-coercive character of this procedure, in that it attempts to persuade states into compliance. This must be, so Sáchica argues,

---

12 The terms 'incompetencia' or 'extralimitación de competencias' can also be found among Andean writers (Sáchica 1985a: 19).

because processes of integration, like the Andean, are not construed upon coercion, but upon the acknowledgement of the benefits that arise from an ever-closer union. Integration, he says, excludes any kind of pressure. The administrative phase before the General Secretariat is shaped by the logic of persuasion and mediation in direction of compliance (Sáchica 1985a: 22).

The Andean preliminary ruling

Andean scholars clearly agree on the importance of the procedure of preliminary rulings as a means for strengthening Andean law. Uribe Restrepo confidently states that without this preliminary mechanism Community law would have virtually no chance of functioning adequately (Uribe Restrepo 1993: 19; Andueza 1985b: 98). Likewise, Luis Sáchica argues that legal integration is only possible as long as national judges give direct effect and prevalence to Community law over national law (Sáchica 1985b: 150).

Like the EC procedure, the Andean preliminary rulings aim to guarantee the uniform application of the Cartagena Agreement within the territorial boundaries of the member states (Art. 32) (Andueza 1985b: 97). Article 33 of TCACJ provides that: 'National judges hearing a case in which one of the provisions comprising the legal system of the Andean Community should be applied or is litigated, may directly request the Court's interpretation of such provisions, providing that the verdict is susceptible to appeal under national law.'

Some scholars give interesting accounts of the legal reasons that supposedly led to the establishment of this specific procedure of interpretation of Andean Community law:

> Reasons of specialisation suggest trusting interpretation of international treaties to international tribunals. The national judge does not have the technical ability to appraise the various international interests that are in play, [nor] to pronounce a ruling that might harmonise and re-establish the cohabitation between states in conflict. These were the reasons that led member countries to create the Court of Justice of the Cartagena Agreement.
>
> (Andueza 1985b: 98)[13]

---

13 'Las razones de especialización aconsejan confiar la interpretación de los tratados a tribunales internacionales. El juez nacional no está en capacidad técnica de apreciar los distintos intereses internacionales en juego, de pronunciar una decisión que los armonice y de restablecer la convivencia entre los Estados en conflicto. Estas fueron las razones que llevaron a los países miembros a crear el Tribunal de Justicia del Acuerdo de Cartagena' (Andueza 1985b: 98) (my own translation).

At this point, it is worth remembering Joseph Weiler's claim in regard to how important it was for the development of EC law that domestic courts were responsive to the implementation of EC law; without Article 177 'the constitutional transformation ushered in by the European Court would have remained with all the systemic deficiencies of general public international law' (Weiler 1991: 2425).

The Treaty instituting the ACJ was revised by the Protocol of Cochabamba in 1996, changing, among other issues, the conditions and requirements for individuals to file a claim before the Court. Some authors consider these changes an incentive for Andean citizens to resort to the ACJ comparable to the standing granted to European individuals: 'As can be seen, the admissibility conditions are, at least on paper, more generous than those set out in art. 73 of the EC Treaty' (da Cruz Vilaça and Sobrino 1998: 34, fn. 47).

From a neofunctionalist perspective, by means of a strategic use of preliminary rulings, actors can further their individual interests in constructed governance arenas (Stone Sweet *et al.* 2001: 17; Stone Sweet and Brunell 2004: 52–5). Actors that have a standing before the Community judge are able to exert influence on the policy-making process, with the aim of changing less favourable norms into more favourable ones. This, in turn, sees a flourishing of constitutional dialogues, through which national courts bargain their final position at the macro level (Slaughter *et al.* 1998). The interaction of national courts with a supranational court was underscored in the Andean literature by Sáchica. The former president of the ACJ asserted, in 1985, that the complementary action between the judiciaries in regard to the procedure of non-compliance constituted an 'evident political dimension', and also the foundations for the effectiveness of the doctrines of direct effect and supremacy (Sáchica 1985a: 24; Andueza 1985b: 104–5).

Andean law itself is still very unclear in regard to the hierarchy between Andean and national law. This is why some observers of the Andean legal system have suggested that there is much incomplete contracting regarding the Andean system, especially the founding treaty (da Cruz Vilaça and Sobrino 1998: 39). Neofunctionalist theorists might expect the ACJ to fill in this lacuna in favour of Andean law. Questions like this motivated Karen Alter and Laurence Helfer to begin the first exhaustive coding of all preliminary rulings in the Andean Community. Their findings reveal that there is indeed a dialogue between the ACJ and national courts taking place:

> It is not widely known that the ATJ is the world's third most active international court, having decided more than 1,400 cases through 2007. More than 90% of these cases are preliminary rulings issued in response to referrals from national courts in the five principal Andean Community member states – Bolivia, Colombia, Ecuador, Peru, and Venezuela. This fact alone suggests that the existence of a preliminary mechanism facilitates dialogue

between national and supranational judges over the meaning and scope of international law.

(Helfer and Alter 2009: 3–4)

This circumstance becomes more intriguing if the numbers of preliminary rulings are compared with other remedies available in the Andean judicial system. Between 1985 and 2007, 1,338 preliminary rulings interpreting Andean law constituted 93 per cent of all ACJ decisions – an impressive number if measured against the 70 non-compliance rulings and 28 nullification rulings (Helfer *et al*. 2009: 15).

With the benefit of hindsight, however, it can be affirmed that the Andean Community did not attain its goals of advancing integration and meeting its deadline for the completion of a common market. Why has this goal not been accomplished? Especially as the Andean Community has shaped a polity design equivalent to that of the European Community, with a supranational court that has the ultimate power to interpret Community law – which, in turn, should have a direct effect as well as supremacy, just like the Luxembourg Court?

The following section will address Andean case law with the neofunctionalist approach. The empirical focus of the analysis lies hereinafter on the performance of the Andean preliminary ruling in two fields of case law: the common policy on intellectual property, which is clearly the field that has motivated the majority of preliminary rulings, and the Andean common market through the liberalisation programme that was established by the Cartagena Agreement. The section unveils the real strategy of the Andean Court, taking stock of the teleological guise adopted by the supranational judge, in light of the European judicial saga.

Common policy on intellectual property: the case of patents

Regulation of intellectual property (IP) rights, especially those related to patents, belong to the competencies of the Andean Community. It has also been a cornerstone for the Andean Group since its inception (Helfer *et al*. 2009: 10), and the Cartagena Agreement itself called for the establishment of a common system for the treatment of trademarks, patents, licences and royalties (CA Art. 55). IP has also been the policy field that has demanded the most jurisprudential activity in Quito. During the period 2004–05, for instance, preliminary rulings related to the common policy on industrial property amounted to 92 per cent of the total sum of preliminary rulings from that period of time (TJCAN 2005: 7). The pattern of reference is also very uniform, as 96 per cent of the referrals originated as challenges to an IP agency's decision to grant or deny an application to register a patent, trademark, a utility model, or other IP right (Helfer *et al*. 2009: 17). The result is that the rulings are highly repetitive, where the references do not address innovative legal issues. They would ordinarily refer to whether two trademarks can cause confusion or to ensure fulfilment of the requirements for patentability. As a consequence, the 'ATJ responds to these requests in kind, regurgitating its analysis and sometimes cutting and pasting paragraphs from its earlier rulings' (Helfer et al. 2009: 17, 26–7).

Introducing the doctrines of supremacy and direct effect

The Andean Commission approved Decision 85 (5 June 1974) with the title 'Regulation for the Applicability of Norms on Industrial Property'.[14] Its source of inspiration was Colombian law, which it followed almost to the letter.[15] This Decision marked a significant phase in Andean jurisprudential history, since it was under its rule that the doctrines of supremacy (*Preeminencia*; case 2-IP-88) and direct applicability (*Aplicabilidad Directa*; case 1-IP-88) were established. Decision 85 sought to give uniformity to national regulations on the concession and protection of rights relating to trademarks, patents and licences. It had a clear bias towards policies stemming from the dependence theory, as it 'subordinated the property rights of investors to the region's economic development goals, treating patents and trademarks as vehicles for transferring technology from foreign firms' (Helfer et al. 2009: 11). But its most remarkable feature was its Article 5c.[16] This prohibited national authorities from granting patents of invention to pharmaceutical products, medicaments, therapeutically active substances, beverages and food, all of them for human, animal or vegetal use. The rule was coherent with the import substitution policy of that time; it must not be forgotten that the Agreement considered technological development as a crucial mechanism for the subregion's development (CA Article 3a *bis*). Multinational pharmaceutical corporations were thereof impeded from getting protection for their products.

The first ruling in this saga is known as the *Stauffer Chemical* ruling (1-IP-88), based on Decision 85. The Stauffer Chemical Company filed a lawsuit against the Industrial Property Division of the Colombian Regulation Authority for Industry and Trade (Superintendencia de Industria y Comercio de la República de Colombia) because the latter failed to register a patent for the invention of a herbicide presented by the former. The authority's refusal motivated the company to file a judicial action before the Supreme Administrative Court (Consejo de Estado) to declare the decree of refusal null

---

14 Reglamento para la aplicación de las normas sobre propiedad industrial.
15 The ACJ recognised this fact in case 3-IP-88.
16 'Artículo 5. No se otorgarán patentes para: ... (c) Los productos farmacéuticos, los medicamentos, las sustancias terapéuticamente activas, las bebidas y los alimentos para el uso humano, animal o vegetal.'

and void, since herbicides were not mentioned by Article 5c. That decree of refusal, Resolution 322, allegedly violated Community law. The Supreme Administrative Court in turn, acknowledging that the question was a matter of Community law, requested a preliminary ruling on the matter of whether herbicides should be understood as being included in the list of non-patentable products, despite not being expressly mentioned by Article 5c.

The Andean Court again invoked a supposedly teleological interpretation to assess the question raised, and argued in favour of 'the preferential use of the functional, systematic and teleological interpretation. The use of the latter has its foundation in the Treaty of Creation of the Court, since its attributions stem from the need to contribute to the common integrationist purpose.'[17] It follows, then, that the concession of industrial property rights should not become an obstacle to the proliferation of technology within the Andean region. According to the Court, a patent configures a monopoly over the exploitation of an invention. In the words of the Court: 'the system of patents must not hinder the Andean Community's process of development, but on the contrary, it must constitute a coadjutant factor'.[18] In other words, herbicides should be allowed free use within the Andean region. Thus, they were considered to be included among the exemptions to patentability listed in Article 5(c) of Decision 85 – teleologically interpreted, that is. Scholars have described these exceptions as 'nurtur[ing] a thriving regional generics industry that produced low-cost medicines' (Helfer *et al.* 2009: 12).

Nevertheless, the supreme interpreter planted a seed in the ruling that would grow with considerable consequences. The Court briefly revealed what it really understood by teleological interpretation: it reasoned that teleological interpretation had to conform to the goals carried in mind by the organ that generated the norm rather than the goals of the treaty itself.[19]

The doctrine established for *Stauffer Chemical* was reaffirmed in the rulings for *Ciba Geigy A.G.*, cases 3-IP-89 and 7-IP-89. In those processes, the plaintiff, Ciba Geigy, judicially proceeded against an administrative act of the Colombian Industrial Property Division, again based on the fact that this authority refused to register the claimants' invention, namely a herbicide. The Industrial Property Division argued that a herbicide was by nature a 'medicament with vegetal use', and therefore one of the exemptions considered in

---

17 'el empleo preferente de los métodos funcional, sistemático y teleológico. La utilización de este último tiene su fundamentación en el mismo Tratado de Creación del Tribunal, ya que sus atribuciones derivan de la necesidad de contribuir a la consecución *del propósito común integracionista*' (Case 1-IP-88, emphasis added).
18 'el sistema de patentes no debe entorpecer el proceso de desarrollo de la Comunidad Andina sino, por el contrario, debe constituirse en un factor coadyuvante' (Case 1-IP-88).
19 'teniendo en cuenta la finalidad perseguida por el órgano generador de la norma' (Case 1-IP-88).

Article 5(c) of Decision 85, in the terms stated for *Stauffer Chemical*. The case was referred again to Quito for a preliminary ruling.

The Andean Court referred back to the importance of using the teleological interpretation over other forms, because it was more consistent with communitarian nature than any other method of interpretation.[20] It consequently drew attention to the historical background of Decision 85. This had been discussed in an earlier case, 7-IP-89, between the same two parties, in which the Court had implicitly referred to 'dependence theory';[21] that is to say, laws on industrial property rights had been established by the developed countries in times when the Andean countries had not yet become industrialised and the possibilities of technology creation were practically non-existent. Moreover, offering protection to exploitation monopolies – the actual goal of such a system, the Court argued – produced undesired effects on the region's economy and favoured the capture of markets by foreign products.[22] The countries belonging to the Andean Group were 'victims of their dependency on industrialized countries and therefore extremely vulnerable, requiring an institutional framework that would protect them'.[23] The Court also elaborated on the limits of this protection, which were outlined by the general goal of the Agreement (Art. 2), consisting of the promotion of a balanced and harmonious development of the member states.[24] Therefore, according to the

---

20 'Esta interpretación, de otra parte, debe atender al elemento sistemático y al teleológico, de preferencia a los elementos gramatical, idiomático, técnico o lingüístico, ya que esa es, precisamente, la hermenéutica que mejor se aviene a la naturaleza propia del derecho comunitario' (Case 3-IP-89).
21 In Spanish 'teoría de la dependencia' (Cardoso and Faletto 1996).
22 'Las leyes de propiedad industrial, inspiradas en las necesidades e intereses de los países desarrollados habían sido implantadas en los países de la región en momentos en que el desarrollo fabril no había realmente comenzado y la posibilidad de creación tecnológica era inexistente. La protección a los monopolios de explotación, objetivo fundamental de estos sistemas de patentes, producía efectos no deseables para la economía de la región y favorecía la captura de los mercados para los productos extranjeros, la tenencia de las patentes por los agentes de la economía transnacional, la ninguna o escasa vinculación de la inventiva local con el proceso productivo real, el entorpecimiento del flujo tecnológico externo por la imposición de cláusulas restrictivas, la posibilidad de fijar precios monopolísticos del aprovechar la patente para eliminar la competencia, etc.' (Case 7-IP-89).
23 [Los países del grupo Andino,] 'víctimas de su dependencia frente a los países industrializados y extremadamente vulnerables, requieren de un marco institucional que los defienda' (Case 7-IP-89).
24 [Las disposiciones de la Decisión 85] 'tienen como objetivo fundamental establecer una relación de consecuencia directa entre el desarrollo socio-económico, en especial el tecnológico, y los derechos que se conceden a los particulares. Es decir, que la protección de estos últimos tiene su justificación moral, económica y jurídica en que los mismos sean mecanismos que promuevan el desarrollo equilibrado y armónico de los Países

Court, herbicides were included in the exemptions to patentability listed by Article 5 of Decision 85.

There is much Andean legal scholarship that is consistent with this. Carlos Sáchica wrote in 1985 that integration schemes like the Andean must take such external factors as the industrial dependence from other countries into consideration if it aspires to achieve its own goals. Nonetheless, dependence from states outside the integration scheme has the effect, according to Sáchica, of hindering integration (Sáchica 1985a: 6). The view of this particular author is especially interesting in the light of the ruling cited above, as he was one of the judges in the first period of the ACJ.

Facing the challenge of pre-emption

The 1980s, sometimes known as the 'lost decade' of Latin America due to the pervasive debt crisis (Blanco 1997), brought significant changes in the direction of liberalisation and deregulation. This was possible due to the leverage that allowed several international organisations – notably the World Bank, the International Monetary Fund, and the Inter-American Development Bank – to press for reforms that followed the 'Washington Consensus'. Correspondingly, this demanded higher levels of protection for IP rights (Helfer *et al.* 2009: 9; Helfer and Alter 2009: 8).[25]

Decision 85 (secondary law) was in place for 17 years, motivating a profusion of case law decisions in the Andean Court of Justice, and was replaced by subsequent short-lived Decisions[26] until Decision 344 was approved on 21 October 1993 by the Commission of the Cartagena Agreement in Bogotá,[27] and came into force on 1 January 1994. The new IP regulation reflected the region's change with regard to economic liberalisation and multilateral agreement on the protection of intellectual property rights (TRIPS). Member states became aware 'that augmented protection for IP would be the price of admission to the new global trading system' (Helfer and Alter 2009: 10).

Decision 344 – also secondary Community law – contained a substantial amendment: the Andean Commission had eliminated the controversial letter (c) of Article 5 (now Article 7), and the prohibition for patenting pharmaceutical

---

Miembros y el mejoramiento persistente del nivel de vida de los habitantes de la Subregión' (Case 3-IP-89).

25 Helfer *et al.* note another factor that might have had an impact on this decisión: the inclusión of IP rules in the discussions held during the Uruguay Round of the WTO, as well as the US threat of trade sanctions (Helfer *et al.* 2009: 11).

26 Decision 311 of 12 December 1991; Decision 313 of 6 February of 1992. Significant jurisprudence has not been found, which might be explained by the short space of time they were in place.

27 Published on the Official Journal No. 142, 29 October 1993.

products was no longer in place. This new regulation was clearly less favourable to the Andean pharmaceutical industry, which had made profits by trading pharmaceuticals without being bound to pay any patent duties or fees to extra-regional companies. According to neofunctionalist predictions, it would not be long before private litigants would make strategic use of preliminary rulings as a mechanism to defy Decision 344, especially since the Court of Justice had upheld the importance of the 'common integrationist purpose' (ruling 1-IP-88).

The expected action came in 1994: case 6-IP-94. The actors were a group of Ecuadorian laboratories that filed a lawsuit against their government for having dictated Decree 1344-A, which regulated at domestic level the abovementioned Decision 344, because it allegedly violated Andean Community law. The presidential decree now facilitated the concession of patents for those inventions that had been prohibited for registration under Decision 85. Moreover, this measure directly affected the interests of the pharmaceutical companies, who argued in their claim that the Ecuadorian pharmaceutical industry would disappear, that it would be ostracised from the integration process and, therefore, the spirit of the Cartagena Agreement would be violated.[28]

The case was referred to the ACJ and summoned to adjudicate on matters concerning the 'spirit of the Agreement'. In its final ruling, the Court started by acknowledging 'the welfare of the Andean inhabitant as being the first goal of the subregional agreement, according to article 1 of the Cartagena Agreement, the first community norm that guides the very philosophy of the integration mechanism'.[29] However, the Court continued by stating that the Andean Community had been striving for common rules that would allow its incorporation – under equal conditions – into a world that did not develop uniformly. Therefore, 'prohibitions regarding pharmaceutical patents that were in place before the validity of Decisions 311, 313 and 344, that is to say, those contained in Article 5 of Decision 85, those prohibitions ceased to be legally effective with the new Andean legislation, and so it follows that the prohibitions in Article 7 of Decision 344 are still valid today'.[30] Moreover, this

---

28 'desaparecería la industria farmacéutica ecuatoriana, quedaría al margen de la integración andina y se violaría el espíritu del Acuerdo de Cartagena' (Case 6-IP-94).
29 'el bienestar del habitante andino, primer objetivo del Acuerdo Subregional, conforme lo establece el artículo 1° del Acuerdo de Cartagena, norma comunitaria primaria que orienta la filosofía misma del mecanismo de integración' (Case 6-IP-94).
30 'en lo tocante a las prohibiciones existentes sobre patentes farmacéuticas antes de la vigencia de las Decisiones 311, 313 y 344, o sea las que existían en el artículo 5° de la Decisión 85, dichas prohibiciones dejaron de tener vigencia a partir de la nueva legislación andina quedando establecido como lógica consecuencia, que las únicas existentes a la fecha, son las contempladas en el artículo 7° de la Decisión 344 hoy vigente' (Case 6-IP-94).

interpretation of Decision 344 would be harmonious with the Paris Convention on the protection of Industrial Property and the Agreement on Trade-Related Aspects of Intellectual Property Rights (TRIPS): 'All of them [are] consistent with the common spirit of defence and protection of rights emerging from intellectual property, and in order to be applied within the Andean Group must therefore show absolute accordance with the spirit of Decision 344 of the Cartagena Agreement.'[31]

This analysis is remarkable because in it, the ACJ draws the principles of Andean Community law from the will of the legislator – in this case, the Commission – and not actually from the founding goals of the Cartagena Agreement, nor from its declared spirit or philosophy of integration, since neither its goals nor its spirit could possibly have been mutated by the mere promulgation of Decision 344.[32] It must be stated, nevertheless, that Latin American literature on Andean Community law overwhelmingly agrees with the assumption that the Court actually followed teleological interpretation.[33]

If we compare this specific finding with the European situation, we see divergence among interpretation methods. Despite the fact that the ECJ has made use of the historical element to interpret some provisions of secondary Community law, in case of conflict with the goals of the treaty (TEC) it is the teleological interpretation that must prevail (Anweiler 1997: 206).[34] As a result, secondary Community law must necessarily be subordinated to the principles that spring from primary law, since otherwise the unity of the legal order would be jeopardised (Zuleeg 1969: 97). In other words, it is not credible to interpret primary Community law according to its *ratio legis*, and simultaneously secondary law with historical-systematic tools of legal interpretation (see case ECJ C-300/89 *Commission v. Council*, and case 45/86 *APS*; Anweiler 1997). In addition, and due to reasons of legal certainty, the historical method of interpretation has been limited to those cases where the will of the legislator can be drawn from explicit documentation incorporated into the piece of legislation, such as an annex or addendum (Schroeder 2004: 183).

In the long term, the jurisprudential line adopted by the ACJ allowed Andean law to make a smooth transit to the later Decision 486. This piece of

---

31 'Todos ellos convergentes con el espíritu común de defensa y protección de los derechos emergentes de la Propiedad Intelectual y que para ser aplicados en los países del grupo andino, deben guardar absoluta concordancia con el espíritu de la Decisión 344 del Acuerdo de Cartagena' (Case 6-IP-94: 17–18).
32 This understanding is bolstered by the text of rulings 3-IP-94 and 6-IP-94 where the ACJ makes the *ratio legis* of integration law equal to the 'will of the legislator'.
33 For instance, Sáchica (1985), Uribe Restrepo (1993) and Vigil Toledo (2004).
34 For this stand, Anweiler cites rulings on case C-215/88 (*Fleischhandel*), case 45/86 (APS), and C-300/89 (*Commission v. Council*). However, the author mentions an opposing current to what he categorises as teleological-objective interpretation.

legislation came into force on 1 December 2000 and replaced Decision 344, as well as its successor, Decision 85. With Decision 486, the Andean Community adapted its Common Policy on Industrial Property to the TRIPS agreement, bolstering rights stemming from industrial property in accordance with multilateral treaties (Bianchi Pérez 2002: 103), and yielding to the interpretation that follows the will of the Community legislator.

Establishing a common market by expansive interpretation

In a passage in *L'esprit des lois*, Montesquieu describes a type of judge who does not use creativity when needing to interpret the meaning of the law. According to the Roman tradition, the function of a judge is to serve as a mere mouthpiece of the law, either absolving or convicting defendants, but never creating new legislation (Montesquieu 1961: 82). The Roman ideal type for a judge is rather an extreme one. Nonetheless, it helps as an analytical counterpoint when interpreting the role played by the ECJ in integration. This is especially the case considering the profusion of literature that stresses the creative work of the court when it chooses among different possible interpretations of the law in its rulings (Dehousse 1998: 72). Neither has the ECJ missed the chance to attempt an extensive interpretation of Community norms whenever the text lacks specificity. In the *Dassonville* ruling (case 8/74), the Court expanded the meaning of Article 30 of the treaty, reasoning that 'banning discriminatory measures' should be understood as prohibiting any norm capable of impeding directly or indirectly, actually or potentially, intra-Community trade. According to this interpretation, it is not so relevant whether a given national measure is overtly discriminatory in nature or not; what is relevant is the impact of this measure on intra-Community trade (Dehousse 1998: 74).

Studying the activity of the ACJ is not a simple task. The challenge here is that neither Andean litigation nor its jurisprudence is reported in scholarly publications, with the sole exception of the issue area of intellectual property rights (Helfer *et al.* 2009: 25). Nevertheless, Andean authors have generally addressed the importance of teleological interpretation. Especially those scholars who would become Andean judges were very straightforward regarding the importance of the goals of the CA. Sáchica wrote in 1985 that the interpretation of the treaty should follow its finality because it was essentially a programmatic text (Sáchica 1985a: 26). Similarly, Andueza argues that the provisions of the Cartagena Agreement are essentially a case of incomplete contracting. Therefore, it is for the Community organs, as well as for member states, to complete Andean provisions. Completing a scheme of economic integration, Andueza adds, requires that the relevant provision be 'programmatic': 'For this reason, the interpretation of the Cartagena Agreement has to be teleological' (Andueza 1985b: 88).

Although the ACJ has been prolific when it comes to issuing preliminary rulings, it has been confronted with questions related to the establishment of the Andean Common Market only in a handful of cases. In fact, of all preliminary rulings that have been recorded by Helfer *et al.*, being a total of 1,338, only 2 per cent (35) were not intellectual property law cases (Helfer *et al.* 2009: 16).

Still, the ACJ found itself confronted with questions that are very similar to those faced by the ECJ. Article 41 of the Cartagena Agreement established a programme that pursued the progressive dismantlement of trade barriers (Programa de Liberación de la Comunidad Andina).[35] Nevertheless, Article 55 of the Agreement allowed a list of exceptions to liberalisation, with goods that were considered sensitive for the economies of member states.[36] However, the text of the Agreement was not explicit about the nature or the scope of these exemptions, and this provided a perfect opportunity for the Court to fill in the gap.

In case 1-IP-90 on preliminary ruling, the plaintiffs Aluminio Reynolds Santo Domingo and the Sociedad Aluminio Nacional S.A. sued the Colombian government, soliciting the annulment of a governmental decree (*Ley 75* of 1986) that imposed a tax of 18 per cent on the CIF value of aluminium imported from Venezuela, a product listed as an exception to the liberalisation plan. The plaintiff claimed that imposing new taxes on transnational trade would go against the spirit of the Cartagena Agreement. Although Article 55 and its list of exceptions to liberalisation could not force member states to reduce or eliminate existing tariffs on these goods, this provision – if interpreted teleologically – prohibited both raising current tariffs levied on them and taxing them with any additional duty. Thus, the existence of lists of exceptions to liberalisation should be interpreted as a mere delay in the process of dismantling trade barriers, something the member states had committed themselves to through the liberalisation programme.

To neofunctionalism, this argument sounds very familiar and reasonable, especially considering that in 1988 the Court had promoted the teleological interpretation of Andean Community law, which allegedly had its foundation in Community primary law and served the integrationist common purpose (*propósito común integracionista*).[37]

---

35 Cartagena Agreement Art. 72 (former Art. 41) 'El Programa de Liberación de bienes tiene por objeto eliminar los gravámenes y las restricciones de todo orden que incidan sobre la importación de productos originarios del territorio de cualquier País Miembro.'
36 This article was amended by Decision 217 of the Commission, and ratified as an amendment of the Cartagena Agreement by virtue of the Quito Protocol of 12 May 1987. Today, it has been abrogated.
37 'En cuanto a la interpretación del derecho comunitario, ratifica el Tribunal en esta oportunidad los criterios establecidos en anterior sentencia, dictada en el Proceso No. 1-IP-87.

On the other hand, the Colombian government fiercely opposed this position, claiming that the Andean Commission itself – i.e. the legislative body – had decided to amend Article 55 of the Agreement introducing the lists of exceptions by Decision 217, being the secondary Community law, arguing that 'systematic interpretation [is] the only valid source when it comes to norms that are part of a coherent legal body like the Cartagena Agreement'.[38] The defendant added that the text of the Cartagena Agreement should be interpreted as obliging states to refrain from raising tariffs *only* on those goods that were part of the general liberalisation programme of Article 41; it follows that the programme cannot be applied to a comprehensive[39] set of goods, either currently or in the future.[40]

In its national procedural stage, the case came before the highest Colombian Administrative Court (Consejo de Estado de la República de Colombia). It was then referred to the Andean Court, requesting a preliminary ruling on Articles 45 (now Art. 76) and 55 (now abrogated) of the Cartagena Agreement, and an answer to the question whether member states should retain the right to raise tariffs on goods that were listed as exceptions to the liberalisation programme.

The Andean Court was confronted with two contradictory interpretations. On the one hand, there was the expansive interpretation, in the style of *Dassonville*, in which the consequences of additional taxation on imported goods were taken into consideration. On the other hand, there was the restrictive interpretation demanded by the Colombian government, claiming that if the text of the Agreement did not specifically prohibit raising tariffs, it should be understood that member states retained their right to do so.

Contrary to what neofunctionalism would expect, the Court accepted the latter argumentation, and pointed out that in this case a norm that restricted the freedom of member states was at stake. This meant, according to the Court, that this norm was also subject to a restrictive interpretation, and that member states were free to decide for themselves on matters of tariffs and

---

Se aplica los métodos de hermenéutica jurídica generalmente aceptados, pero corresponde, llegado el caso, el empleo preferente de los métodos funcional, sistemático y teleológico. La utilización de este último tiene su fundamentación en el mismo Tratado de Creación del Tribunal, ya que sus atribuciones derivan de la necesidad de contribuir a la consecución del propósito común integracionista' (Case 1-IP-88).

38 'interpretación sistemática como la única válida tratándose de normas que hacen parte de un cuerpo legislativo coherente como es el Acuerdo de Cartagena' (Case 1-IP-90).
39 'Universal', in the words of the Colombian government.
40 Cartagena Agreement Art. 72 (former Art. 41) 'El Programa de Liberación de bienes tiene por objeto eliminar los gravámenes y las restricciones de todo orden que incidan sobre la importación de productos originarios del territorio de cualquier País Miembro.'

restrictions related to these exempted goods.[41] Therefore, the Cartagena Agreement by no means prohibited them from levying new taxes or giving these goods favourable treatment.[42] The Court went on to state, 'it must not be forgotten, finally, that norms that limit freedom must be interpreted restrictively, as the exception to the general rule they are, according to a universally accepted principle of interpretation'.[43]

However, the judges did not explain how this interpretation could be compatible with Article 3 of the Cartagena Agreement, which states that in order to achieve the objectives of the treaty a more advanced trade liberalisation programme should be used than the agreements reached in the Treaty of Montevideo of 1980. While it must not be overlooked that the Court had previously accepted the liberalisation programme as the most important mechanism to achieve the common integrationist goals, its restrictive reasoning indicates that the Andean Court yielded to the position of international law that stands against eventual loss of sovereignty of the states (cf. Weiler 1982: 270).

Although preliminary rulings on the issue of the liberalisation programme are scarce, in 1993 the doctrine of restrictive interpretation was again invoked in the discussion of case 3-IP-93, which was initiated by the Sociedad de Aluminio Nacional against the Colombian Customs Authority (Dirección de Aduana de Colombia), on the same grounds and directed against the same decree, namely the *Ley 75* of 1986. In this case, the Court came back to the precedent and pointed out that restrictive interpretation should be used when it comes to the liberalisation programme, 'since the clear goal of those norms is that of limiting the freedom which governments initially have for the purpose of levying taxes, in accordance with their loyal knowledge and understanding'.[44]

The Court once again discarded any expansive interpretation in the style of *Dassonville*.[45] Consequently, member states retained the right to impose taxes

---

41 'los países miembros son autónomos para decidir sobre gravámenes y restricciones en relación con productos reservados o exceptuados' (Case 1-IP-90).

42 'el Acuerdo de Cartagena en ningún caso les prohíbe imponer nuevos gravámenes o conceder dichos productos un tratamiento más favorable' (Case 1-IP-90).

43 'No debe olvidarse, finalmente, que las normas que limitan la libertad deben ser interpretadas restrictivamente, como excepción que son a la regla general, según un principio de interpretación universalmente aceptado' (Case 1-IP-90).

44 'ya que el claro objetivo de dichas normas es el de limitar la libertad que inicialmente se encuentran los gobiernos para imponer gravámenes según su leal saber u entender' (Case 3-IP-93).

45 Cartagena Agreement Art. 76 (former Art. 45) 'El Programa de Liberación será automático e irrevocable y comprenderá la universalidad de los productos, salvo las disposiciones de excepción establecidas en el presente Acuerdo, para llegar a su liberación total en los plazos y modalidades que señala este Acuerdo'.

'Este principio de hermenéutica viene en respaldo de la interpretación de los Artículos 45 y 54 del Acuerdo de Cartagena, adoptada por el Tribunal según las consideraciones

and other duties on imports coming from the region, as long as they were listed as exemptions to the liberalisation programme. From the point of view of contributing towards the consolidation of a common market, this interpretation goes clearly in the opposite direction (for the same argument, see Marwege 1995: 250). Moreover, it strengthens the decision-making capacities of the member states in the field of taxation of goods.

If we take a look at European integration, we see that the ECJ has been confronted with the possibility of restricting Community policies for the sake of the freedom of member states, but has interpreted differently the treaty's objectives concerning restrictions of the relevant policy. Hence, the latter has had to yield to the former. For instance, in case 6/72 *Continental Can* (par. 24), the ECJ ruled that eventual restrictions imposed on competition policy find their limit in the general principles of the legal order, contained in Articles 2 and 3 of the treaty (Anweiler 1997: 211). Moreover, in case 3/62 *Commission v. Luxembourg*,[46] the European Court used the teleological interpretation and ruled that restrictive interpretation was to be used in those cases where the question at stake was about eventual exemptions to the policy of free movement of goods (Anweiler 1997: 232).

It has been argued that this dynamic approach can be found in periods of inertia and stagnation of the Commission and the Council of the EU (Rasmussen 1986: 178). This, in turn, reminds us that within the Andean region the deadlines for the establishment of the Customs Union have been repeatedly postponed by intergovernmental decisions. Despite an evident stagnation of the integration process, the ACJ has refused to follow an expansive course of action.

que anteceden, ya que el claro objetivo de dichas normas es el de limitar la libertad en que inicialmente se encuentran los Gobiernos para imponer gravámenes según su leal saber y entender. Tales limitaciones, que obviamente requieren de consagración expresa, han de ser interpretadas restrictivamente, como en este caso lo ha hecho el Tribunal'
(Process 3-IP-93, citing process 1-IP-90).

46 'it follows, then, from the clarity, certainty and unrestricted scope of articles 9 and 12, from the general scheme of their provisions and of the treaty as a whole, that the prohibition of new customs duties, linked with the principles of the free movement of products, constitutes an essential rule and that in consequence any exception, which moreover is to be narrowly interpreted, must be clearly stipulated' (ECJ case 3/62, p. 432).

Chapter 6

What legal engineers do not get
Rights politics and the pitfalls of concept stretching

The comparison made in previous chapters suggests that legal copies or transplants are often not as complete as intended, no matter how sophisticated they are. Rather, the opposite is true in that, regardless of how legal transplants are designed and implemented, they will always be legal artefacts that produce compartmentalised legal effects instead of profound societal transformation. No legal engineering can be comprehensive enough to produce a full economic or legal development on its own.

However, it is claimed that legal reforms like the Andean Court of Justice are not inherently negative. They can make an important contribution and there is much that we can learn from these experiences, as long as we remember that the law entails a complex of norms embedded in social behaviour. If we are to transplant a fully fledged court, there will always be important tenets of the donor that we will be leaving behind.

The case of the Andean Court of Justice is an example of how important it was for the European integration to discuss in depth the fundamental rights between judges, practitioners and academics. These rights were largely lacking in the Andean Community of the 1980s and, therefore, the capabilities to start a judicial revolution *à la européen* were low. Nonetheless, the comparison shows that courts still have room for circumscribed legal changes, even if the scope conditions are not optimal. Recent reports show how the Andean Court of Justice has been able to form a limited but valuable island of rule of law in the field of intellectual property (IP) (Helfer and Alter 2009). These interconnections can be positively exploited as long as the road towards development is a not understood as a mono causal path, suitable of being solved through legal engineering, but a slow and incremental process (North 1990).

Taken together, these findings confirm Amartia Sen's claims that law and judicial reforms are contingent on social characteristics and should, therefore, take note of the enhancement of people's capabilities (Sen 2006) as well as the improvement of the democratic rule of law.

Assessing empirical variations between the courts

The comparison between the goals from which the European Union and the Andean Pact originated reveals considerable differences. In turn, these differences had an indirect influence in the observable case law handed down by both tribunals, the ECJ and the ACJ.

The legacy of post-war Europe and the hard lessons that were drawn determined a strong normative agenda that sought to prevent future wars (Wiener and Diez 2004). In addition, the protection of the individual became an important element, not only of European law-making, but also of the nascent constitutional judiciary that had found inspiration in the organically grown system of judicial review of the US Supreme Court (Kramer 2004). Together with the establishment of a common market as a means to control the market of raw materials necessary for conducting war, the integration process was linked with fundamental rights that sought to prevent states from abusing individuals.

The Andean process of integration shows steady goals across time, but also changing strategies on how to attain them. In its inception, the Cartagena Agreement included strong critical claims. The dominance of dependence theory sought to enable developing states to attain industrial and commercial autonomy by protecting their internal market from extra-regional competitors. It was thought that this general goal would provide the necessary conditions for economic development, being the Andean Community's ultimate purpose. Through economic development, the Andean people would see their living conditions increased. The concretisation of this leitmotiv (Uribe Restrepo 1990) was entrusted to Andean regional institutions. The welfare and well-being of the Andean population in general was conceived as a collective aim.

The protection of the individual, however, never played a central role in the Andean scheme – at least, not in regard to the Andean Community. To be sure, the protection of human rights has taken a stellar place in the inter-American stage during the last two decades, led by national constitutional judges and reinforced by the Inter-American Court of Human Rights (Góngora-Mera 2011). This is probably due to a notable history of dictatorship and human rights violation. Nevertheless, and contrary to the persistent efforts of the ECJ to become a guarantor of fundamental rights and freedoms, the ACJ never undertook any measure that would link the establishment of a common market with the protection of individual rights. The Andean Court did not create a bill of rights that could be enforceable by Andean citizens and it did not draw them from the Latin American catalogues that were available.

The radical change of strategies that came with the SAI (Andean Integration System) did not change the ultimate goal of economic development. It only provided new perspectives on how to compete in the competitive world markets. This reinvention did not introduce the dimension of fundamental rights or fundamental freedoms. However, in the field of intellectual property rights, the ACJ radically departed from its own case law. IP rights became a focal point of Andean jurisprudence, which became the world's most active international court (Helfer *et al.* 2009).

The comparative perspective reveals that European integration has been confirming its normative goal during the last 50 years, whereas the Andean Community is still striving for a goal that has proven elusive. The research also shows that the impressive similarities between both regional courts are not an accident. The outstanding role that the ECJ played in the establishment of the European legal system appeared as a possible solution to the challenges that the Andean Community was facing during the late 1970s and 1980s.

As discussed in Chapter 4, the process of transplantation of the ECJ was an act of legal engineering, understood as the task of designing and building new legal structures that should serve a specific purpose. The function that a specific building block (using the wording of Cashin Ritaine 2008) should fulfil in the process of legal integration was generally drawn from European legal scholarship and applied with no prior deconstruction or re-engineering. The structure of the Court, and the competences for making authoritative interpretation of Andean law, are an exact emulation of its European counterpart. Procedures are almost identical: those of nullification, non-compliance and preliminary rulings. The latter is especially relevant as it allows for the doctrines of supremacy and direct effect to be tailored. According to some Andean commentators, the Andean polity provides conditions for private litigants that are even more generous than those of the EC treaty (da Cruz Vilaça and Sobrino 1998).

The transplantation of the ECJ is, therefore, consistent with legal narratives on the 'magic triangle': that is, the procedure of preliminary rulings, plus the doctrines of supremacy and direct effect. This idea is strengthened by the fact that the ECJ's doctrine of supremacy of community law was formally included in the treaty of the ACJ. Therefore, it is unthinkable that the Andean legislator sought anything else than a proficient emulation of the ECJ and its case law.

As for the motivations for establishing a supranational court, there are slight differences between European and Andean integration. Mainly due to the heroic narrative on the judicial transformation of the European legal system, the first goal behind the establishment of the ECJ is often overlooked. The Court was intended to operate as a control mechanism that could check community organs – especially the Commission – and protect states' interests against undue encroachment into national affairs (Alter 2001). That the ECJ would develop its doctrines and demand further powers was not in the minds of the drafters of the treaty (Cappelletti 1989).

Unlike the European founding fathers, the ACJ's role as a control mechanism was not primordial. Interestingly, it was precisely its role as a promoter of legal integration that persuaded Andean decision-makers to emulate the ECJ. The epistemic network around the ECJ strongly advocated for an equivalent court. The inclusion of the doctrine of supremacy into the treaty of the ACJ is also an achievement of the Euro-Andean advocates. By means of expansive rulings, the ACJ was supposed to tackle the endemic problems of non-compliance that made the Andean region and Latin America so infamous. In terms of a properly functioning common market, a uniform application of Andean law was deemed to be necessary.

With regard to the function of settling disputes in Europe, although there are some approaches that have stressed the need to prevent retaliation and trade wars (Weiler 1994: 526), the scenario where member states would intensely sue each other was not in the minds of the drafters (Kuper 1998: 4). However, the asymmetries between economic importance of member states and their respective rates of compliance with European law became a conspicuous issue. The most compliant member states intensified pressure on the 'worst cheaters' (Alter 2001: 16). As a consequence, sanctionary powers were (re)established in 1993.

In the case of the Andean Community, literature and data on non-compliance procedures suggest that it was not the scenario of trade wars that motivated the establishment of a court, but rather a window of opportunity that was strategically used in the shadow of a persistent state of non-compliance with Andean commitments. Instead of an outburst of commercial retaliation, endemic non-compliance had given birth to a decision-making style that was based on a sense of brotherhood and the lowest common denominator. 'Concerted' multilateralism (Frohmann 1990; Tomassini 1990) in regional issues was conducted through a set of measures that combined high-level jargon stressing the common cultural legacy with less than binding agreements that were highly deferential to state sovereignty. The persistent claim that conflicts should be solved in a 'gentlemanlike' fashion – and at the highest possible level – is contradictory with the idea of unrestrained trade wars.

Variations in case law

Research reveals that the most significant differences are in the implications of case law, even though the Andean Court of Justice followed the ECJ's case law almost by the book. The ACJ introduced concepts that clearly have their origins in EC case law, such as supremacy and direct effect. It did not shy away from citing European case law and proclaiming that Andean law was following the same European path. It also introduced constitutional jargon in connection with the doctrines that might suggest a departure from traditional public international law. Yet, Andean law strongly deviates from European law as the ACJ does not see itself as the guarantor of fundamental rights. This was by no means an arbitrary claim. European legal scholars have shown that the Euro-law game was a consequence of several challenges that originated at national level.

These challenges pointed to the fact that as the EC was claiming to be the higher law and to possess exclusive regulatory authority in some fields, it was not granting the same level of protection of rights as national law. Such concerns were the product of the doctrines of pre-emption in combination with the doctrine of supremacy. The ECJ reacted with its already mentioned case law on the protection of fundamental rights. If the states were to maintain the authority to protect fundamental rights, it would have certainly led to uneven application of EC law, since the member states had different standards.

The ACJ, on the other hand, proclaimed supremacy without the doctrine of pre-emption. The ACJ refused to expand the regulatory authority of the Community despite explicit demands by private litigants, and despite the programmatic norms to which member states were bound. As a consequence, supremacy of Andean law was limited to those norms that had been agreed in explicit terms by the member states. No question regarding conflicts between common market policies and fundamental rights came before the Court, as the limited understanding of supremacy did not spark any concerns at national level, nor constitute any threat to rights holders. It did not force its way into such cases, either.

Neofunctionalism and the Andean engine of integration

As illustrated above, all the conditions for legal integration, as laid down by neofunctionalism, for the advancement of legal integration were present in the Andean Community. These include a supranational court with authority over community law; institutions that would enable the Court to ensure uniform interpretation of Community law; the introduction of doctrines that establish supremacy of Community law vis-à-vis national law, as well as its direct effect; and individuals' access to supranational justice through their own national courts. Furthermore, these national courts would assume the task of enforcing the ACJ's interpretation of Community law, even against their own government.

The neofunctionalist hypothesis assumed an ever-expanding authority that would upgrade common interests. In the case of legal integration, the reference to common goals with strong normative content like 'proper functioning of the common market', 'prohibition of arbitrary discrimination', and 'free movement of goods' would lead people to shift their expectations. At the same time, the authority of the supranational court would increase. The hypothesis assumed a court that would always push the process forward. Even when faced with resistance, it would find a way to circumvent political clashes using the advantages of possessing technical knowledge and procedures. If technical decisions were to be politicised, the Court would have the means to outplay member states thanks to the different time horizons of judges and government officials. Although the speed might change, it would always head forward, just like an engine. Neofunctionalism, however, does not offer an explanation for the case of an engine restraining itself.

In its case law on patents, the ACJ refused to engage in expansive decision-making. Although there was a demand side that expected to benefit from a judicial review, the Court decided to follow principles of traditional international public law. In other words, it became deferential to national sovereignty. As this new course of action is not an instance of circumventing strategies, it becomes impossible for neofunctionalism to explain the outcome. Nevertheless, the Andean saga confirms some of the neofunctionalist predictions. The court was indeed confronted with the same questions that the ECJ had to face. This is particularly notable for the issue of pre-emption. Although scholarship on federalism had already suggested the inevitability of this topic in federal courts, it is a new insight that the sequence can be ignited at supranational level with the conditions laid down by neofunctionalists. The challenges to national law and national regulatory authority are conveyed by private litigants acting in their own interest. In the Andean case, the mechanism works up to the point where the Court faces the question of pre-emption. From that moment, neofunctionalism cannot sustain its assumptions.

Intergovernmentalism and the kite model

Considering that the theoretical debate between neofunctionalism and intergovernmentalism was held at a meta-level, one might expect that if one grand theory failed, it would confirm the rival theory. But, while neofunctionalism flunked the test, intergovernmentalism did not pass it either.

Intergovernmentalism, and particularly neorationalism, expected a more servant role of the Court. Eventual activism would receive correcting measures on behalf of the member states. Conversely, if judicial behaviour was in line with member states' interests, no correcting measures would follow. The flaw in this hypothesis is that it assumes a court – an agent – would persistently push for expansion of its competences, in order to satisfy its own interests. This is the reason why member states had established control mechanisms. The delegated powers of the court would go only as far as the member states would allow. The model can be exemplified with the action of flying a kite. As the kite rises up into the sky, the kite-flyer is controlling the action with a tether. The kite is supposed to fly high, but always within the reach of the tether. If a strong wind pulls the kite further, the master can allow it to glide farther away or hold it. However, if there is no wind for the kite to fly, the tether becomes pointless. Neorationalism hereby assumes a court that has to be checked constantly by member states. The ACJ, however, decided not to fly in spite of the long tether.

Even after the rulings, the member states decided to increase the binding effect of their commitments by including them into their national constitution. Moreover, even after the Court had exercised self-restraint, the member states – through the Commission – decided to expand the powers of the Court in the fields of labour arbitration. Therefore, and returning to the metaphor, if the kite lies on the floor but the kite-flyer has unrolled several yards of tether, it would be a very unconvincing argument to say that it is the wish of the master that the kite remains on the ground.

Towards an alternative explanation

Supranational entrepreneurship

With the analysis of the empirical data available in the jurisprudence of the ACJ, one could be inclined to admit the prevalence of explanations that are based on neorationalist intergovernmentalism rather than on neofunctionalism. With reference to the situation in Europe during the 1960s, Karen Alter wrote:

> National governments did not appear unhappy with this situation. They seemed to like being able to maintain protectionist policies and claim they were committed to building a Common Market. Indeed, some governments seemed to expect legal bodies to defer to them in interpreting European law. Governments, after all, had negotiated the treaties. Thus they knew what they meant.
>
> (Alter 2001: 216)

Some Andean evidence seems to uphold this claim. In the first years of operation of the ACJ, national governments were not fond of being subjected to non-compliance procedures. Although member states failed to implement Andean Decisions, governments blocked the Junta from filing non-compliance suits (Helfer and Alter 2009: 8). Against this background, the assumption according to which supranational courts are agents that serve the member states' interests, and that their effective authority depends on the acceptance of its rulings on behalf of the principal, becomes plausible.

Helfer and Alter noted some differences between Andean and European judges, and offered an explanation to the question why the ACJ was so unknown to scholars of international adjudication and regional integration:

> In the Andean context, national judges do not pose far reaching or provocative questions that would provide the ATJ with opportunities to expand the scope and reach of Andean law. Rather, they are mostly passive intermediaries situated between the ATJ and domestic administrative agencies charged with protecting intellectual property ... national judicial support cannot be taken for granted.
>
> (Helfer and Alter 2009: 4)[1]

---

1 In order to contextualise this citation, it should be noted that the authors were highlighting the role of national agencies as promoters and consumers of supranational law: 'interlocutors

If that assertion is true, it would explain the low number of rulings with constitutional content despite the Court's impressive docket. In other words, it would corroborate the assertion that the ACJ is an active court but not an activist one (see Helfer and Alter 2009); and yet, it leaves the question open as to why the ACJ would not seek further empowerment. Even if we admit that Andean national judges are less 'provocative' than their European fellows, the rulings on the *Aluminio* case pose a second challenge. Despite the low number of cases that implied constitutional issues vis-à-vis the overwhelming number of cases that could be watered down to a mere technical interpretation of IP rules, there were indeed instances for expansive ruling. According to the foregoing evidence, the few 'provocative' references presented by national judges – that is, the questions that boiled down to the validity of community law in the domestic sphere – were decided in favour of member states. This weakens the explanation as to why the absence of expansive rulings is due to the 'parsimony' of national judges at the moment of formulating questions to the ACJ. The question remains, why would the ACJ not try to expand the scope of supranational law in the few instances it found itself in?

For neofunctionalism, this latter finding is also highly problematic, as one critical assumption, namely the expansive nature of supranational courts, fails the test in the Andean case with no satisfactory explanation. Early neofunctionalism postulated some supranational agency as a necessary element for spillover (Haas 1968: 710), but never laid down the conditions under which supranational entrepreneurship would not take place. Neofunctionalism always assumed that supranational institutions are constantly looking to advance integration, and that 'in so doing usually manage to upgrade [their] own powers at the expense of the member governments' (Haas 1968: 152).

Neorationalist explanations, therefore, seem to explain this puzzle better, at least initially. If the Court is indulgent with member states, and these states do not flout courts' decisions or do not override court rulings through treaty revisions, then – according to the neorationalist argument – it should be assumed that member states' preferences are being served (Garrett 1995: 178). Nevertheless, this neorationalist explanation remains equally unsatisfactory in the light of the Andean evidence, which becomes visible with the principal-agent (P-A) approach, as outlined below.

First, P-A approaches insist that one of the reasons that lead member states to delegate authority to a supranational court is to solve monitoring problems (Garrett 1995: 172; Garrett and Weingast 1993). However, if we first accept the neorationalist explanation that the ACJ's decisions followed the preferences

and compliance constituencies for international judicial rulings' (Helfer and Alter 2009: 4). However, this interesting finding does not alleviate the neofunctionalist predicament, as one of its critical assumptions, namely the empowerment of the judiciary, remains hitherto questioned.

of member states, and then realise that the Court curtailed its own monitoring competences, we face a contradiction, since the agent would have sought to leave the monitoring problem unsolved. That is precisely what happened in the *Stauffer Chemical* ruling on the Andean patents, as it introduces European legal concepts, but at the same time the Court waters them down to doctrines faithful to classic international public law.

Second, if by establishing a court the states aimed at overcoming a credibility problem (Thatcher and Stone Sweet 2002: 4; Tallberg 2002: 29), it remains unexplained how it could possibly be in the interests of member states for the Court to rule on the prevalence of secondary Community law over treaty goals. If, in the eyes of the Court, states remain sovereign to alter the course of integration by means of secondary law, then the credibility gain is close to zero. Perhaps an eventual sovereignty loss might be avoided, but the act of delegation to the Court would not make any sense if it was going to shrink its own competences.

Third, neorationalists have concurred with neofunctionalists that courts can be understood as strategic rational actors. For both theories supranational courts' preferences apparently seek to extend (European) Community law and their authority to interpret it (Garrett 1995: 173). Simultaneously, courts allegedly seek to enhance their reputation through constraining the behaviour of a powerful member state, as long as the government is expected to accept the decision (Garrett 1995: 178, 80). However, in the Andean case, we see that the Court has undermined the scope of Community law in the region, and it did so even in cases where the products subject to litigation corresponded to a minor sector of the economies, namely herbicides or aluminium.[2] In none of the cases explored here, which seem to be the most relevant in terms of doctrinal importance, did the court rule against any member state in order to enhance its reputation or legitimacy. The Andean case does not fit either theory, as it challenges several assumptions on which both competing theories have rested.

Inter-court competition

A further challenge is posed by the patterns of references to the ACJ. According to the coding offered by Helfer and Alter, the bulk of references are issued by a small number of national courts. Out of a total amount of 1,338 preliminary ruling references between 1987 and 2007, Colombian courts initiated 64 per cent.

---

2 According to current statistics (2006), imports of herbicide and unwrought aluminium account for less than 0.21 and 0.57 per cent of total imports to Colombia (source: UN's Economic Commission for Latin America, division of international trade and integration. <http://www.cepal.org/comercio>).

Moreover, of the 860 references sent by Colombian courts, the Consejo de Estado was responsible for 63 per cent (Helfer and Alter 2009: 15).

References are, therefore, predominantly emanating from higher courts. This pattern is different from the European one, in that higher national courts often do not have a superior and, therefore, there is no need to circumvent any superior court. Judicial competition cannot be assessed with the same framework that scholars used in studies on European legal integration. The dialogue that has taken place between the ACJ and national judges is predominantly horizontal, because there is no superior court to any of them. On the contrary, European theories of integration have constantly assumed that competition between courts involves at least some degree of verticality. In other words, at least one dialoguing court has a superior.

Although the above-mentioned claim that Andean national judges are not prone to formulate provocative questions in their references seems to be a plausible observation, I argue that horizontal dialogues pose an institutional constraint on expansive rulings, and therefore contribute to shaping the content of Andean preliminary rulings. National judges frame parsimonious questions to the ACJ because higher courts have no interest in expanding ACJ competences. If considered as actors, higher courts do not have any reason to challenge the status quo. The best outcome for national higher courts is that institutions remain exactly the same, as their credibility and their image increases due to their obedience to the law. The dominant tradition of international public law, and especially the principle of national sovereignty, entails high levels of judicial discretion for higher courts vis-à-vis any other court, be it national or supranational. By assuming that courts generally prefer higher levels of judicial discretion instead of lower levels, we are being loyal to notions of judicial interests that have also been applied to the European situation (Alter 2001).

Consistent with that argument is the fact that higher courts are not threatened if questions referred to the ACJ do not challenge existing distributions of judicial discretion and authority within the state. Such referrals do not threaten any existing national judicial tradition; on the contrary, they might be of considerable benefit. Just as the claim that the governments of member states increase their reputation when they project an image that corresponds to a state that complies with its international obligations, a court might also benefit from an image that suggests it complies with the agreements entered upon by their states. This assumes that there are costs for courts that overtly challenge international treaties. Therefore, if higher courts can project an image of compliance with international law by repeatedly referring cases to the ACJ, but maintaining the control of the scope and content of the referrals, it attains both goals: increased credibility, as well as keeping high levels of judicial discretion.

The problem with the Andean case is that neither the neofunctionalist nor the intergovernmentalist approach seems to convincingly explain the case of the Andean Community. Rather, it becomes necessary to frame a new set of assumptions in order to overcome the flaws that have become apparent and to understand the choices made by the ACJ.

Framing a functional comparison based on regulatory models

The functional comparison, where every actor is assumed to fulfil a role that can be used as a baseline for comparing both regional settings, has broad theoretical implications. To start with, it allows a comparison of partial systems or structures, for instance litigation by the procedure of preliminary rulings. Comparisons of partial systems are relevant, because the roles that we attach to partial systems during our observations are not necessarily identical to the roles played by the whole system. This is epistemically relevant because it highlights only those facts that are relevant in the light of the functions we attach to our partial structures. Such a research strategy allows us to gather and evaluate the evidence with a new prism.

In addition, a comparison based on functions or roles enables us to construct precise models that can organise the inquiry and the evaluation of empirical findings. In what follows the judicial saga is presented through two competing models that are primarily taken from the theory on the ECJ. However, the merit of these heuristic artefacts is that they tell us much more about the ACJ and its case law as current institutional comparisons. In this exercise, functional differences between both settings come to the forefront.

Two competing regulatory models: decentralised vs. centralist

Measuring judicial discretion is a challenging task, as it is difficult to know what occurs inside a judge's mind. When it comes to a legal order that is developing, the central questions hinge on the possibility of incorporating new principles into that new order. If precise rules have not been written by the legislator, judges enjoy a considerable amount of discretion, since they are to decide *which* principle enters the community legal order (Canor 1998: 65).

The two sets of data – on the issues of a common market and intellectual property rights, respectively – testify to two dilemmas with which the Andean Court was confronted.

In the case of the exceptions to the establishment of a common market, namely the *Aluminio Reynolds* case, the legal facts and argumentations show a conflict between a policy and a legal principle. On one hand, there is a Community policy that aims at the liberalisation of the market. On the other hand, there is an established principle of international law, according to which states should not be held liable for obligations when the circumstances under which they engage are not clearly and expressly stated in the agreement.

If we try to comprehend the dilemma, we see that the two arguments come from different arenas. Private litigants file their arguments from a private domain, while member states refuse to abandon their status as subjects of international law. Each tries to force the contender to enter the arena from which they hold their own argument. There is disagreement as to which set of rules prevails in a situation of conflicting systems: Community law in its economic constitutional dimension, or international law with its view of the Cartagena Agreement remaining a traditional international treaty. We should not be surprised by this, since it has often been the case in the history of European integration that actors engage in these conflicts with disparate normative expectations. This is by no means alien to judicial developments. Legal arguments displayed by both litigant parties might seem very reasonable from a strategic point of view. Yet, it is one thing to understand the litigants' argumentations; it is another to explain the Andean judicial saga in theoretical terms.

The first thing to do is to acknowledge that the legal dilemma of the ACJ is not identical to the political dilemma it was confronted with. What appears in the eyes of a litigation lawyer to be a normative problem of weighting the efficacy of a given community's policies against the freedom of member states is for political scientists rather a difficult dilemma regarding the allocation of regulatory power. In other words, the normative argumentation contained in the legal cases tells us little about the instrumental effectiveness of the law for furthering integration.

Interpretative theories suggest that principles usually constitute limits on judicial discretion, as judges cannot abuse incomplete contracting and remain bound to general principles of law. However, in the special case where a judge is to decide on two alternative principles – two legal 'realities' – it constitutes an opportunity for expansion (Canor 1998). The implications of each possible alternative can be demonstrated through two competing models for understanding the allocation of regulatory authority: decentralised and centralised.

The decentralised model of regulatory authority

A decentralised model of regulatory authority assumes that there is a clear division between competences that belong to the national level, and competences that belong to Community level. This was the Colombian government's position in the aluminium dispute in *Aluminio Reynolds*. In such a view, Community competences are strictly limited to those areas that have previously been assigned to it by member states. Because these competences are being transferred gradually, a centralised model of regulatory authority does not assume that states have renounced all competences from the outset.

The guiding principle for this model reads: every competency that has not been explicitly transferred to the Community remains at national level. For every step towards further integration, a new dividing line between both fields of competence should be drawn by the member states through the intergovernmental Community organ: the Andean Commission. If the matter under litigation is about goods that are listed as exemptions to liberalisation or integration, then it is a question that falls within the regulatory field of the member states by default. Because of this clear division of competences, it is for the states and not the Court to decide *if* or *how* these exempted goods should be taxed. This model is very close to traditional readings of the treaties that we find in international law: that is to say, against eventual losses of state sovereignty (Weiler 1982: 270).

The centralist model of regulatory authority

The centralist model is very close to what private litigants claimed in the different stages of the Andean saga, and corresponds to a regulatory model inspired by the EC's experience. If member states commit themselves to creating an organisation with supranational attributions with a view to establishing a common market, then it can only be assumed that it is beyond the capabilities of individual member states to achieve this task on their own. By creating the Community and establishing a commitment institution (Mattli 1999b), member states recognise the regulatory authority of the Community regarding transnational trade, and purposely retain only specific items or exemptions that correspond to domestic rather than commercial criteria. Thus, since Community law must be allowed to grow gradually, materialising through statutes that begin replacing national law, there is no dividing line separating the two fields of authority because the jurisdiction of the commitment institutions is growing. When it comes to the common market, member states cede sovereignty to the Community which, in turn, starts regulating a policy area. If the member states have decided from the outset that certain barriers should not yet be dismantled, then the Community must respect this even in the centralist model.

However, this does not mean that the states retain regulatory authority over these goods. On the contrary, they can only choose between using this privilege and renouncing it; they cannot regulate it. Therefore, every issue arising outside of specific exemptions, or every grey area that has not clearly been claimed by the member states, falls within the higher regulatory field of the Community. What the claim of the private litigants implied in political terms was that the Community should take full control of the regulatory authority that it was entitled to exert in this policy field, and that national regulation dealing with tariffs higher than those already in place at the moment when the list of exceptions was established should be replaced with Community regulations: in this case, the Court's criteria. Miguel Maduro called this the centralist model (Maduro 2002).

For this dilemma of institutional choice to be solved, considerable judicial discretion is necessary. For its part, the ECJ faced this dilemma too. In the cases *ERTA* and *Dassonville*, the Court confined member states' actions to ever smaller fields. *ERTA* presented the Court with two 'realities' (Canor 1998): one dominated by the principle of state sovereignty, the other represented by centralised regulatory authority. While the ECJ used the doctrine of pre-emption to incorporate the centralised model into EC law, the ACJ chose to underpin the principle of state sovereignty to ascertain the decentralised model. Interestingly, both claim to have used the teleological method of interpretation.

In the foregoing cases, since the Andean Court was required to make a decision with institutional implications, it was expected to offer a plausible justification for its decision. This is what MacCormick has called 'second-order justification', giving reasons that justify choices between rival rulings (MacCormick 1978: 101). In *Dassonville*, by contrast, the ECJ did not justify its choice. Instead, it resorted to what is called 'formal reasoning' (Maduro 2002: 22): that is, a syllogistic argumentation that presents the decision of the Court as the only possible legal decision. Yet, by doing so, the Court does not answer *why* this choice was taken, since it does not acknowledge that a significant choice between two institutional alternatives was at stake. According to Maduro:

> the adoption of formal reasoning as a model of justification in the Court's decisions is, in part, a consequence of legal traditions in Member States that are, nevertheless, becoming outdated. For the European Court of Justice, the adoption of formal reasoning responded to the need to establish its judicial authority by preserving an image of neutrality and impartiality.
> (Maduro 2002: 22)

This brings us back to one of the significant divergences between the case loads. *Dassonville* was about non-tariff barriers to trade. The struggle over who was to be in charge of the policy domain of tariffs had been settled long ago, as the foundational doctrines had already been issued. The European doctrines underpinned the centralist model for regulatory authority. Now it was about shaping general principles within an economic constitution. The principal question was not who governed Article 30 of the TEC, but rather which cases fell within the range of Article 30.

Clearly, the Andean Court would have had a more daunting task if it was to follow in the footsteps of the ECJ. If the Andean Court was to perform any formal reasoning on which it could base a decision favourable to private litigants on the road to an economic constitution, it had to settle a crucial question: who would have ultimate policy authority in the field of a common market? In other words, who would hold the governing stick of intra-community trade policy – the Community or member states? Admittedly, it is impossible for us to know if the Court seriously considered this alternative of upholding the centralist model; but if it did there was no realistic way to bring it about. Since the *Aluminio Reynolds* case could not realistically have had any other outcome than it actually did, the choice made by the Court is hardly surprising.

The consequence of not upholding the centralist model is that it becomes almost impossible for the Court to frame general principles in the policy field of intra-regional trade. As mentioned, if any given principle cannot be applied to all goods or cases – or, at least, the vast majority – it renounces any claim of abstraction and remains specific to these goods. In turn, if a principle is not abstract enough to spill over to other policy areas, judicial discretion is severely curtailed. Furthermore, the only doctrines that were actually shaped, namely direct effect and supremacy, were consistent with the interests of the other stakeholders – the member states. However, principles that are conditions and aims of a common market, such as freedom of movement or non-discrimination (see the concept of *Basisfunktion* for free movement of goods in Frenz 2004: 13), are inherently abstract, and were therefore impossible for the Andean Court to tailor for the area of intra-regional trade policy once the centralist model was discarded. Thus, the Court's leeway became even smaller.

By representing the Andean dilemma through these two heuristic models, it is possible to identify a crucial difference between them and the experience made with the 'Euro-law game'. And yet, considering the disruptive potential of EC-like doctrines of direct effect and supremacy, how was it possible to introduce them so gently, without raising even initial opposition of member states? First, the doctrines were shaped in a policy field that entirely belongs to the Community's competences: industrial property rights. Therefore, no takeover was necessary. Second, the rulings (*Stauffer Chemical* 1-IP-88 and *Ciba Geigy* 3-IP-89) were not issued against a member state, but in favour of the Colombian government's position, since they declared that herbicides were non-patentable products, a position defended vigorously by the member states. It can therefore be assumed that, at that stage, the Court did not represent much of a threat to Andean governments. On the contrary, the judicial discourse appeared clearly cooperative with member states and bolstered the policy of import substitution. If the Court was to confirm the position of member states, there was no chance for the national judiciary to defy the status quo of their relationship with their respective governments, nor was there any space for inter-court negotiation within a national-supranational framework as foreseen by neofunctionalism.

Putting these developments into context is very helpful to understand its significance. Just one year after the rulings on direct effect and supremacy were announced (both on 25 May 1988), the question of the common market came before the Court (ruling of 18 May 1990). It is now clear to us that the Court had neither the time nor the leverage to favour the centralist model that claimed for regulatory authority to be taken over by the Community, since no judicial collaboration with national lower courts, or any genuine transnational constituency (as suggested for Europe in Slaughter 2000a: 248), or any 'compliance constituency' that would advocate for the strengthening of the Andean legal system (Helfer *et al.* 2009: 5) had previously been established. The evidence presented in Chapter 5 suggests that, contrary to predominant legalistic assumptions, Andean doctrines did not evolve out of a gradual functional process. They did not irrupt either, because they did not challenge the underlying decentralised model of regulatory authority. The doctrines were introduced rather gently, simultaneously, and with considerable deference to the preferences of national higher courts. However, because the Andean-law game did not defy the decentralised model, it could never shape doctrines that were comprehensive and abstract enough in order to be applicable to a majority of cases. If doctrines on Andean intra-regional trade law cannot be applied to all regional trade, they will be severely inadequate in fulfilling the functional purpose of driving integration ahead.

Most of the scholarship on legal integration shares the underlying assumption that national judges are interested in defying the status quo of their relationship within the state. In other words, they want to have a say in more transcendent matters; they want to engage with more complex cases (Weiler 1994, 1985). Neofunctionalism postulates that supranational entrepreneurship rises as community organs demand loyalties. In the case of the ECJ, national lower courts and private litigants were willing to direct their loyalties to the new centre of power. However, as I have shown, Andean higher judges were not as open to shifting loyalties to the ACJ, primarily because they were demanding loyalties for themselves. I argue that this was the case because of their hierarchy within the national judicial system.

In the light of the impressive IP docket, 'the most frequent collaborator' was a higher court, namely the Colombian Consejo de Estado (Helfer *et al.* 2009: 27), a collaboration based more on repetition than on constitutional dialogue. Furthermore, as reported by Helfer and Alter, the ACJ missed the opportunity to rely on a supranational-friendly IP agency when it had the chance. The Peruvian administrative tribunal INDECOPI carried out judicial functions in IP law and sought to engage in a dialogue with the Court. This agency had considerable independence due to the fact that its budget was funded mainly by IP registration fees and fines; and, inasmuch as Andean law provided IP regulation, INDECOPI applied them and solved disputes arising from trademark and patent registrations (Helfer and Alter 2009: 11). When INDECOPI attempted to refer a question to Quito, the ACJ denied access on the grounds that INDECOPI was not an actual judicial body. Even though the ACJ attempted to reverse this position in 2007 (Helfer *et al.* 2009: 45), the Andean saga seemed to have been resolved by that time.

Nonetheless, Helfer, Alter and Guerzovich suggest that the repetitiveness of ACJ judgments might have served an end, which is 'to inculcate habitual compliance with its rulings in countries where the domestic rule of law is weak', and IP agencies have been the engine driving these interactions

(Helfer *et al.* 2009: 28). However, as these authors admit, the issues that are repeatedly referred to the ACJ do not necessarily entail questions related to the expansion of supranational law. Instead, they contain issues related to guidelines on the originality and patentability of trademarks and patents. In an overwhelming majority of cases, disputes arise as a consequence of an IP agency's decision to grant or to deny a certain patent, trademark or licence.

Although these agencies regularly apply Andean IP law, they do not necessarily have an inherent bias towards Andean integration. Neither are they competing with other agencies within their own states. If we look at the patterns that are available, we see that in half of the cases that have originated preliminary rulings, private actors complain against the agencies because they did not register a patent, trademark or licence despite their novelty or originality. The rest of the cases are often the opposite: that is, private actors holding a prior patent or licence complain against IP agencies because they agreed to register or grant a patent that supposedly is not original. The interaction that emerges boils down to an ATJ-IP agency dialogue (Helfer and Alter 2009: 31).

Although this dialogue seems to contribute to the diffusion of Andean IP law among practitioners and interested actors, it does not provide the ATJ with the space and leverage foreseen by neofunctionalism. The repetition of rulings about originality or novelty of particular patents might have been relevant for the establishment of pockets of rule of law, but it does not contribute to the alleged expansion of supranational courts and Community law. To be sure, the focus on IP agencies tells us much about the constellation of domestic actors, but it does not explain why the ACJ did not follow the expansive logic predicted by neofunctionalism.

This is why the ACJ-IP agency approach relies on explanations based on the 'passivity and reluctance' of national courts: 'even in IP disputes, judges are rarely bold or creative when interacting with their Andean colleagues. Instead, they are dutiful technocrats, requesting referrals in ways that are unlikely to produce expansive rulings' (Helfer and Alter 2009: 38). This argument stresses the lack of 'provocative questions' as a cause for the ACJ non-expansive logic. However, the weight of this explanation lies in the assumption that the ACJ would indeed have been prone to issuing expansive rulings if only national judges had framed the questions more boldly. I argue that the ACJ had the opportunity to engage in expansive ruling. The opportunities were certainly few, but in all of these cases it was not because of reticent national judges that the ACJ issued restrictive rulings. Every decision made in the saga meant that alternative choices had to be discarded if the Court was to maintain a coherent discourse. This is a limitation courts normally face (Canor 1998).

The dispute between Ecuadorian Laboratories and the Ecuadorian government is one of those cases, and it is in sharp contrast to the type of dispute between a private litigant and a national IP agency. The former kind of dispute involved the challenge of national law, and contained a question regarding the scope of Andean law. Such a demand entails a particular constellation of questions, because it seeks to clarify the scope of both national and supranational law. Scholars often refer to this type of conflict as one of 'incomplete contracting'. A supranational court is entitled to address constitutional issues without stepping beyond the boundaries of its own powers; in other words, without incurring *ultra vires*. Conversely, the 'detailed and precise' Andean IP rules make it less likely that the issues of incomplete contracting arise, as opposed to non-IP Andean law, which 'often contain loopholes or hortatory language that preserve national discretion' (Helfer *et al.* 2009: 43). Thus, the few instances where litigation hinged around incomplete constitutional contracting become even more relevant.

Explaining expansive jurisprudence in regional integration: rights politics

Scholars are increasingly focusing on the expansion of opportunities for individuals and interest groups to bring rights claims to courts and the implication for democracy (Cichowski and Stone Sweet 2003; Conant 2006). It is argued that the expansion of judicial power is related to the expansion in rights protection (Stone Sweet 2000). According to this view, courts are used by a growing number of private litigants as opportunities for political participation through law enforcement and rights litigation, especially due to the liberalisation of legal-standing rules (Cichowski 2006a). Hence, a broader jurisdiction, as well as a greater number of explicit social rights bases, contributes to higher rates of rights litigation (Conant 2006: 85–6). As I show below, rights litigation, especially fundamental freedoms litigation, also provides an opportunity for participation, as it allows the individual to challenge member states in their role as protectors of rights and freedoms, and provoke the reallocation of fragments of authority with the complicity of the courts.

Fundamental rights and freedoms are precisely examples of incomplete contracting. They are supposed to find application even if they are not explicitly mentioned by the treaty. This situation offers a notable opportunity for judicial creativity (Everling 1983: 155). Even strong legalistic debates have tried to incorporate these concerns, asking whether fundamental rights are part of European law only once they have been concretised by the ECJ, or if they already find application before an explicit judicial declaration (Rengeling 1992: 8).

Furthermore, by involving individuals in a triad of fundamental freedoms, or 'interests triangle' (Pernice 1990: 2410), authority is fragmented whereby interests remain plural. This particular 'political fragmentation can empower judges because it creates disputes about who possesses authority, and also it may increase political gridlock, which subsequently can impede the ability of political actors to rein in courts' (Cichowski 2006b: 12). As fundamental freedoms are basically directed against states, interests have a conflict potential. But the member states–individual antagonism is not limited to two parties. The Court has the option to side with one of the parties or mediate in solomonic terms, splitting the difference. Whichever claim the Court decides to uphold, it has considerable implications for authority, as in the midst of judicial conflict authority has been contested, and thereby also fragmented. Once the Court has settled the dispute by declaring a judicial solution, authority coheres again. Whether the post-conflict authority remains identical to its pre-conflict stages is dependent on the Court's choice, especially if it decides to uphold one of the positions.

The first alternative leads to the status quo. According to this pattern, the Court can also choose to uphold the claim of the member state, against the individual. As in rights litigation, the authority has been fragmented through an adversarial venue of participation (the idea of participation through rights litigation before the ECHR was suggested by Conant 2006: 77; for participation through Art. 234 TEC, see Börzel 2006). The judicial process, siding with the member state, entails that the scattered fragments of authority are reintegrated into the domestic order. The cards are not reshuffled, but placed in their initial positions. This gives rise to a normative narrative that things have never changed. The outcome is not expansion, but maintenance of the status quo. This was the pattern followed by the ECJ in the cases of *Stork*, *Geitling* and *Sgarlata*.

There is a second alternative that leads to expansion. It requires that the Court upholds the individual's claim for more protection of his or her freedoms. If this happens, the fragmentation of authority – ideally invoked by the litigant – crystallises and either the domestic legal order will suffer a transfer of competences or it might have to share authority with the Community. Although authority over rights coheres again, the cards have been shuffled again in favour of the Community and the individual, awaiting the next round. This pattern is, therefore, inherently expansive. Along with the reallocation of authority over fundamental rights and freedoms, the court conveys a constitutional rhetoric on grounds of the new arrangement and shapes a new political landscape. Constitutionalisation has advanced hand in hand with judicial rights politics by means of constitutional judicial review (the case is made for the ECHR in Shapiro 2002a: 155).

South American scholarship and the community of fate

In this section, I present the current state of Andean scholarship on Andean legal integration. I do not claim this to be exhaustive, but I am reasonably confident that there is a significant consensus on the ideas presented. I have not been able to find any author contradicting the essence of my claims on Andean scholarship: that its analysis has incurred in 'concept stretching'.

To be sure, as Andean literature is not the object of study here, and rather constitutes a secondary or 'soft' source (Moravcsik 1997a), it remains an interpretative exercise.

When comparing two legal systems, it is not easy to agree on the role that legal education and legal scholars play within the analysis. Whether they are an inherent part of law is hard to say in general terms (Sacco 1991: 30; on a German view on the teaching of European legal studies see Franzius 2005).[3] Scholars have written quite profusely on regional integration in Latin America. But even from the beginning of the 1980s, when the Andean Court of Justice was established – and especially the 1990s, when the Andean Integration System (SAI) and MERCOSUR[4] were established – literature on regional integration and the ACJ became strikingly homogeneous. Legal scholarship overtly dominates this field and textual analysis is the most usual methodology.

Similar to the rulings of the ACJ, most Latin American scholars converge in calling this category 'community law'[5] or 'integration law'.[6] They seem to agree on the idea that law serves the purpose of materialising integration. It strikes the reader, especially the European comparativist, that the bulk of this scholarship does not engage Andean integration critically. In other words, a legal work that asks whether regional integration is something that is inherently *good* or *bad*, or questions whether Andean law is in harmony with fundamental principles of Andean national orders, still remains to be written. Legal integration appears as something 'natural' and self-evident for a region that strives for economic development.

This observation coincides with Mols' contention about a Latin American 'ideology of integration' (Mols 1993). The fact that Andean judicial institutions resulted as a reception of EC institutions is not problematised, either. Andean jurists do not raise doubts about the appropriateness of alien institutions because, in their eyes, the Andean system does not appear to have been fertilised, or granted validity by European law. The awareness of alterity seems to be missing to a great extent, and the EC experience seems, therefore, to be

---

3 Legal reasons given by judges and scholars, as well as their conclusions, are among the 'legal formants' that Rodolfo Sacco sees in each legal system.
4 The EC-inspired Andean Integration System was established on 10 March 1996 by the Trujillo Protocol. MERCOSUR was established by the Treaty of Asunción on 26 March 1991.
5 Sobrino 2001: 34–5; Tangarife 2001b: 161; Perotti 2001: 105 (although Perotti refers to legal uniformity through preliminary rulings as being essential for any integration process); Ekmekdjian 1994: 271–2; Sáchica 1985a: 9; Andueza 1985a: 34–5; Sáchica 1985c: 52; Hurtado Larrea 1985: 70. Andueza goes even further and highlights the differences he observes between a community law system and a federal system (Andueza 1985b: 85).
6 Díaz Barrado: 'Con carácter general lo que podemos reseñar es que se aprecian, en el ordenamiento andino, desde la perspectiva formal, las características propias de un ordenamiento jurídico de integración' (Díaz Barrado 1999: 57; Bayá 2004: 26).

a valuable confirmation of the rightfulness and natural character of these kinds of processes,[7] rather than a causal factor for them.[8] Although cases of EC law are cited in much Andean literature, they are not included as normative reasons – as part of a syllogism – but rather as examples of how Andean law should progress if it is to become a complete system.[9] It is as though they belonged to the same category, with both regions being part of a 'community of fate', or *Schicksalsgemeinschaft*.[10] In 1996, Trevor Hartley suggested, for the European case, that the arguments of the ECJ presented the treaties as '"genetically coded" to develop into the constitution of a fully-fledged federation', where the judges were 'doing no more than their duty in developing the law in the desired direction, even if some laggard member states are reluctant to accept such developments' (Hartley 1996: 107). To be clear, some Andean authors have acknowledged the similarity of the ACJ and ECJ, but none has pointed to its nature of transplanted legal institution.[11]

---

7 Luk Van Langehove noticed and criticised a quasi-teleological aspect of some discourses regarding regionness: 'becoming a region is presented as almost a natural and unavoidable process' (Van Langehove 2003).
8 Even Francisco Orrego Vicuña, a critic of uncontrolled expansion of supranational thinking, called for a closer look at the 'European process' (Orrego Vicuña 1977: 80).
9 Alan Watson warned against the unsound assumption that each legal system 'during its youth passes through a similar process before peculiarities of the nation are imposed upon its juridical order', naming it a peril of comparative law (Watson 1993: 12).
10 Gebhard Rehm uses this term to refer to the political features that bind a nation, and that allows for differentiation in relation to others that do not share the same fate (Rehm 2008: 23).
11 At first glance, Francisco Orrego Vicuña, Laura Dromí San Martino and Daniel Perotti seem to be interesting exceptions to the Latin American mainstream. Orrego Vicuña, on the one hand, expresses his dissatisfaction with the misfit between theory and practice within the Latin American integration projects; but his suggestion, though innovative, does not fully escape the assumption of a higher legal order when he claims that flexibility of primary law and functionality of secondary law are possible within integration schemes. Rather, he challenges the assumption that the state is unable to deal with modern problems (Orrego Vicuña 1977: 75–6). He does not call for the recognition of the alterity of many institutions, but, on the contrary, a close following of the European example of carefully weighing both political and technocratic considerations within the institutional settings of the regional integration projects (p. 80). Perotti chose to make a thorough description of the similarities and differences between the ACJ and the ECJ that strike the reader when going through the text of the statutes that govern both courts. But neither connection nor function seems to govern the analysis, rendering the argument spineless and trivial. When justifying the need for both the procedure of preliminary rulings and the doctrine of *l'acte claire* in the Andean system, he turns to European scholars (Perotti 1999: 211, 215). In his conclusion, he limits himself to justifying that his claim in favour of the ACJ is based on the facts of 'experience', for which the ECJ is a vivid example (p. 237). See also Dromí San Martino 2002. Alberto Zelada recalls that the Junta examined the antecedents and

If we reconstruct the canons that form this assumed ideal order of community law, we realise that South American scholars converge on some components. In brief, these assumed components are supranationality,[12] supremacy,[13] and direct effect.[14]

The bulk of the existing literature on Andean legal integration suggests that Latin American scholars clearly tend to contribute to the shaping of a notion of what a fully fledged economic union looks like. Against this idea of an economic union, they measure the progress of projects of regional integration in Latin America, notably the Andean Community and to some extent MERCOSUR. Nevertheless, sustaining that they are making a bold comparison with the European Union would not be accurate, either; on the contrary, almost all of them recognise the importance of context and the social differences that would make impracticable any attempt to introduce a strict European copy into the Latin American context. But the continuous reference to what the Andean Community will look like when it finally reaches its ultimate stage, or the persistent claim that elements like cession of sovereignty, direct effect and supremacy are inherent to any community legal system, reveals a preconceived ideal normative order that drives the bulk of Latin American scholars, a notion of Community law. Be that as it may, the allocation of relevant properties of this normative order has not been theoretically driven, but appears to be a consequence of intuitive operation. Alan Watson warned against this peril, suggesting that it could lead us to gross misstatements, such as treating lions and ants as similar and comparable just because they are both 'warm blooded, have six legs and are always winged [sic]'.[15]

Concept stretching and theory building

The categories constructed by Andean writers do not contemplate dynamic objects of study. The fact that a unit of analysis might change over time and

---

experiences of the ECJ, and that 'these elements had influence over the content of the final ideas elaborated by the Junta' (Zelada Castedo 1985: 127–8).

12 Hurtado Larrea (1985: 70), who also claims that supranationality is the principle of community law. See also Jorge Luis Suárez Mejías (2006: 80), who makes supranational a synonym of communitarian when he speaks about the Andean system; further to direct effect and supremacy, he adds legal certainty and the legal liability of member states.

13 Sobrino 2001: 56; Camacho Omiste 2001: 113 (though this author tends to confuse supranationality with multilaterality); Tangarife 2001a: 129–30; 2001b; Bayá 2004: 26; Ekmekdjian 1994: 71; Moya Domínguez 2006: 257; Sáchica 1985a: 8, 24; Suárez Mejías 2006 (using the term 'aplicación preferente' at 80–1).

14 Andueza 1985a: 33–43; Rico Frontaura 2001; Tangarife 2001b: 166; Bayá 2004: 68; Ekmekdjian 1994; Moya Domínguez 2006: 257; Sáchica 1985a: 8; Suárez Mejías 2006 (using the term 'aplicabilidad directa' at 80–1).

15 Watson 1993: 12, criticising Pringsheim's 'Ancient Law'.

fit a new category, yet to be created, is a challenge for Andean literature on the ACJ. Instead, comparisons of mechanisms, laws or institutions that allegedly belong to a same categorical level are abundant; they are all elements of 'regional integration'. Legal mechanisms that have proven successful in European integration are transplanted into other regions, and then compared against each other.

The objection to this kind of theorising is that it uses a common vocabulary, or integration jargon, and turns theories into concepts that are later used in scholarly writings. This faulty strategy creates the illusion of making cases comparable in situations where they would ordinarily be incomparable.

As shown in Chapter 5, semantic similitude between rulings of both courts, using concepts like direct effect, supremacy, or teleological interpretation, has led to some misconceptions, and the tendency of Andean law to follow principles of international public law instead of those of European Community law has significant implications with regard to the integration outcome. However, not only would Andean jurisprudence inhibit further integration, it would also bolster a conceptual frame that would become dominant in the work of South American scholars of regional integration.

Concepts are containers of data and information, and in order to be precise they ought to be very clear in both their connotation (what criteria they are fulfilling) and their denotation (the cases to which they apply). Recognising similitude is not enough to take concepts forged in one case and apply them in another case. Concepts do not travel so easily.

What should the scholar do when he or she intends to compare concepts that show similitude precisely because they are the product of diffusion or transplantation? Giovanni Sartori suggests that any operation with concepts should follow the dictates of the ladder of abstraction. Moving along the ladder of abstraction takes place whenever we utilise taxonomic criteria in our classification. When we add a taxonomic requirement for our set of cases, we are excluding those cases that do not share a particular attribute. We are excluding them because we are purposely making the concept more specific. Conversely, if we are to extend the concept to more cases, we have to drop some taxonomic requirements imposed on our cases; the criteria for sorting them out is, then, *per genus et differentiam* (Sartori 1995: 268). It should be noted that climbing up the ladder of abstraction does not make the concept less precise; it will in fact be equally precise because we will know with certainty what cases belong to the category that has become more general.

The epistemological predicaments of comparative regional studies are closely related to the question of whether the EC is a unique case; whether it represents $n=1$. The case for uniqueness implies that 'shoehorning' them into some preconceived theoretical framework is a futile task, because there are no current analogies available (Caporaso 1997: 1). But uniqueness is not an attribute inherent to phenomena in the empirical world, but rather a property allocated by the eye of the observer.

> To say that the EC is unique is simply a shorthand for saying that we have not yet developed the categories, abstract enough, to see the EC as an instance of a more general class of phenomena. Nevertheless, generalization by itself, without an improvement in explanatory capacity, would be a hollow victory. Thus the central question is, 'What categories are abstract enough to generate comparable cases, and not so general that they prevent useful comparisons?' (Caporaso 1997: 2)

As a consequence, if the comparativist intends to apply a particular concept to an additional case, what he or she should do is make the concept more general. If, however, the concept is applied to a wider number of cases without making it more abstract, we are stretching it (Sartori 1995: 274, 91–302). The result of stretching suggests that not only are we not certain whether the concept is applied in identical terms, as in the first case, but we do not know whether the concept can be equally applied to other cases too. In other words, stretched concepts are less precise.

Thus, Latin American legal scholars who have written on Andean integration have formed heuristic categories called 'regional integration' and 'integration law' where any integration arrangement is assumed to fit in. By so doing, similarities come to the forefront, especially institutions and legal frameworks. Unfortunately, such scholarship is driven by isomorphism in its purest form. It has not been constructed by the classificatory logic. This posits a particular difficulty, as every element of this category 'regional integration' is analysed with the logic of grades, instead of the logic of taxonomy. In other words, the 'plus–minus' criterion takes precedence over the 'inclusion–exclusion' criteria; the question of 'how much' is answered prior to the question of 'what'. This canon had led most of the literature on Latin American integration to treat the topic as the study of a continuum, a matter of degrees instead of qualities. In this continuum, the European case is the end of the road, the goal that the rest of the world is trying to reach.

Chapter 7

Epilogue and excursus
The Andean way towards constitutionalisation

The narrative provided in this book reveals that the significance of the Andean Court of Justice has persistently been misjudged. I have argued that because the ACJ is a paradigmatic example of a legal transplant, it has been very difficult to know and understand it. Many assumptions about how a supranational court works and affects its environment were blindly taken from the trajectory of its forerunner, the European Court of Justice (ECJ). Policy-makers and legislators assumed that, being the same institution, the ACJ would unfold the same effects that the ECJ became famous for in the EC. In turn, Andean judges assumed that copying doctrines would mean that their rulings would have the same impact upon national law. Latin American legal scholars have also misunderstood the nature of this Court, mainly because they stretched the concepts contained in EC law so as to apply them to Andean law.

I have shown that this way of comparing is not sound, and have provided evidence that reality does not fit with the normative assumptions the Andean literature has been relying on. The taxonomy that has resulted from decades of misconceptualisation of the Court is flawed. In terms of its case law, its trajectory and its role within economic integration, the ACJ and the ECJ do not belong to the same category. I have termed the blind belief that they do belong to the same category the 'community of fate' (*Schicksalsgemeinschaft* in German).

The evidence suggests a plurality of factors that have inhibited the ACJ from becoming an engine of integration. To begin with, the ACJ persistently favoured member states with its doctrines. Furthermore, the ACJ did not seek collaboration with lower national courts; on the contrary, most of the pseudo-constitutional dialogues were held with higher national courts. This fact alone is a clear divergence from the Euro-law game because it alters the patterns of inter-court competition that motivates the most prominent hypothesis on European integration.

Moreover, the patterns of incorporation of Andean case law are also peculiar. They were not introduced in phases, but simultaneously. This hasty procedure was mainly due to the European epistemic influence, examined in

Chapter 4. The advocates of a supranational court trusted that the mere introduction of the 'magic triangle' – that is, the doctrines of direct effect and supremacy plus the procedure of preliminary rulings – would spur legal integration. They neglected the multiplicity of factors that can determine the trajectory of a court. There was no gradual process of legal socialisation; there was no instance where regulatory authority could be negotiated with member states or other subnational actors. And yet, this precipitation provoked every decision to fit the underlying models that determined the allocation of authority. In the Andean case, the brief judicial saga enshrined the decentralised model of regulatory authority. Chapter 6 showed how this choice is an additional barrier hindering general supranational doctrines from blossoming.

Each of these factors merits a separate analysis, to be sure, and each analysis would require a separate book. I have nonetheless presented them within the perspective of a meta-theoretical debate around regional integration. The analysis of legal integration in the Andean Community represents a remarkable setting for testing the hypothesis promoted by the rival theories of intergovernmentalism and neofunctionalism. Testing their claims regarding European legal integration reveals much about the role of the ACJ. Indeed, the examination allows me to contest the traditional narratives on the significance of the Court and the impact of its case law on the process of regional integration.

The evidence presented in this book showcases Andean integration in a completely new light, with goals that remain constant but with strategies that change according to factors that come predominantly from outside the region. Accordingly, the process of Andean integration can be broken down into three distinctive periods, although the third period is still evolving. Its inclusion is an interpretation of current events, and should be regarded as an outlook: a glimpse into what the near future of the Community might look like.

The foundational period (1969–72)

The most important intellectual contribution for the movements that were arising in the region during the mid-twentieth century came from the UN Economic Commission for Latin America and the Caribbean (ECLAC or CEPAL). This institution supported the critical ideas of Raúl Prebisch, among others, and strived for the overcoming of the dependence of Latin American economies on the developed world. This was the stellar moment of 'dependence theory', which claimed that Latin American states could benefit from economies of scale that would take place thanks to the expansion of their markets, and also by protecting them from extra-regional markets.

The Cartagena Agreement (CA) emerges in this historical context, driven by the desire of Andean states to accelerate the process of economic integration within the Latin American Free Trade Association (LAFTA or ALALC).

The evidence presented in Chapter 4 suggests that there was a growing dissatisfaction with the biggest member states, Brazil and Argentina, because they allegedly regarded the Agreement as a mere trade instrument, while the smaller states emphasised its potential for sparking economic development. This is the point at which Chile, Colombia, Ecuador, Peru and Venezuela – a conglomerate that would be known as the Andean Group – signed the CA on 26 May 1969.

The Cartagena Agreement was considered an offshoot of LAFTA's Treaty of Montevideo of 1960, and it offered the possibility for other Latin American states to join the Andean Group. Member state officials put much effort into analysing the legal implications of this project, because there was a latent fear that the endeavour could be interpreted as a contravention to LAFTA. This explains why the genesis of what is known today as the Andean Community had to be approved by a unilateral act of a third entity: the declaration of compatibility issued by the Executive Committee of LAFTA (Villagrán Kramer 1989). At its inception, the Andean Group was so embedded within LAFTA that in case of conflicts between member states, LAFTA's dispute resolution mechanism had to be resorted to should the Andean Commission not be able to mediate (Zelada Castedo 1985: 126).

The period of institutional expansion and stagnation (1972–96)

I suggest that this period had two particular traits: first, a clear initial impulse towards establishing new institutions and organs that were not in the original plans of the founding members of the Cartagena Agreement, sometimes even against the dominant economic doctrines of that time; and second, the strong influence of epistemic and professional currents that were linked to European integration and European Community law. This is the phase where the major doctrines of the ECJ penetrate Andean Community law.

The first milestone of this expansive phase was the creation of the Andean Court of Justice. The constitutive treaty was signed on 28 May 1979, and the Court began its work in January 1984, after a long delay for ratification. The considerable time that elapsed before its ratification conceals the true origin of the tribunal. The majority of observers claim that the tribunal was established precisely because of the compliance problems within the Community; however, as shown in Chapter 4, the first impetus for the creation of the Court can be found in the year 1972, when several Andean governments were challenged by domestic national organs that were looking to expand their influence over the pace of regional integration.

For example, the Colombian Supreme Court, ruling on a lawsuit on the unconstitutionality of the Cartagena Agreement, was claiming for itself the right to scrutinise Andean secondary law. It is interesting to note that this ruling followed a strategy that was used by the ECJ; that is, it rejects the particular lawsuit, but introduces a doctrine that will unfold its effects for the future: the *Marbury v. Madison* strategy (Burley and Mattli 1993). The Colombian Supreme Court noticed that if there was no other organ to exert the legality control of Andean acts, then it would be called upon to assume that task.

In another example, the Chilean parliament challenged its government for the control over regional integration. In a decision by the Senate, the competence to approve and sanction norms of Andean Community law was claimed by parliament, especially the statutes of the nascent Corporación Andina de Fomento (CAF). It also reclaimed the faculty to examine whether the decisions made by CAF were in harmony with Chilean laws.

With these two challenges to the regulatory autonomy of the organs of the Cartagena Agreement, Andean governments understood the costs of not having a mechanism of dispute resolution, especially an organ that could get to grips with objections emanating from domestic institutions.

The second milestone of institutional expansion was the adoption of the treaty that established the Andean Parliament on 25 October 1979, which came into force in 1984. This treaty did not consider the Andean Parliament as a main organ of the 'Andean Pact'; in fact, there has been considerable conjecture about this measure, especially considering its goal of gaining legitimacy (Alter, Helfer and Saldías 2012). Yet, despite the proliferation of institutions, the development strategy based on critical theories and import substitution suffered a severe blow towards the end of the 1970s because of the severe economic crisis that would endure for the following decade. The suffocation that would come with the debt crisis is infamously known as the 'lost decade' of Latin America.

Towards constitutionalisation (1996 onwards): an excursus

Towards the end of the 1980s, and with the demise of the Cold War, Latin America experienced a change of political and economic paradigms. States that formerly adhered to import substitution began opening to global markets in the search for sources of funding and foreign investment. From then on, the credo would read that no economic growth would be possible without attracting investment from outside (Franko 2007: 236). The imperatives of the Washington Consensus were progressively permeating the convictions of national legislators, thereby fostering an amicable environment for incoming foreign direct investment (Faúndez 2010). Several regional integration schemes adapted to this changing environment and began regarding themselves as a means to increasing the attractiveness of Latin America for those investors that were expecting credible institutional frameworks (cf. Mattli 1999 or: 155). This period reflects the changes in the world order, especially the impact of the World Trade Organisation, and the European transition from the Single European Act towards the Maastricht Treaty. The transformation of regional integration arrangements is a partial consequence of the changes at global level (Helfer *et al.* 2009).

ECLAC's axioms adapted to the new strands of thought and new regional scenario. Policy-makers were increasingly persuaded that Latin American markets were not big enough to promote the long-ambitioned development. And yet, there was the fear that a unilateral opening with no preferential access for states within the region could cause even more harm, because the major trade blocs would not necessarily correspond by opening their own markets. The term 'open regionalism' became fashionable; it promoted complementation among regional blocs with a view to opening themselves to world markets (ECLAC 1994). Latin American states would pursue their incorporation into the new world economic order through existing blocs.

Against this backdrop, the Community began to transform itself. Institutions that had been created outside or parallel to the Community, but had become a pillar of the integration process, were now formally incorporated into the Cartagena Agreement. The Trujillo Protocol formally incorporated the Andean Presidential Council (CPA), the organ that gathers the presidents of the member states with the mission of giving the Community its major political orientation. It also incorporated the Andean Council of Foreign Relations Ministers (CAMRE), the mission of which was to formulate the member states' external policy, while the Junta was transformed into the General Secretariat, and subordinated to the executive requirements of the CPA, CAMRE, and the Commission. The conglomerate of Andean institutions was now mutually linked through the Andean Integration System (SAI), and the Andean Pact was formally renamed as the Andean Community (CAN).

Analysts of Latin American regionalism have not been very enthusiastic about the progress of Andean integration. The establishment of the SAI in 1996 did not change their minds. As this book has shown, the functionalist strategies of achieving full integration through an ECJ-style 'engine of integration' did not live up to expectations, despite massive incorporation of the EC judicial doctrines into Andean community law. There was no spillover into cognate fields; neither was there any constitutional dialogue between domestic and supranational courts. However, there seems to have been some noteworthy developments that came with the inclusion of the CPA and CAMRE into the Community, which should be followed carefully.

There has been an ongoing proliferation of Andean legal norms that do not aim at the establishment of a common market, but rather at flanking economic integration by underpinning the respect for democracy, human rights and good governance. The majority of Andean legal scholars have persistently criticised the dominance of intergovernmental law-making in the Andean process. However, the density and the content of this law-making are currently setting the foundation for what could be termed an incipient process of constitutionalisation of the Andean legal order.

With reinforced competences, Andean presidents and national foreign affairs ministers have become active in what they term the Andean External Policy.[1] This set of policies is not limited to extra-regional affairs; on the contrary, it includes much intra-regional policies. The difference of this rationale to the integration ideology of the 1960s is that member states increase their control over new policy fields such as human rights, rule of law, democracy and good governance.[2] These are all fields that would, according to the neo-functionalist hypothesis, be functionally negotiated between the ACJ and subnational actors. As recent evidence is beginning to suggest, Andean foreign affairs ministers have been very effective in advancing an incipient constitutional agenda.

Constitutionalisation should hereby not be understood as the drafting of a written constitution. In my argumentation, constitutionalisation is a process that binds political power through legal arrangements. To be sure, there are other possible means for the term constitutionalisation; it can mean, for instance, the common pledge to found a polity or a new legal order (Murphy 1993), or the hierarchical systematisation within a legal system (Preuss 1996). I understand that constitutionalisation can also mean the process of harnessing political power and subjecting it to a rational and legitimate set of rules, that can only be modified by sovereign peoples (Möllers 2003). Power can be bound and harnessed at the national level, but also at the supranational level, and maybe even at the global level (Pernice 2006). There is increasing evidence that suggests that Andean member states are binding themselves in constitutional fields and through constitutional tools, by pooling political power in the newly established Andean human rights and democracy regime at the Andean level. Contrary to traditional international public law, however, through this constitutionalisation process, the Andean member states pool the sanctions at Andean level, too, and adapt their home constitutions to the growing set of Andean norms.

In June 2000, CAMRE adopted an additional protocol to the Cartagena Agreement,[3] whereby member states committed themselves to democracy, recognising that 'full validity of the democratic institutions and the rule of law are essential conditions for political cooperation, as well as for the process of economic, social, and cultural integration' (Art. 1). The protocol envisions that, in a case of disruption of the democratic order in any member state, Andean peers would hold consultations with the aim of re-establishing democracy. In the

---

1 Decision 458 of the Andean Council of Foreign Affairs Ministers.
2 See the research project 'Governance Export by Regional Organizations', funded by the German Research Council, Sonderforschungsbereich SFB 700 'Governance in Areas of Limited Statehood'; <http://www.sfb-governance.de/en/teilprojekte/projektbereich_b/b2/index.html>.
3 Additional Protocol 'Compromiso por la Democracia', 10 June 2000, Andean Council of Foreign Affairs.

case of a serious breach, the protocol mandates the suspension of the privileges granted by the Community. Andean states further embedded this 'democratic clause' into the region through a joint agreement with MERCOSUR in the summit of 2000 in Brasilia.

Shortly after this additional protocol, Andean presidents signed the Act of Carabobo in June 2001, reinforcing their commitment to democratic governance and binding themselves to solving eventual threats by 'constitutional means'. The context of this declaration is compelling, as the Peruvian President Alberto Fujimori and the former Chilean dictator Augusto Pinochet were indicted and prosecuted for crimes of corruption and violations of human rights respectively. The region was in suspension.

In terms of human rights protection, the Act of Carabobo and the Declaration of Machu Picchu of 2001[4] are the first attempts to draft a proto-catalogue of fundamental rights and freedoms focusing on equality within the region. The culmination of this endeavour would come in 2002, when the Andean presidents adopted an Andean Charter of Human Rights.[5] The charter contains a remarkably comprehensive catalogue of rights based mainly on binding international public law. It contains rights that are traditionally protected by national constitutions, but also includes new types of rights and new subjects of rights. Rights of women, children, adolescents, older adults, persons with disabilities, ethnic minorities, workers, migrants and refugees are only some examples of the new approaches of the charter compared to national constitutions.

None of these fields of rights has been addressed by the ACJ, contrary to the experience with EC case law during the 1970s, where the ECJ established in *Stauder* that 'fundamental human rights were enshrined in the general principles of Community Law and protected by the Court'.[6] Conversely, the ACJ has so far never linked human rights and democracy with the implementation of Andean Community law. The process of constitutionalisation has been driven by member states, especially Andean presidents and their foreign affairs ministers.

The hypothesis of an Andean process of constitutionalisation requires much scholarly vetting and appraisal. There is much still to be written and discussed. The available evidence for a constitutional claim is still very modest. Andean scholars and comparatists are facing a new challenge in understanding the ACJ in its own terms and finding out what this apparently exceptional court is really an instance of.

---

4 Declaration of Machu Picchu on 'Democracy, Rights of Indigenous Peoples and Fight Against Corruption', 29 July 2001.
5 Andean Charter for the Protection and Promotion of Human Rights, Guayaquil, 26 July 2002.
6 See Chapter 2.

Policy-makers and legal engineers face a different challenge. There are lessons to be drawn from the Andean saga, which should be internalised before political and economic pressures begin demanding a new generation of institutional transplants.

A dear colleague once shared an idea with me that can sum up much of the claims made in this book. The simplicity of the idea is only matched by its wisdom. In her words: 'Copies are always less complete than we think.'

Bibliography

Alter, Karen. 1998. 'Who are the Masters of the Treaty? European Governments and the ECJ', *International Organisation* 52(1) (Winter): 121–46.
———. 2001. *Establishing the Supremacy of European Law: The Making of an International Rule of Law in Europe*. Oxford and New York: Oxford University Press.
———. 2006. 'Private Litigants and the New International Courts', *Comparative Political Studies* 39 (1 February): 22–49.
———. 2008. 'Jurist Advocacy Movements in Europe and the Andes: How Lawyers Help Promote International Legal Integration', Center on Law and Globalization Research Paper No. 08–05.
Alter, Karen, Helfer, Laurence R. and Saldías, Osvaldo. 2012. 'Transplanting the European Court of Justice: The Experience of the Andean Tribunal of Justice', *American Journal of Comparative Law* 60(3): 629–64.
Andueza, José Guillermo. 1985a. 'La Aplicación Directa del Ordenamiento Jurídico del Acuerdo de Cartagena', in BID-INTAL (ed.) *El Tribunal de Justicia del Acuerdo de Cartagena*. Buenos Aires: BID-INTAL.
———. 1985b. 'La Interpretación Prejudicial y el tribunal de Justicia del Acuerdo de Cartagena', in BID-INTAL (ed.) *El Tribunal de Justicia del Acuerdo de Cartagena*. Buenos Aires: BID-INTAL.
———. 1986. *El Tribunal del Pacto Andino*. Quito: Ediciones del Tribunal de Justicia del Pacto Andino.
Anweiler, Joachim. 1997. *Die Auslegungsmethoden des Gerichtshofs der Europäischen Gemeinschaften*. Frankfurt am Main: Peter Lang.
Arellano, Félix. 2004. 'Comunidad Andina: de la Zona de Libre Comercio a la Unión Aduanera. Los Nuevo Temas', *Aldea Mundo* 8(16): 5–15.
Balassa, Bela A. 1962. *The Theory of Economic Integration*. London: Allen and Unwin.
———. 1972. 'El segundo decenio para el desarrollo y la integración económica regional', *Revista de la Integración* 11 (May): 5–19.
Bayá, María de la Cruz. 2004. *Derecho y Procesos de Integración*. Cochabamba-Bolivia: Editorial Alexander.
Berkowitz, Daniel, Pistor, Katharina and Richard, Jean-François. 2003. 'The Transplant Effect', *American Journal of Comparative Law* 51(1): 163–204.
Beutler, Bengt. 1991. 'Grundrechtsschutz', in V. D. Groeben, J. Thiesing and C.-D. Ehlermann (eds) *Kommentar zum EWG-Vertrag*. Baden-Baden: Lutzeyer.
Bianchi Pérez, Paula. 2002. 'Exigencia de Protección penal de bienes de la Propiedad Industrial. Especial referencia a la decisión 486 de la Comisión de la comunidad

Andina', *Anuario de Derecho, Facultad de Ciencias Jurídicas y Políticas de la Universidad de Los Andes, Mérida-Venezuela* 24.
BID-INTAL (ed.). 1985. *El Tribunal de Justicia del Acuerdo de Cartagena*. Buenos Aires.
Blanco, Ronald José. 1997. 'La Integración y sus Enfoques en América Latina', *Aldea Mundo* (November): 37–41.
Bondia García, David. 1999. 'El Compromiso de los Estados Miembros de la Comunidad Andina con el Mantenimiento del Orden Democrático. ¿Compromiso Real o Retórica?', in *XVIII Jornadas de la Asociación Española de Profesores de Derecho Internacional y Relaciones Internacionales*. Madrid: Boletín Oficial del Estado.
Börzel, Tanja A. 2002. 'Why do States not Obey the Law?', in *ARENA*. University of Oslo.
———. 2005. 'Mind the Gap! European Integration between Level and Scope', *Journal of European Public Policy* 12(2): 217–36.
———. 2006. 'Participation Through Law Enforcement: The Case of the European Union', *Comparative Political Studies* 39(1): 128–52.
Börzel, Tanja A. and Risse, Thomas. 2009. 'The Transformative Power of Europe: The European Union and the Diffusion of Ideas'. KFG Working Paper No. 1. Available at: www.transformeurope.eu
Breyer, Stephen. 2006. *Judicial Activism: Power Without Responsibility?* Schwarz Lectures. University of Chicago.
Burley, Anne-Marie and Mattli, Walter. 1993. 'Europe before the Court: A Political Theory of Legal Integration', *International Organisation* 47(1) (Winter): 41–76.
Camacho Omiste, Edgar. 2001. 'El Marco Constitucional y el Principio de la Supranacionalidad', in *Integración y Supranacionalidad: Soberanía y Derecho Comunitario en los Países Andinos*. Lima: Secretaría General de la Comunidad Andina.
Canor, Iris. 1998. *The Limits of Judicial Discretion in the European Court of Justice: Security and Foreign Affairs*. Baden-Baden: Nomos.
Caporaso, James. 1997. 'Does the European Union Represent an n of 1?', *ECSA Review* X (3) (Fall): 1–5.
Caporaso, James, Jupille, Joseph and Checkel, Jeffrey T. 2002. 'Integrating Institutions: Theory, Methods, and the Study of the European Union', ARENA Working Paper WP 02/27.
Cappelletti, Mauro (ed.). 1989. *The Judicial Process in Comparative Perspective*. Oxford: Clarendon Press.
Cappelletti, M., Seccombe, M. and Weiler, J. H. H. 1985. *Integration through Law: European and the American Federal Experience, Vol. 1: Methods, Tools and Institutions*. Berlin/New York: Walter de Gruyter.
Cardoso, Fernando Henrique and Faletto, Enzo. 1996. *Dependencia y desarrollo en América Latina: Ensayo de interpretación sociológica*. Santiago de Chile: Siglo XXI (27 ed.).
Cashin Ritaine, Eleanor. 2008. 'Legal Engineering in Comparative Law – An Introduction', in E. Cashin Ritaine, L. Franck, S. Lalani (eds) *L'ingénierie juridique et le droit compare. Legal Engineering and Comparative Law: Rapports des collaborateurs à l'occasion du 25e anniversaire de l'Institut suisse de droit comparé*. Publications de l'Institut Suisse de Droit Comparé.
Cichowski, Rachel A. 2006a. 'Courts, Rights, and Democratic Participation', *Comparative Political Studies* 39(1): 50–75.

———. 2006b. 'Introduction: Courts, Democracy, and Governance', *Comparative Political Studies* 39(1): 3–21.
Cichowski, Rachel A. and Stone Sweet, Alec. 2003. 'Participation, Representative Democracy and the Courts', in B. Cain, R. Dalton and S. Scarrow (eds) *Democracy Transformed? Expanding Opportunities in Advanced Industrial Democracies*. Oxford: Oxford University Press.
Claes, Monica and De Witte, Bruno. 1996. 'The European Court and National Courts: Report on the Netherlands', EUI Working Paper.
Comunidad Andina, Secretaría General. 2006. *Comunidad Andina: Avances y Perspectivas: Informe de la Secretaría General de la Comunidad Andina 2005–2006*. Lima: Documento informativo SG/di 800.
Conant, Lisa. 2001. 'Europeanization and the Courts: Variable Patterns of Adaptation among National Judiciaries', in M. G. Cowles, J. Caporaso and T. Risse (eds) *Europeanization and Domestic Change*. Ithaca, NY: Cornell University Press.
———. 2002. *Justice Contained: Law and Politics in the European Union*. Ithaca, NY: Cornell University Press.
———. 2006. 'Individuals, Courts, and the Development of European Social Rights', *Comparative Political Studies* 39(1): 76–100.
———. 2007. 'Review Article: The Politics of Legal Integration', in U. Sedekmeier and A. Smith (eds) *The JCMS Annual Review of the European Union in 2006*. Oxford: Blackwell.
Couso, Javier. 2004. 'Consolidación Democrática y Poder Judicial: Los Riesgos de la Judicialización de la Política', *Revista de Ciencia Política* 24(2): 29–48.
Craig, Paul and de Búrca, Gráinne. 2008. *EU Law: Text, Cases, and Materials*, 4th edn. New York: Oxford University Press.
Cremona, M. 1999. 'External Relations and External Competence: The Emergence of an Integrated Policy', in P. Craig and G. de Búrca (eds) *The Evolution of EU Law*. Oxford: Oxford University Press.
Cross, Frank and Lindquist, Stefanie A. 2007. 'The Scientific Study of Judicial Activism', *Minnesota Law Review* 91(6).
da Cruz Vilaça, J. L. and Sobrino, José Manuel. 1996. 'Del Pacto a la Comunidad Andina: El Protocolo de Trujillo de 10 de marzo de 1996 ¿simple reforma institucional o profundización en la integración subregional?', *Gaceta Jurídica de la CEE* 26: 83–138.
———. 1998. 'The European Union and the Transformation of the Andean Pact into the Andean Community', *European Foreign Affairs Review* 3: 13–52.
Dahrendorf, Ralf. 1973. *Plädoyer für die Europäische Union*. Munich: Piper.
Dehousse, Renaud. 1998. *The European Court of Justice: The Politics of Judicial Integration*. Basingstoke: Macmillan/New York: St Martin's Press.
Dehousse, Renaud and Weiler, Joseph H. 1990. 'The Legal Dimension', in W. Wallace (ed.) *The Dynamic of European Integration*. London: Pinter.
Deutsch, Karl W. 1953. 'The Growth of Nations', *World Politics* 5(2).
———. 1954. *Political Community at the International Level*. New York: Doubleday.
———. 1962. 'Towards Western European Integration: An Interim Assessment', *Journal of International Affairs* XVI.
Dezalay, Yves and Garth, Bryan G. 1996. *Dealing in Virtue: International Commercial Arbitration and the Construction of a Transnational Legal Order*. Chicago: Chicago University Press.

———. 2002. *The Internationalization of Palace Wars: Lawyers, Economists and the Contest to Transform Latin American States*. Chicago: Chicago University Press.

Díaz Barrado, Cástor. 1999. 'Iberoamérica ante los Procesos de Integración: Una aproximación general', in *XVIII Jornadas de la Asociación Española de Profesores de Derecho Internacional y Relaciones Internacionales*. Madrid: Boletín Oficial del Estado.

Dieckmann, Johann. 2005. *Einführung in die Systemtheorie*. Munich: Wilhelm Fink.

DiMaggio, Paul and Powell, Walter. 1983. 'The Iron Cage Revisited: Institutional Isomorphism, and Collective Rationality in Organizational Fields', *American Sociological Review* 48(2): 147–60.

Dreyzin de Klor, Adriana. 2007. 'La primera Opinión Consultiva en MERCOSUR ¿Germen de cuestión prejudicial?' *Revista española de derecho europeo* 23: 437–61.

Dromí San Martino, Laura. 2002. *Derecho Constitucional de la Integración*. Facultad de Derecho, Universidad Complutense, Madrid.

Easton, David. 1965a. *A Framework for Political Analysis*. Englewood Cliffs, NJ: Prentice-Hall.

———. 1965b. *A Systems Analysis of Political Life*. New York: Wiley.

ECLAC. 1994. *Open Regionalism in Latin America and the Caribbean: Economic Integration as a Contribution to Changing Production Patterns with Social Equity*. Santiago, Chile: ECLAC.

Ekmekdjian, Miguel Ángel. 1994. *Introducción al derecho comunitario latinoamericano: con especial referencia al Mercosur*. Buenos Aires: De Palma.

Emmes, Manfred and Mols, Manfred. 1993. 'Integration, Kooperation und Konzertation in Lateinamerika', in *Regionalismus und Kooperation in Lateinamerik und Südostasien im Zusatz ein politikwissenschaftlicher Vergleich*. Münster.

Engle, Harold E. 1957. *A Critical Study of the Functionalist Approach to International Organization*. Unpublished PhD dissertation, Columbia University.

Everling, Ulrich. 1983. 'Der Gerichtshof als Entscheidungsinstanz', in J. Schwarze (ed.) *Der Europäische Gerichtshof als Verfassungsgericht und Rechtsschutzinstanz*. Baden-Baden: Nomos.

Farrell, Henry and Héritier, Adrienne. 2005. 'A Rationalist-institutionalist Explanation of Endogenous Regional Integration', *Journal of European Public Policy* 12(2): 273–90.

Faundez, Julio. 2010. 'Rule of Law or Washington Consensus: The Evolution of the World Bank's Approach to Legal and Judicial Reform', in Amanda Perry-Kesaris (ed.) *Law in the Pursuit of Development*. London: Routledge.

Fawcett, Louise. 1995. 'Regionalism in Historical Perspective', in L. Fawcett and A. Hurrell (eds) *Regionalism in World Politics: Regional Organization and International Order*. Oxford: Oxford University Press.

Ferris, Elizabeth. 1979. 'National Political Support for Regional Integration: The Andean Pact', *International Organization* 33(1): 83–104.

Franko, Patrice. 2007. *The Puzzle of Latin American Development*, 3rd edn. Lanham, MD: Rowman and Littlefield.

Franzius, Claudio. 2005. 'Europawissenschaft in der Ausbildung', in G. Schuppert, I. Pernice and U. Haltern (eds) *Europawissenschaft*. Baden-Baden: Nomos.

Frenz, Walter. 2004. 'Europäische Grundfreiheiten', in *Handbuch Europarecht 1*. Berlin: Springer.

Frischhut, Markus. 2003. *Die Rolle der Judikative in der Ausformung der Verbandsgewalt supranationaler Organisationen: EuGH, Andengerichtshof, Supreme Court und Conseil Constitutionnel im Vergleich*. Frankfurt am Main: Peter Lang.

Frohmann, Alicia. 1990. *Puentes sobre la turbulencia: concertación política latinoamericana en los 80*. Santiago: FLACSO.

Galanter, Marc. 1974. 'Why the "Haves" Come Out Ahead: Speculations on the Limits of Legal Change', *Law and the Society* (Fall): 95–160.

García Amador, Francisco V. 1977. *El ordenamiento jurídico andino: Un nuevo derecho comunitario*. Buenos Aires: De Palma.

Garrett, Geoffrey. 1995. 'The Politics of Legal Integration in the European Union', *International Organisation* 49(1) (Winter): 171–81.

Garrett, Geoffrey and Weingast, Barry. 1993. 'Ideas, Interests, and Institutions: Constructing the European Community's Internal Market', in J. Goldstein and R. O. Keohane (eds) *Ideas and Foreign Policy*. Ithaca, NY: Cornell University Press.

George, A. L. and Bennett, A. 2004. *Case Studies and Theory Development in the Social Sciences*. Cambridge, MA and London: MIT Press.

Golub, Jonathan. 1996. 'The Politics of Judicial Discretion: Rethinking the Interaction Between National Courts and the European Court of Justice', *West European Politics* 19: 360–85.

Góngora-Mera, Manuel. 2011. *Inter-American Judicial Constitutionalism: On the Constitutional Rank of Human Rights Treaties in Latin America through National and Inter-American Adjudication*. San José (CR): Instituto Interamericano de Derechos Humanos.

Grabitz, Eberhard (ed.). 1984. *Abgestufte Integration: Eine Alternative zum herkömmlichen Integrationskonzept*. Kehl am Rhein: Engel.

Haas, Ernst. 1958. *The Uniting of Europe: Political, Social, and Economic Forces, 1950–57*. Stanford, CA: Stanford University Press.

———. 1961. 'International Integration: The European and the Universal Process', *International Organisation* 15(3): 366–92.

———. 1964a. *Beyond the Nation-state: Functionalism and International Organization*. Stanford, CA: Stanford University Press.

———. 1964b. 'Technocracy, Pluralism, and the New Europe', in S. R. Graubard (ed.) *A New Europe?* Boston, MA: Houghton Mifflin.

———. 1967. 'The Uniting of Europe and the Uniting of Latin America', *Journal of Common Market Studies* 5(1): 315–43.

———. 1968. *The Uniting of Europe: Political, Social, and Economical Forces, 1950–1957*. Stanford, CA: Stanford University Press.

———. 1970. 'The Study of Regional Integration: Reflection on the Joy and Anguish of Pretheorizing', *International Organization* 24 (Autumn): 607–46.

———. 1972. 'El estudio de la integracion regional: reflexiones acerca de la alegría y la angustia de pre-teorizar', *Revista de la Integración* 10 (May): 85–139.

———. 1991. 'Does Constructivism Subsume Neo-functionalism?', in T. Christiansen, K. E. Jørgenen and A. Wiener (eds) *The Social Construction of Europe*. Thousand Oaks: Sage Publications.

———. 2000. 'Interview', 30 October.

Haas, Ernst and Schmitter, Philippe. 1964. 'Economics and Differential Patterns of Political Integration: Projections about Unity in Latin America', *International Organization* 18(4): 705–37.

Haas, Peter. 1992. 'Introduction: Epistemic Communities and International Policy Coordination', *International Organization* 46(1): 1–36.
Haltern, Ulrich. 2004. 'Integration Through Law', in A. Wiener and T. Diez (eds) *European Integration Theory*. Oxford: Oxford University Press.
Hartley, Trevor (ed.). 1988. *The Foundations of European Community Law*, 3rd edn. Oxford: Clarendon Press.
———. 1996. 'The European Court, Judicial Objectivity and the Constitution of the European Union', *Law Quarterly Review* 112: 95–109.
———. 2001. 'The Constitutional Foundations of the European Union', *Law Quarterly Review* 117: 225–46.
Heathcote, Nina. 1966. 'The Crisis of European Supranationality', *Journal of Common Market Studies* 5(2): 140–71.
Helfer, Laurence and Alter, Karen. 2009. 'The Andean Tribunal of Justice and its Interlocutors: Understanding Preliminary Reference Patterns in the Andean Community', *NYU Journal of International Law and Politics* 41: 871–930.
Helfer, Laurence and Slaughter, Anne-Marie. 1997. 'Toward a Theory of Effective Supranational Adjudication', *Yale Law Journal* 107(2): 273–391.
Helfer, Laurence, Alter, Karen and Guerzovich, Florencia. 2009. 'Islands of Effective International Adjudication: Constructing an Intellectual Property Rule of Law in the Andean Community', *The American Journal of International Law*. 103: 1.
Herrera, Felipe. 1976. 'America Latina y la cooperación del Tercer Mundo'. *Integración Latinoamerican*, 2 (May).
Hirst, Monica. 1992. 'Condicionantes y motivaciones del proceso de integración y fragmentación en América Latina', *Integración Latinoamericana* (January–February).
Hobe, Stephan and Kimminich, Otto. 2004. *Einführung in das Völkerrecht*. Tübingen/Basel: A. Francke.
Hoffmann, Stanley. 1966. 'Obstinate or Obsolete? The Fate of the Nation-state and the Case of Western Europe', *Daedalus* 93(3): 862–915.
———. 1987. 'Reaching for the Most Difficult: Human Rights as a Foreign Policy Goal', in S. Hoffmann (ed.) *Janus and Minerva: Essays in the Theory and Practice of International Politics*. Boulder, CO: Westview Press.
Horwitz, Morton. 2009. 'Constitutional Transplants', *Theoretical Inquiries in Law*, 10(2): 535–60.
Hufbauer, Gary Clyde and Kotschwar, Barbara. 1998. 'The Future of Regional Trading Arrangements in the Western Hemisphere', in *The US-Canada Free Trade Agreement*. Michigan State University.
Hummer, Waldemar. 1979. 'Regionale Integrationsideologie und innerstaatliche Legitimationsbedürfnisse', in D. Benecke, M. Domitra and M. Mols (eds) *Integration in Lateinamerika, Beiträge des Simposiums der Arbeitsgemeinschaft Deutsche Lateinamerika-Forschung*. Munich.
———. 1980. 'Neueste Entwicklungen im fortschreitenden Integrationsprozeß in Lateinamerika', *Jahrbuch des Öffentlichen Rechtes der Gegenwart* 29: 527–63.
Hunt, J. and Shaw, J. 2009. 'Fairy Tale of Luxembourg? Reflections on Law and Legal Scholarship in European Integration', in D. Phinnemore and A. Warleigh-Lack (eds) *Reflections on European Integration: 50 Years of the Treaty of Rome*. Basingstoke: Palgrave Macmillan.

Hurrell, Andrew. 2005. 'The Regional Dimension in International Relations Theory', in M. Farrell, B. Hettne and L. Van Langenhove (eds) *The Global Politics of Regionalism. Theory and Practice*. London: Pluto Press.
Hurtado Larrea, Eduardo. 1985. 'Los Incumplimientos y la Acción Asignada a la Competencia del Tribunal', in BID-INTAL (ed.) *El Tribunal de Justicia del Acuerdo de Cartagena*. Buenos Aires: BID-INTAL.
Ibañez, Joseph. 1999. 'El Nuevo Regionalism Latinoamericano en los Años Noventa', in *Iberoamérica ante los procesos de Integración*. Actas de las XVIII Jornadas de la Asociación Española de Profesores de Derecho Internacional y Relaciones Internacionales.
INTAL. 1972. 'Estudio sobre procedimientos para solucionar conflictos', *Derecho de la Integración* 11 (October): 121–31.
INTAL. 1973a. 'Colombia: Seminario sobre aspectos jurídicos de la integracion', *Derecho de la Integración* 12 (March): 178.
INTAL. 1973b. 'Primer Congreso de Abogados del Grupo Andino', *Derecho de la Integración* 12 (March): 179–81.
Jellinek, Georg. 1914. *Allgemeine Staatslehre*, 3rd edn. Berlin: O. Häring.
Jenkins-Smith, Hank and Sabatier, Paul. 1994. 'Evaluating the Advocacy Coalition Framework', *Journal of Public Policy* 14(2): 175–203.
JUNAC (Junta del Acuerdo de Cartagena). 1972. *Informe de la Junta sobre el establecimeinto de órgano jursidiccional del Acuerdo de Cartagena*. COM/VI-E, Lima.
———. 1973. 'Informe de la Junta sobre el establecimiento de un órgano jurisdiccional del Acuerdo de Cartagena', *Derecho de la Integración* 13 (July): 135–50.
———. 1979. *Evaluación del Proceso de Integración 1969–1979 Grupo Andino*. Lima: Editorial Universo S.A.
———. 1983. *Sobre el cumplimiento de los compromisos derivados del Acuerdo de Cartagena y de las Decisiones de la Comisión*. Lima: Editorial Universo S.A.
Katzenstein, Peter J. 1989. 'International Relations Theory and the Analysis of Change', in E.-O. Czempiel and J. N. Rosenau (eds) *Global Changes and Theoretical Challenges*. Lexington, MA: Lexington Books.
Keener, E. Barlow. 1987. 'The Andean Common Market Court of Justice: Its Purpose, Structure and Future', *Emory Journal of International Dispute Resolution* 1: 39–71.
Kelsen, Hans. 1928. *Das Problem der Souveränität und die Theorie des Völkerrechts*. Tübingen: Mohr.
Keohane, Robert O. 1984. *After Hegemony: Collaboration and Discord in the World Political Economy*. Princeton, NJ: Princeton University Press.
———. 1986. *Neo-Realism and Its Critics*. New York: Columbia University Press.
Keohane, Robert O. and Hoffmann, Stanley. 1991. 'Institutional Change in Europe in the 1980s', in R. O. Keohane and S. Hoffmann (eds) *The New European Community: Decisionmaking and Institutional Change*. Boulder, CO: Westview Press.
Keohane, Robert O., Slaughter, Anne-Marie and Moravcsik, Andrew. 2000. 'Legalized Dispute Resolution: Interstate and Transnational', *International Organization* 54(3): 457–88.
King, Gary, Keohane, Robert O. and Verba, Sidney. 1994. *Designing Social Inquiry: Scientific Inference in Qualitative Research*. Princeton, NJ: Princeton University Press.
Kirchhof, Paul. 1999. 'The Balance of Powers between National and European Institutions', *European Law Journal* 5: 225–42.

Kmiec, Keenan D. 2004. 'The Origin and Current Meaning of "Judicial Activism"', *California Law Review* 92(5): 1441–77.
Koopmans, Tim. 1978. 'Legislature and Judiciary: Present Trends', in M. Cappelletti (ed.) *New Perspectives for a Common Law of Europe*. Brussels: Bruylant.
Kramer, Larry. 2004. *The People Themselves: Popular Constitutionalism and Judicial Review*. Oxford/New York: Oxford University Press.
Kumm, Matthias. 1999. 'Who is the Final Arbiter of Constitutionality in Europe? Three Conceptions of the Relationship between the German Federal Constitutional Court and the European Court of Justice', *Common Market Law Review* 36: 351.
Kuper, Richard. 1998. *The Politics of the European Court of Justice*. London: Kogan Page.
Lecourt, Robert. 1976. *L'Europe des juges*. Brussels: Bruylant.
Lagrange, Maurice. 1968. 'La interpretación unitaria del derecho de las Comunidades Europeas: aspectos de la interpretación prejudicial', *Derecho de la Integración* 3 (October): 51–80.
La Porta, Rafael, López de Silantes, Florencio, Shleifer, Andrei and Vishny, Robert. 1998. 'Law and Finance', *Journal of Political Economy* 106: 1113–55.
Legrand, Pierre. 1997. 'Against a European Civil Code', *Modern Law Review* 60(1): 44–63.
Likhovski, Assaf. 2009. 'Argonauts of the Eastern Mediterranean: Legal Transplants and Signaling', *Theoretical Inquiries in Law* 10(2): 619–51.
Lindberg, Leon N. 1963. *The Political Dynamics of European Economic Integration*. Stanford, CA: Stanford University Press.
———. 1965. 'Decision Making and Integration in the European Community', *International Organization* 19(1).
———. 1966. 'Integration as a Source of Stress on the European Community System', *International Organization* (Spring): 233–65.
———. 1994. 'Comment on Moravcsik', in S. Bulmer and A. Scott (eds) *Economic and Political Integration in Europe: Internal Dynamics and Global Contexts*. Oxford: Blackwell.
Lijphart, A. 1975. 'The Comparable-Cases Strategy in Comparative Research', *Comparative Political Studies* 8(2): 159–77.
Lodge, Juliet. 1978. 'Loyalty and the EEC: The Limits of Functionalist Approach', *Political Studies* 26.
López Medina, Diego E. 2004. *El derecho de los jueces*. Bogotá: Ediciones Universidad de Los Andes.
Luhmann, Niklas. 1964. *Funktionen und Folgen formaler Organisation*. Berlin: Duncker & Humblot.
MacCormick, Neil. 1978. *Legal Reasoning and Legal Theory*. Oxford: Clarendon Press.
———. 1999. *Questioning Sovereignty*. Oxford: Oxford University Press.
Maduro, Miguel Poiares. 2002. *We, the Court: The European Court of Justice and the European Economic Constitution*. Oxford: Hart.
———. 2003. 'Europe and the Constitution: What if this is as Good as it Gets?', in J. H. H. Weiler and M. Wind (eds) *Constitutionalism Beyond the State*. Cambridge: Cambridge University Press.
Mahoney, Paul G. 2001. 'The Common Law and Economic Growth: Hayek Might be Right', *Journal of Legal Studies* 30(2): 503–25.

Malamud, Andrés and Schmitter, Philippe. 2007. 'The Experience of European Integration and the Potential for Integration in South America', IBEI Working Paper 2007/6.
Mancini, Federico. 1989. 'The Making of a Constitution for Europe', *Common Market Law Review* 26: 595–614.
Mancini, Federico and Keeling, David T. 1992. 'From CILFIT to ERTA: The Constitutional Challenge Facing the European Court', *Yearbook of European Law* 11: 1–13.
Márquez, Iván Gabaldón. 1985. 'Algunos Comentarios sobre el Estatuto del Tribunal de Justicia del Acuerdo de Cartagena', in BID-INTAL (ed.) *El Tribunal de Justicia del Acuerdo de Cartagena*. Buenos Aires: BID-INTAL.
Marwege, Renata. 1995. *Der Andengerichtshof. Das Rechtsschutzsystem des Andenpaktes mit vergleichenden Bezügen zum Recht der Europäischen Gemeinschaft*. Berlin: Duncker & Humblot.
Mattli, Walter. 1999a. 'Explaining Regional Integration Outcomes', *Journal of European Public Policy* 6(1): 1–27.
———. 1999b. *The Logic of Regional Integration: Europe and Beyond*. Cambridge: Cambridge University Press.
———. 2005. 'Ernst Haas's Evolving Thinking on Comparative Regional Integration: Of Virtues and Infelicities', *Journal of European Public Policy* 12(2): 327–48.
Mattli, Walter and Slaughter, Anne-Marie. 1996. *Constructing the European Community Legal System from the Ground Up: The Role of Individual Litigants and National Courts*. Florence: European University Institute.
———. 1998. 'Revisiting the ECJ', *International Organisation* 52(1) (Winter): 177–209.
Medina, Manuel. 1989. 'La Integración Internacional', *Derecho de la Integración Economica Regional*. Buenos Aires: BID-INTAL.
Merton, Robert King. 1957. *Social Theory and Social Structure: Toward the Codification of Theory and Research*. Glencoe, IL: Free Press.
Mertz, Elisabeth. 2007. 'The Language of Law School: Learning to "Think" Like a Lawyer'. Oxford: Oxford University Press.
Mitrany, David. 1933. *The Progress of International Government*. New Haven, CT: Yale University Press.
———. 1948. 'International Affairs', *International Affairs* XXIV.
———. 1966. *A Working Peace System*. Chicago: Quadrangle Books/Society for a World Service Federation.
Möllers, Christoph. 2003. 'Verfassungsgebende Gewalt – Verfassung – Konstitutionalisierung', in A von Bogdandy (ed.) *Europäisches Verfassungsrecht. Theoretische und dogmatische Grundzüge*. Berlin/Heidelberg: Springer.
Mols, Manfred. 1993. 'Zur Genese und Begründungslogik des modernen internationalen Regionalismus in Lateinamerika', in *Regionalismus und Kooperation in Lateinamerika und Südostasien Zusatz ein politikwissenschaftlicher Vergleich*. Münster.
Montaño Galarza, César. 2004. 'Constitución ecuatoriana e integración andina: la situación del poder tributario del Estado', *Anuario de Derecho Constitucional Latinoamericano* Décimo año: 949.94.
Montesquieu, Charles L. 1961 [1741]. *De l'Esprit des Lois*. Paris: Éditions Garnier Frères.

Moravcsik, Andrew. 1991. 'Negotiating the Single European Act: National Interests and Conventional Statecraft in the European Community', *International Organization* 45 (Winter): 19–56.

———. 1993. 'Preferences and Power in the European Community: A Liberal Intergovernmentalist Approach', *Journal of Common Market Studies* 31(4).

———. 1994. 'Why the European Community Strengthens the State: Domestic Politics and International Cooperation', Harvard University Center for European Studies Paper No. 52.

———. 1995. 'Liberal Intergovernmentalism and Integration: A Rejoinder'. *Journal of Common Market Studies* 33(4): 611–28.

———. 1997a. 'Does the European Union Represent an n of 1?' *ECSA Review* X(3) (Fall): 1–5.

———. 1997b. 'Taking Preferences Seriously: A Liberal Theory of International Politics', *International Organisation* 51(4) (Autumn): 513–53.

———. 1998. *The Choice for Europe*. Ithaca, NY: Cornell University Press.

———. 2005. 'The European Constitutional Compromise and the Neofunctionalist Legacy', *Journal of European Public Policy* 12(2): 349–86.

Moya Domínguez, María Teresa. 2006. *Derecho de la Integración*. Buenos Aires: Ediar S.A.

Murphy, Walter. 1964. *Elements of Judicial Strategy*. Chicago: Chicago University Press.

———. 1993. 'Constitutions, Constitutionalism, and Democracy', in D. Greenberg and S. N. Katz (eds) *Constitutionalism and Democracy: Transitions in a Contemporary World*. New York and Oxford: Oxford University Press.

Mutimer, David. 1989. '1992 and the Political Integration of Europe: Neofunctionalism Reconsidered', *Journal of European Integration* 13(4): 75–101.

Nanclares, Andrés. 2001. *Los jueces de mármol*. Medellín: La Pisca Tabaca Editores.

Naroll, Raoul. 1961. 'Two Solutions to Galton's Problem', *Philosophy of Science* 28(1).

Nelken, David and Feest, Johannes (eds). 2001. *Adapting Legal Cultures*. Oxford: Hart.

Nicolaysen, Gert. 1991. *Europarecht*. Baden-Baden: Nomos.

North, Douglass. 1990. *Institutions, Institutional Change and Economic Performance*. Cambridge: Cambridge University Press.

Nye, Joseph. 1965. 'Patterns and Catalysts in Regional Integration', *International Organization* 19(4): 870–84.

———. 1969. 'Integración regional comparada: concepto y medición', *Revista de la Integración* 5 (November): 50–86.

———. 1971. 'Comparing Common Markets: A Revised Neofunctional Model', in L. N. Lindberg and S. A. Scheingold (eds) *Regional Integration*. Cambridge, MA: Harvard University Press.

O'Leary, Timothy F. 1984. 'The Andean Common Market and the Importance of Effective Dispute Resolution Procedures', *International Tax & Business Lawyer* 1: 101–28.

Orellana Ayora, Manuel. 1989. 'El ordenamiento jurídico del Auerdo de Cartagena', in A. Zelada Casteło (ed.) *Derecho de la integración cónomica regional: Lecturas seleccionadas*. Buenos Aires: BID-INTAL.

Orrego Vicuña, Francisco. 1970. 'La incorporación del ordenamiento jurídico subregional al derecho interno: Análisis de la práctica chilena', *Derecho de la Integración* 7 (October): 42–67.

———. 1972. 'La incorporación del ordenamiento jurídico subregional al derecho interno. Análisis de la práctica y jurisprudencia de Colombia', *Derecho de la Integración* 11 (October): 39–60.

———. 1973. 'Contemporary International Law in the Economic integration of Latin America', in Joël Rideau (ed.) *Les aspects juridiques de l'integration economique: Colloque de 1971*. Leiden: Sijthoff.

———. 1974. 'La creación de un tribunal de justicia en el Grupo Andino', *Derecho de la Integracion* 15 (March): 31–46.

———. 1977. 'Los presupuestos jurídicos de un proceso de integración económica efectivo', *Revista Derecho de la Integración* (March).

———. 1981. 'Análisis de la práctica latinoamericana en materia de solución de controversias durante la década de 1970 y sus implicaciones para el futuro', in F. Orrego Vicuña and J. Irigoin Barrene (eds) *Perspectivas del derecho internacional contempráneo, experiencias y visión de América Latina*. Santiago de Chile: Instituto de Estudios Internacionales de la Universidad de Chile.

Ortiz, Richard. 2004. 'Institutionelle Ansätze und die Präsidentialismusdebatte in Lateinamerika – Die *Heidelberger Schule* und der historisch-empirische Ansatz', *Lateinamerika Analysen* 7 (February): 89–120.

Padilla, David. 1979. 'The Judicial Resolution of Legal Disputes in the Integration Movements of the Hemisphere', *Lawyers of the Americas* 11(1): 75–95.

Paolillo, Felipe and Ons-Indart, Carlos. 1971. 'Estudio de los procedimientos de hecho utilizados para la solución de conflictos en la ALALC', *Derecho de la Integración* 9 (October): 19–74.

Parsons, Talcot. 1951. *The Social System*. New York: Free Press.

Pentland, Charles. 1973. *International Theory and European Integration*. New York: Free Press.

———. 1981. 'Political Theories of European Integration: Between Science and Ideology', in D. Lasok and P. Soldatos (eds) *The European Communities in Action*. Brussels: Bruylant.

Pernice, Ingolf. 1979. *Grundrechtsgehalte im Europäischen Gemeinschaftsrecht*. Baden-Baden: Nomos.

———. 1990. 'Gemeinschaftsverfassung und Grundrechtsschutz – Grundlagen, Bestand und Perspektiven', *Neue Juristische Wochenschrift* 43: 2409–20.

———. 2001. 'Der Beitrag Walter Hallseins zur Zukunft Europas: Begründung und Konsolidierung der Europäischen Gemeinschaft als Rechtsgemeinschaft', WHI-Paper 9/01.

———. 2006. 'The Global Dimension of Multilevel Constitutionalism: A Legal Response to the Challenges of Globalisation', in *Völkerrecht als Wertordnung/Common Values in International Law: Festschrift für Christian Tomuschat*. Kehl am Rhein: Engel.

Perotti, Alejandro Daniel. 1999. 'Los tribunales comunitarios en los procesos de integración. El caso del Tribunal de Justicia de la Comunidad Andina', *Revista Dikaion* 8 (July): 186–241.

———. 2001. 'Algunas consideraciones sobre la Interpretación Prejudicial Obligatoria en el Derecho Andino', *Gaceta Jurídica de la Unión Europea y de la Competencia* 213 (May/June).

Pescatore, Pierre. 1967. 'Distribución de competencias y de poderes entre los Estados miembros de las Comunidades Europeas', *Derecho de la Integración* 1 (October): 108–52.

——. 1974. *The Law of Integration: Emergence of a New Phenomenon in International Relations, based on the experience of the European Communities*. Leiden: Sijthoff.

—— (ed.). 1985. *References for Preliminary Rulings under Article 177 of the EEC Treaty and Co-operation, between the Court and National Courts*. Luxembourg: European Court of Justice.

Phillips, Nicola. 2005. 'The Americas', in A. Payne (ed.) *The New Regional Politics of Development*. Basingstoke: Palgrave Macmillan.

de Piérola, Nicolás. 1987. 'The Andean Court of Justice', *Emory Journal of International Dispute Resolution* 2: 11–38.

Pohl, Heinrich. 1929. *Völkerrecht und Außenpolitik in der Reichsverfassung*. Berlin: Dümmler.

Pollack, Mark. 1997. 'Delegation, Agency and Agenda Setting in the EC', *International Organization* 51(1): 99–134.

——. 2004. *The New Institutionalism and European Integration*. Oxford: Oxford University Press.

Preuss, Ulrich K. 1996. 'The Political Meaning of Constitutionalism', in R. Bellamy (ed.) *Constitutionalism, Democracy and Sovereignty: American and European Perspectives*. Aldershot: Avebury Ashgate.

Puchala, Donald. 1972. 'Of Blind Men, Elephants, and International Integration', *Journal of Common Market Studies* 10(3): 267–84.

Putnam, Robert. 1988. 'Diplomacy and Domestic Politics', *International Organization* 42(3): 427–60.

Rasmussen, Hjalte. 1980. 'Why is Article 173 Interpreted Against Private Plaintiffs?', *European Law Review* 5: 112–27.

——. 1986. *On Law and Policy in the European Court of Justice: A Comparative Study in Judicial Policymaking*. Dordrecht: M. Nijhoff.

Rawlings, Richard. 1993. 'The Eurolaw Game: Some Deductions from a Saga', *Journal of Law and Society* 20 (Autumn): 309–40.

Rehm, Gebhard M. 2008. 'Rechtstransplantate als Instrument der Rechtsreform und –transformation', *Rabels Zeitschrift* 72: 1–42.

Rengeling, Hans-Werner. 1992. *Grundrechtsschutz in der Europäischen Gemeinschaft*. Munich: C. H. Beck.

Rico Frontaura, Víctor. 2001. 'El Derecho de la Integración en la Comunidad Andina', in *Integración y Supranacionalidad: Soberanía y Derecho Comunitario en los Países Andinos*. Lima: Secretaría General de la Comunidad Andina.

Rideau, Joel (ed.). 1973. *Les aspects juridiques de l'intégration économique. Colloque 1971*. Leiden: Sijthoff.

Ringhand, Lori. 2007. 'The Rehnquist Court: A by the Numbers Retrospective', *University of Pennsylvania Journal of Constitutional Law* 9(4): 1033–81.

Risse, Thomas. 2005. 'Neofunctionalism, European Identity, and the Puzzles of European Integration', *Journal of European Public Policy* 12(2): 291–309.

Rodriguez Lemmo, María Alejandra. 2002. 'Study of Selected International Dispute Resolution Regimen with an Analysis of the Decisiones of the Court of Justice of the Andean Community', *Arizona Journal of International and Comparative Law* 19(3): 863–929.

Rosamond, Ben. 2000. *Theories of European Integration*. New York: St Martin's Press.

——. 2005. 'The Uniting of Europe and the Foundation of EU Studies: Revisiting the Neofunctionalism of Ernst B. Haas', *Journal of European Public Policy* 12(2): 237–54.

Sacco, Rodolfo. 1991. 'Legal Formants: A Dynamic Approach to Comparative Law', *American Journal of Comparative Law* 39(1): 1–34.
Sáchica, Luis Carlos. 1985a. 'El Ordenamiento Jurídico Andino y su Tribunal de Justicia', in BID-INTAL (ed.) *El Tribunal de Justicia del Acuerdo de Catagena*. Buenos Aires: BID-INTAL.
———. 1985b. *Introducción al derecho comunitario*. Quito: Colección de Estudios del Tribunal de Justicia del Acuerdo de Cartagena.
———. 1985c. 'La Acción de Nulidad en el Ordenamiento Jurídico Andino', in BID-INTAL (ed.) *El Tribunal de Justicia del Acuerdo de Catagena*. Buenos Aires: BID-INTAL.
Salazar, Felipe. 1978. 'Solución de conflictos en organizaciones interestatales para la integración económica y otras formas de cooperación económica', *Derecho de la Integración* 28/29: 11–33.
Salazar Santos, Felipe. 1973. 'The Andean Group: Fact or Fiction?', in *Current Legal Aspects of Doing Business in Latin America: The New Challenge of Latin American Nationalism to Foreign Investment – Present and Future*, American Bar Association Conference, 4–5 May, New York.
Saldías, Osvaldo. 2008. Comparative Community Law: Latin American Scholarship on Regional Intergration and the Peril of Legal Functionalism. *UCLA Pacific Basin Law Journal* 26: 1.
Saldías, Osvaldo. 2010. 'Can We Explain the Emergence of Legal Cultures? A Methodological Approach on the Example of the Andean Court of Justice', *Journal of Comparative Law* 5(2).
Sánchez Chacón, Francisco Javier. 2001. 'El Tribunal de Justicia de la Comunidad Andina: Estructura y Competencias', *Aldea Mundo* 5(9): 38–44.
Sangmeister, Hartmut. 2001. 'Zehn Jahre MERCOSUR: Eine Zwischenbilanz', *Ibero-Analysen* 9 (March).
Sanguinetti, Julio Luis. 1994. 'MERCOSUR: las alternativas del diseño institucional definitivo', *Integración Latinoamericana* 201 (June).
Sartori, Giovanni. 1995. *Politica: Logica y Metodo en Las Ciencias Sociales*. México: Fondo de Cultura Económica.
Scharpf, Fritz. 1988. 'The Joint-Decision Trap-Lessons from German Federalism and European Integration', *Public Administration* 66: 239.
———. 1995. 'Negative and Positive Integration in the Political Economy of Welfare States', *Jean Monnet Chair Papers*. Florence: EUI.
Scheingold, Stuart A. 1971. 'The Law in Political Integration: The Evolution and Integrative Implications of Regional Legal Processes in the European Community', Occasional Papers in International Affairs No. 27. Cambridge, MA: Center for International Affairs, Harvard University.
Schilling, Theodor. 1996. 'The Autonomy of the Community Legal Order: An Analysis of Possible Foundations', *Harvard International Law Journal* 37(2) (Spring): 389–409.
Schimmelfennig, Frank. 2004. 'Liberal Intergovernmentalism', in A. Wiener and T. Diez (eds) *European Integration Theory*. Oxford: Oxford University Press.
Schmidt, Jan Peter, and Piscitello, Daniel Pavón. 2007. 'In the Footsteps of the ECJ: First Decision of the Permanent MERCOSUR-Tribunal', *Legal Issues of Economic Integration* 3: 283–93.

Schmitter, Philippe. 1969a. 'La dinámica de contradicciones y la conducción de crisis en la integración centroamericana', *Revista de la Integración* 5 (November): 87–151.

———. 1969b. 'Three Neo-Functional Hypotheses about International Integration', *International Organisation* 23(1) (Winter): 161–6.

———. 1971. 'A Revised Theory of Regional Integration', in L. N. Lindberg and S. A. Scheingold (eds) *Regional Integration: Theory and Research*. Cambridge, MA: Harvard University Press.

———. 2003. 'Neo-neofunctionalism', in A. Wiener and T. Diez (eds) *European Integration Theory*. Oxford: Oxford University Press.

———. 2005. 'Ernst B. Haas and the Legacy of Neofunctionalism', *Journal of European Public Policy* 12(2): 255–72.

Schroeder, Werner. 2004. *Die Auslegung des EU-Rechts*, Vol. 3. Munich: C. H. Beck.

Sen, Amartia. 2006. 'What is the Role of Judicial Reform in the Development Process?', *World Bank Law Review: Law Equity and Development* 2: 33–51.

Shapiro, Martin. 1980. 'Comparative and Comparative Politics', *Southern California Law Review* 53 (January).

———. 2002a. 'The Success of Judicial Review and Democracy', in M. Shapiro and A. Stone Sweet (eds) *On Law, Politics and Judicialization*. Oxford: Oxford University Press.

———. 2002b. 'Judicial Delegation Doctrines: The US, Britain, and France', *West European Politics* 25(1): 173–99.

Slaughter, Anne-Marie. 1998. 'Court to Court', *American Journal of International Law* 92(4): 708–12.

———. 2000a. 'A Liberal Theory of International Law', *American Society and International Law Proceedings* 94: 240–8.

———. 2000b. 'Judicial Globalization', *Virginia Journal of International Law* 40: 1103–24.

———. 2003. 'A Global Community of Courts', *Harvard International law Journal* 44 (Winter): 191–219.

Slaughter, Anne-Marie, Stone Sweet, Alec and Weiler, Joseph. 1998. *The European Court and National Courts: Doctrine and Jurisprudence: Legal Change in its Social Context*. Oxford: Hart.

Smith, Adam. 2003 [1776] *The Wealth of Nations*. New York: Bantam Classics.

Sobrino, José Manuel. 2001. 'Derecho de Integración, Marco Conceptual y Experiencia de la Unión Europea', in *Integración y Supranacionalidad: Soberanía y Derecho Comunitario en los Países Andinos*. Lima: Secretaría General de la Comunidad Andina.

Söderbaum, Frederik. 2008. *Consolidating Comparative Regionalism: From Eurocentrism to Global Comparison*. GARNET Annual Conference, University of Bordeaux.

Stein, Eric. 1981. 'Lawyers, Judges, and the Making of a Transnational Constitution', *American Journal of International Law* 75(1): 1–27.

Streinz, Rudolf. 1989. *Bundesverfassungsgerichtlicher Grundrechtsschutz und Europäisches Gemeinschaftsrecht: die Überprüfung grundrechtsbeschränkender deutscher Begründungs- und Vollzugsakte von Europäischem Gemeinschaftsrecht durch das Bundesverfassungsgericht*. Baden-Baden: Nomos.

Stone Sweet, Alec. 2000. *Governing with Judges: Constitutional Politics in Europe*. Oxford: Oxford University Press.

———. 2004a. 'The European Court and Integration', in A. Stone Sweet (ed.) *The Judicial Construction of Europe*. Oxford: Oxford University Press.
——— (ed.). 2004b. *The Judicial Construction of Europe*. Oxford: Oxford University Press.
Stone Sweet, Alec and Brunell, Thomas. 2004. 'Constructing a Supranational Constitution', in A. Stone Sweet (ed.) *The Judicial Construction of Europe*. Oxford: Oxford University Press.
Stone Sweet, Alec, Sandholtz, Wayne and Fligstein, Neil (eds). 2001. *The Institutionalization of European Space*. Oxford: Oxford University Press.
Suárez Mejías, Jorge Luis. 2001. *Integración y Supranacionalidad en la Comunidad Andina: proceso decisorio, sistema jurisdiccional y relación con los derechos nacionales*. Dissertation. Madrid: Universidad Complutense de Madrid.
———. 2006. *La Responsabilidad Patrimonial del Estado y el Derecho Comunitario*. Caracas: Editorial Sherwood.
Taccone, J. J. and Nogueira, U. (eds). 2005. *Informe Andino: Desarrollos del Período 2002–2004*. Buenos Aires: Instituto para la Integración de América Latina y el Caribe/BID-INTAL.
Tallberg, Jonas. 2002. 'Delegation to Supranational Institutions: Why, How, and with What Consequences?', *West European Politics* 25(1): 23–46.
Tangarife, Marcel. 2001a. 'La Supranacionalidad en el Constitucionalismo Latinoamericano: El caso de los Países Miembros de la Comunidad Andina', in *Integración y Supranacionalidad: Soberanía y Derecho Comunitario en los Países Andinos*. Lima: Secretaría General de la Comunidad Andina.
———. 2001b. 'Sistema Jurisdiccional en el Proceso Andino', in *Integración y Supranacionalidad: Soberanía y Derecho Comunitario en los Países Andinos*. Lima: Secretaría General de la Comunidad Andina.
Taylor, Paul. 1983. *The Limits of European Integration*. New York: Columbia University Press.
Thatcher, Mark and Stone Sweet, Alec. 2002. 'Theory and Practice of Delegation to Non-Majoritarian Institutions', *West European Politics* 25(1): 1–22.
TJCAN (Tribunal de Justicia de la Comunidad Andina). 2005. *Informe Anual del 01/07/2004–30/06/2005*. Quito: Publicaciones del Tribunal.
Tomassini, Luciano. 1990. *Nuevas formas de concertación regional en América Latina*. Buenos Aires: Grupo Editorial Latinoaméricana.
Triepel, Heinrich. 1958 [1899]. *Völkerrecht und Landesrecht*. Meisenheim/Glan: Hain.
Tylor, Edward Burnett. 1889. *On a Method of Investigating the Development of Institutions; Applied to Laws of Marriage and Descent*. London.
Uribe Restrepo, Armando. 1993. *La interpretación prejudicial en el derecho andino*. Quito: Tribunal de Justicia del Acuerdo de Cartagena.
———. 1990. *El derecho de la integración en el Grupo Andino*. Quito.
Vacchino, Juan Mario. 1985. 'Introducción', in BID-INTAL (ed.) *El Tribunal de Justicia del Acuerdo de Cartagena*. Buenos Aires: BID-INTAL.
Van Langehove, Luk. 2003. 'Theorising Regionhood', UNU-CRIS Occasional Paper.
Vauchez, A. 2008. '"Integration-through-Law": Contribution to a Socio-history of EU Political Commonsense', EUI Robert Schuman Centre for Advanced Studies Working Paper 2008/10.
Vendrell, Francisco José. 1975. 'La Organización del Acuerdo de Cartagena', *Derecho de la Integración* 18/19: 59–79.

Vigil Toledo, Ricardo. 2004. 'La consulta prejudicial en el Tribunal de Justicia de la Comunidad Andina', *Anuario de Derecho Constitucional Latinoamericano* (Décimo año): 939–48.

Villagrán Kramer, Francisco. 1973. 'Sistematización de la estructura juridical del Acuerdo de Cartagena', *Revista Jurídica Latinoamericana* 6: 11–34.

———. 1989. 'Sistematización de la estructura jurídica el Acuerdo de Cartagena', in A. Zelada Castedo (ed.) *Derecho de la integración económica regional, lecturas seleccionadas*. Buenos Aires: BID-INTAL.

Watson, Alan. 1993. *Legal Transplants: An Approach to Comparative Law*, 2nd edn. Athens, GA: University of Georgia Press.

———. 2000. 'Legal Transplants and European Private Law', *Electronic Journal of Comparative Law* 44 (December). Available at: www.ejcl.org/ejcl/44/44-2.html

Weiler, J. H. H. 1981. 'The Community System: The Dual Character of Supranationalism', *Yearbook of European Law* (1): 257–306.

———.1982. 'Community, Member States and European Integration: Is the Law Relevant?', *Journal of Common Market Studies* 21: 39–56.

———.1985. 'The European Court, National Courts and References for Preliminary Rulings. The Paradox of Success: A Revisionist View of Article 177 EEC', EUI Working Paper 85/203.

———. 1986. 'Eurocracy and Distrust: Some Questions concerning the Role of the European Court of Justice in the Protection of Fundamental Rights within the Legal Order of the European Communities', *Washington Law Review* 61: 1103–42.

———. 1991. 'The Transformation of Europe', *Yale Law Journal* 100(8): 2403–83.

———. 1993. 'Journey to an Unknown Destination: A Retrospective and Prospective of the European Court of Justice in the Arena of Political Integration', *Journal of Common Market Legal Studies* 31.

———. 1994. 'A Quiet Revolution: The European Court of Justice and its Interlocutors', *Comparative Political Studies* 26(4): 510–34.

———. 2002. 'A Constitution for Europe? Some Hard Choices', *Journal of Common Market Studies* 40(4): 563–80.

———. 2003. 'In Defence of the Status Quo: Europe's Constitutional Sonderweg', in J. H. H. Weiler and M. Wind (eds) *Constitutionalism Beyond the State*. Cambridge: Cambridge University Press.

Wessels, Wolfgang. 1997. 'An Ever Closer Fusion: A Dynamic Macropolitical View on Integration Processes', *Journal of Common Market Studies* 35(2).

Wiener, Antje. 2003. 'Towards a Transnational Nomos: The Role of Institutions in the Process of Constitutionalization', Jean Monnet Working Paper 9/03.6.

Wiener, Antje and Diez, Thomas. 2004. 'Introducing the Mosaic of Integration Theory', in A. Wiener and T. Diez (eds) *European Integration Theory*. Oxford: Oxford University Press.

Wincott, Daniel. 1995a. 'Political Theory, Law and European Union', in J. Shaw and G. More (eds) *New Legal Dynamics of European Union*. Oxford: Clarendon Press.

———. 1995b. 'The Role of Law or the Rule of the Court of Justice? An "Institutional" Account of Judicial Politics in the European Community', *Journal of European Public Policy* 2(4): 583–602.

———. 1995c. 'Institutional Interaction and European Integration: Towards an Everyday Critique of Liberal Intergovernmentalism', *Journal of Common Market Studies* 33(4).

Wöhlcke, Manfred. 1989. *Der Fall Lateinamerik: Die Kosten des Fortschritts*. Munich: C. H. Beck.
Zafonte, Matthew and Sabatier, Paul. 1998. 'Shared Beliefs and Imposed Interdependencies as Determinants of Ally Networks in Overlapping Subsystems', *Journal of Theoretical Politics* 10(4): 473–505.
Zelada Castedo, Alberto. 1985. 'El Control de la Legalidad, la Solución de Controversias y la Interpretación Uniforme del Derecho Común en el esquema de Integración del Grupo Andino', in BID-INTAL (ed.) *El Tribunal de Justicia del Acuerdo de Cartagena*. Buenos Aires: BID-INTAL.
Zucker, Lynne G. 1987. 'Institutional Theories of Organization', *Annual Review of Sociology* 13: 443–64.
Zuleeg, Manfred. 1969. 'Die Auslegung des Europäischen Gemeinschaftsrecht', *EuR*: 97–108.
Zweigert, Konrad and Kötz, Hein. 1996. *Einführung in die Rechtsvergleichung*, 3rd edn. Tübingen: Mohr Siebeck.

Index

acquis communautaire 91
Act of Carabobo 143
Acuerdo de Integración Subregional 85
Advocacy Coalition (Framework) 64, 66
ALADI 2
ALALC (LAFTA) 4, 84–5, 92–3, 138
Alter, K. 79, 81, 100, 119
Aluminio Reynolds Santo Domingo 109, 111, 120, 123–4, 127
Andean 143; *Andean Common Market* 4, 6, 85, 91, 93, 101, 109, 123, 126–7, 141; Andean Group 63, 71, 73, 84–91, 92, 101, 104, 107, 139; Andean law 6, 32–3, 79–81, 92–6, 99–101, 115–16, 130–3, 137; Andean Pact 6, 61, 68, 76, 84–5, 88–9, 92, 114, 140–1; Andean Parliament 89–90, 140; Andean scholarship 97, 105, 131, 132, 136
Andueza, J-G. 80, 86, 95, 97–8, 108
annulment procedure 75, 82
aplicación directa (*aplicabilidad directa*) 96, 102
APS 107
Argentine 2, 67, 84, 139

Balassa, B. 67
Banana policy 86
Battle by proxy 23
big six 9
black boxes 36
Bolivarian dream 86
Brazil 2, 84, 139
Brunell, T. 25, 48
Brussels University 71

CAFTA 2
CAMRE 88, 141–2
CARICOM 2, 3
Cartagena Agreement 4, 61–3, 71, 73–5, 85, 86–9, 92, 94–6, 98–9, 101, 105, 106–11, 114, 124, 138–42
Caudillo 50
Central American Common Market CACM 70, 77–8
Central American Economic and Social Community CAESC 3, 77–8
Central American Integration 69, 77–8
Charles de Gaulle 33, 36, 38
Chile 68, 74, 140; Chilean Parliament 63, 73–5, 140; Chilean Senate 73–5, 140
Ciba Geigy A.G. 103, 127
Ciudad de Guatemala 71
Civil Law 59–60
Cold War 140
Colegio Mayor de Nuestra Señora del Rosario 71
Colombia 69, 71, 74–5, 84–5, 87–8, 100, 102, 139; Colombian Consejo de Estado 102–3, 110, 122, 128; Colombian Customs Authority 111; Colombian government 63, 74–5, 109–10, 127; Colombian Industrial Property Division 102–3; Colombian Regulation Authority for Industry and Trade 102; Colombian Supreme Court 63, 74–5, 95, 139, 140
Comité Ejecutivo Permanente 92
Commission v. Council 107
Commission v. Luxembourg 112

Commission v. UK 53
Common Agricultural Policy 38
Common Law 59
Community law 4, 8, 17, 22, 27, 32–3, 48–56, 75, 79–80, 82, 91, 95–6, 99, 101, 103, 105, 107, 109–10, 115, 117, 120–1, 124, 129, 132, 134, 135, 139–41, 143
community of fate 131, 133, 137
comparative law 63
Concertación 62–3
'concerted' multilateralism 116
Conseil d'Etat 44
Consejo de Ministros de Relaciones Exteriores 92
constitutional dialogues 48, 56, 100, 137, 141
constitutionalisation 7, 27, 50, 52, 54, 84, 131, 137, 140–3
Continental Can 112
Corporación Andina de Fomento (CAF) 73–4, 140
Costa v. ENEL 17, 49–50, 91
Council of the EU 44–5, 88, 112
CPA Andean Presidential Council 141
criollos 1
crisis (70s) 78, 140
crisis (80s) 2, 105
crisis (legitimacy) 27
cross-fertilisation 79, 132

Dassonville 108, 110–11, 126
Decision 217 110
Decision 344 105–8
Decision 486 107–8
Decision 85 102–6, 108
Declaración de Bogotá 84
Declaración de los Presidentes de América 85
Declaration of Machu Picchu 143
dependence theory 2, 102, 104–5, 114, 138
Derecho de la Integración 67–9, 71
deviation of power 98
Diez, T. 14
DiMaggio, P. 65
direct applicability 72, 93, 96–7, 102

direct effect 4, 8, 22, 32–3, 47–9, 52, 54, 57, 79, 80–1, 84, 91, 99, 100–2, 115–17, 127, 134–5, 138
dualism 46–7

ECLAC United Nations' Economic Commission for Latin America and the Caribbean 1, 138, 141
ECOWAS Economic Community of West African States 70
ECSC 17, 39, 44–5, 47
Ecuador 81, 84–5, 88, 100, 139
Effet utile 52
El Salvador 77–8
engine of integration 5, 7–8, 22, 91, 117, 128, 137, 141, 144
epistemic communities 27, 63–6
ERTA 52, 126
Euratom 17
Euro-law game 116, 127, 137
European Community EC 8–57, 70, 86, 89, 91, 97, 117, 135, 136–7; European Community law 8–57, 61, 81, 96, 100, 117, 126, 133, 137; European Community Law Art. 177 100; European Community law Art. 234 24, 131; European Community law Art. 30 108, 126; European Community Law Single European Act SEA 33, 35, 37, 141; European Commission 21, 39, 44–6, 69, 88–9, 112, 115; European Convention for the Protection of Human Rights 56; European Court of Human Rights ECHR 131; European Economic Community EEC 17, 49; European integration 1, 3, 6, 8–10, 14, 18, 21–2, 26, 33–4, 36–9, 41, 44, 47, 67–8, 83, 112–13, 115, 124, 135, 137; European Monetary Union 15; European Parliament 21, 26, 90; European Social Charter 56
Europeanisation 31

Federal union of states 94
Fernandez Saavedra, G. 71
Frontaura, V. 95

Fujimori, Alberto 143
functional equivalents 13
fundamental freedom(s) 56–7, 114–15, 130–1, 143
fundamental rights 50, 53–7, 59, 97, 113–14, 116–17, 130–1, 143

Gabaldón Márquez, I. 80
Galanter, M. 25
Garrett, G. 40–1
GATS 53
GATT (General Agreement on Tariffs and Trade) 70
Gaudet, M. 71, 80
Geitling 54, 131
General Advocate of the EC 97
General Attorney of Venezuela 94
German Basic Law 56, 59
German Constitutional Court 31, 56
Golub, J. 31
Group of Three 2
GS General Secretariat 88–9, 92–3, 97–9, 141

Haas, E. 4, 6, 9, 10, 12–13, 16–18, 20, 24, 67–8
Hague Academy of International Law 68, 82
Helfer, L. 100, 109, 119, 121, 128
herbicides 103, 105, 121, 127
high authority 18, 44
high politics 36, 38
Hoffmann, S. 28, 36
Honduras 77–8
Hummer, W. 86
Hurtado Larrea, E. 80, 96

ideology of integration 86, 132
import substitution 2, 88, 102, 127, 140
INDECOPI 128
INTAL 67–73, 75–8, 80, 82–3
integration law 68, 132
integration through law 8, 44
intellectual property 101, 105, 109, 113, 119; intellectual property rights 105, 107–8, 115, 123

Inter-American Court of Human Rights 114
Inter-American Development Bank 67, 105
inter-court competition 31, 121–3, 137
Interessendreieck (Interests triangle) 57, 130
intergovernmentalism 6, 33–42, 95, 118–19
International Court of Justice 2
International Monetary Fund 5, 66, 105
International Public Law 26, 32, 46–7, 50, 89, 94, 96, 121, 135, 142–3
Internationale Handelsgesellschaft 55
interpretation 9, 22, 32–3, 45, 47, 54–5, 75, 91, 94, 96, 99, 107–8, 110–11, 117, 120, 126, 138; functional interpretation 110; historical method 107; teleological interpretation 22, 47, 81, 103–4, 107–9, 112, 135

Jacques Delors 21
Jean Monnet 10, 21
Jellinek, G. 46
judicial activism 25–30
judicial globalisation 79
Junta (Andean Group) 58, 62, 66–81, 88–9, 93–4, 96, 98, 119, 141

Keeling, D. 22
Kelsen, H. 97
Keohane, R. 36
kite model 118–19
Kramer Villagrán, F. 69

LAFTA (Latin American Free Trade Association) 13, 70, 73, 84, 138–9
Lagrange, M. 67, 69, 80
law as a shield, law as a mask 23, 27
lawyers 6, 31, 44, 46, 63, 65, 71, 81, 124
legal engineering 8, 113, 115
legal transplant 6, 58–9, 60, 64, 76, 79–80, 82, 113, 115, 133, 135, 137, 144
Les Verts 51

Leuven 67
lex posteriori derogat 32, 50
liberal intergovernmentalism 38, 41
Lima 71
Lindberg, L. 14, 38
logic of appropriateness 6
Louis, J-V. 71, 80
low politics 8, 14, 36, 38

MacCormick, N. 126
Maduro, M. 125–6
magic triangle 22–3, 32, 43, 115, 138
Mancini, F. 22, 45
Marbury v. Madison 140
Marwege, R. 93, 96
Mattli, W. 11, 17, 23–4, 31, 40–1, 43
Medina, M. 95
MERCOSUR 2, 4–5, 61, 132, 134, 143
Mestizo 1
Mitrany, D. 16
Mols, M. 95, 132
monism 46
Monnet method 10, 21
Montesquieu, C. 108
Moravcsik, A. 37–8, 41–2
morbus latinus 5

NAFTA 2
Napoleon's Civil Code 59
neofunctionalism 6, 8–43, 58, 84, 109–10, 117–20, 127–30, 138
neorationalism 39–42, 118–21
noción de pertenencia 1
Nold 56
non-compliance procedure 70, 72, 78, 90, 98, 100–1, 115, 119
norm diffusion (law diffusion) 59–60, 63, 129
nuclear option 51
Nye, J. 67

Olivier, G. 69
Orrego Vicuña, F. 68, 71

pacta sunt servanda 97
Paolillo, F. 69
Paraguay 2

Paris Convention on the Protection of Industrial Property 107
Pedro Gual 87
Peña, F. 67–9, 71
Peru 84–6, 88, 100, 139, 143
Pescatore, P. 67, 69–71, 80
petitio principi 41
PICAB 2
Pico Mantilla, G. 79, 81
Piérola, N. 81, 86, 88, 94
Pinochet, Augusto 143
pluralism 10–11, 31
Pollack, M. 51
Powell, W. 65
pre-emption 52, 56, 105, 117–18, 126
Prebisch, R. 138
preeminencia 102
preliminary ruling(s) 4, 22, 24–5, 32, 47–8, 70, 72, 78–81, 84, 90–1, 99–104, 106, 109–11, 115, 121–3, 129, 132–3, 138
primary law 97, 107, 109
principal-agent theory (P-A) 29, 42, 119, 120
private litigants 24, 32, 45, 106, 115, 117, 124–5, 128–9, 130
propósito común integracionista 109
Protocol of Cochabamba 100
protocolo para la Solución de de Controversias 85
Punta del Este, Uruguay 85

ratio legis 107
Reagan administration 5
realist intergovernmentalism 35–6
regional integration 138–41
regulatory authority 117–18, 124–8, 138
regulatory models 123–30
resolutions 92–3, 96–8
Revista de la Integración 67
Revista Integración Latinoamericana 67
rights politics 113, 130–1
Roberto Monaco 68
Rodríguez Lemmo, A. 96
Roman Law 59, 108
rule of law 6–7, 22, 28, 48, 51, 113, 128–9, 142

Sáchica, L-C. 80, 86, 92–4, 97, 98–100, 105, 108
SAI Andean Integration System 88, 114, 132, 141
Salazar Santos, F. 63, 71
Sartori, G. 135
Schaulson, J. 69, 71
Scheingold, S. 39
Schmitter, P. 13
secondary law 51, 75, 92–3, 97, 105, 107, 110, 121, 139
Sen, A. 113
Serie Publicaciones INTAL 67
Sgarlata 54, 131
Shapiro, M. 41
SIECA 77, 79
Simmenthal 51, 95–6
Simón Bolivar 87
Slaughter, A-M 17, 24, 31, 43, 79
sociological functionalism 10
soft rationalist ontology 39
Solange II 56
spillover 11–24, 37, 41, 120, 141
Stauder case 55, 143
Stauffer Chemical 102–4, 121, 127
Stein, E. 44–5, 68
Stone Sweet, A. 25, 27, 29, 46, 48
Stork 54, 131
Suárez Mejías, J-L. 95
supranational law, court 5, 21–5, 30, 32–3, 42, 70, 79–80, 82, 88, 90, 100–1, 115, 117, 119–21, 129, 130, 138, 141
supranationality 3, 35, 89, 134
supremacy 4, 8, 17, 22, 32–3, 47–9, 51, 52, 54–5, 70, 79–81, 84, 91, 101–2, 115–17, 127, 134–5, 138
Supreme Court (US) 40, 114
Swiss Civil Code 59

technical self-determination 12
Thatcher, Margaret 38
theory-building 10, 134

Treaty of Maastricht 41, 141
Treaty of Montevideo 73–4, 84–5, 92, 111, 139
Treaty of Rome 8, 27, 33, 39, 44–5, 47, 54–5
Triepel, H. 46
TRIPS 53, 105, 107–8
Trujillo Protocol 88, 141
two-tier Europe 38

ultra vires 98, 130
unintended consequences 8, 18, 33
Unión aduanera imperfect 4, 91
University of Berkeley 68
University of Madrid 67–8
University of Michigan 68
Uribe Restrepo, A. 86, 92, 99
Uruguay 2, 85
US Congress 41
USA 36

Vacchino, J. 80
Van Gend & Loos 17, 49, 54, 91
Venezuela 3, 81, 84–5, 88, 94, 97, 100, 109, 139
Vidal Perdomo, J. 69, 71
voluntad política (integración) 1, 6, 39, 45, 84, 98

Washington Consensus 66, 105, 140
Watson, A. 134
Weiler, J. 24, 26, 30, 52, 100
Weingast, B. 40–1
Western Europe 10, 12
Wiener, A. 14
window of opportunity 59, 72, 76, 82, 116
World Bank 5, 66, 105
World War II 54
WTO World Trade Organization 53, 140

Zelada Castedo, A. 80
Zusammengehörigkeitsbewusstsein 1

For Product Safety Concerns and Information please contact our EU representative GPSR@taylorandfrancis.com
Taylor & Francis Verlag GmbH, Kaufingerstraße 24, 80331 München, Germany

www.ingramcontent.com/pod-product-compliance
Lightning Source LLC
Chambersburg PA
CBHW051646230426
43669CB00013B/2458